The Myopia and Other Plays by David Greenspan

CRITICAL PERFORMANCES

Presenting key texts by contemporary theater and performance artists along with illuminating commentary by leading critics

Series Editors: Una Chaudhuri and Robert Vorlicky
Founding Editors: Lynda Hart and Paul Heritage

TITLES IN THE SERIES

FROM THE UNIVERSITY OF MICHIGAN PRESS

The Myopia *and Other Plays by David Greenspan*
by David Greenspan, edited by Marc Robinson

The Reverend Billy Project: From Rehearsal Hall to Super Mall with the Church of Life After Shopping
by Savitri D and Bill Talen, edited by Alisa Solomon

Say Word!: Voices from Hip Hop Theater
edited by Daniel Banks

Sex, Drag, and Male Roles: Investigating Gender as Performance
by Diane Torr and Stephen Bottoms

From Inner Worlds to Outer Space: The Multimedia Performances of Dan Kwong
edited by Robert Vorlicky

FROM CONTINUUM PUBLISHERS

Of All the Nerve: Deb Margolin Solo
edited by Lynda Hart

Hardcore from the Heart: The Pleasures, Profits, and Politics of Sex in Performance
by Annie Sprinkle, edited by Gabrielle Cody

Rachel's Brain and Other Storms: The Performance Scripts of Rachel Rosenthal
edited by Una Chaudhuri

The Myopia and Other Plays by David Greenspan

Edited and with an Introduction by
Marc Robinson

The University of Michigan Press / Ann Arbor

Published in the United States of America by
The University of Michigan Press
Manufactured in the United States of America
♾ Printed on acid-free paper

2015 2014 2013 2012 4 3 2 1

A CIP catalog record for this book is available from the British Library.

Library of Congress Cataloging-in-Publication Data

Greenspan, David, 1956–
The myopia and other plays / by David Greenspan ; edited and with an introduction by Marc Robinson.
p. cm. — (Critical performances)
ISBN 978-0-472-07173-9 (cloth : acid-free paper) —
ISBN 978-0-472-05173-1 (pbk. : acid-free paper)
I. Robinson, Marc, 1962– II. Title.
PS3557.R39642M96 2012
812'.54— dc23 2012005034

ISBN 0-472-02851-1 (e-book)

Acknowledgments

For *The HOME Show Pieces,* Randy Rollison and Didi Balle at HOME for Contemporary Theatre and Art and JoAnne Akalaitis at the New York Shakespeare Festival; for *Dead Mother,* Joseph Papp at the New York Shakespeare Festival and André Bishop and Tim Sanford at Playwrights Horizons; for *She Stoops to Comedy,* Tim Sanford and Sonya Sobieski at Playwrights Horizons; for *The Argument,* David Herskovits at Target Margin Theater and Susan Wyman, who kindly allowed me to adapt the work of her father, Gerald F. Else; for *The Myopia,* Melanie Joseph at The Foundry Theatre and director Brian Mertes; to my agent, Judy Boals, who has long supported my theater endeavors; to Marc Robinson for many years of encouragement; and finally to my partner, William Kennon, who has, time and again, contributed to my artistic development.

—David Greenspan

I am grateful to the Fund for Lesbian and Gay Studies and the History of Art department at Yale University for generously supporting this volume. Thank you, too, to Jacob Gallagher-Ross for his assistance in preparing the manuscript. Una Chaudhuri and Robert Vorlicky have been sensitive series editors; their advice has been invaluable. At University of Michigan Press, LeAnn Fields, Scott Ham, and Marcia LaBrenz shepherded the manuscript into print with their characteristic grace; I am also grateful to the Press's anonymous reader. David Herskovits of Target Margin Theater and Melanie Joseph of The Foundry Theatre helped immeasurably from the very beginning of this project. Erika Rundle, as ever, was unsparing in her support. Finally, I am thankful to David Greenspan for his energetic collaboration, his patience with queries large and small, and—especially—his inspiring work.

—Marc Robinson

Contents

Introduction by Marc Robinson 1

The HOME Show Pieces 30

Dead Mother, or Shirley Not All in Vain 86

She Stoops to Comedy 146

The Argument 196

The Myopia, an epic burlesque of tragic proportion 218

An Interview with David Greenspan 263

Chronology 277

Introduction

MARC ROBINSON

It may seem perverse to approach David Greenspan, a mannerist actor and often baroque writer, through his least theatrical qualities. Yet for all his strategic excesses, he is also a sincere minimalist, and his theater's omissions may be particularly revealing of his priorities. Spectators at a recent production encountered one such landscape of abstention. A warmly lit white platform seemed to hover just above the stage floor in dark space. The theater's brick back wall framed a hanging door, presumably an exit to a loading dock. An armchair upholstered in rich brown leather, its plain wooden arms and legs suggestive of work rather than leisure, sat center stage; it was the only piece of furniture in the open field. On the floor beside the chair was an aluminum water bottle that further hinted at the strenuous labor about to begin. About to—but not yet. The opening moments of *The Myopia,* as produced by New York's Foundry Theatre in 2010, were generously proportioned, allowing a long connoisseurial look at emptiness, a deep registering of the pregnant tension—its currents almost visible in the air—before the performance began. The inaugural pause also allowed us to turn back toward ourselves and track our variable surges of expectation, the senses sharpening as they awaited the rupture of the stage calm.

Of course many productions start this way, but Greenspan's immaculate opening took on added meaning once it became clear that it would be only the first of many refusals. He wasn't in any obvious character when he finally walked onstage. Purposeful without affect, efficient and unself-conscious, he sat in the armchair and took a drink from the canteen. Only his exceeding care in screwing the top back on hinted at the intensity to follow. His restraint sharpened into renunciation during the play's first dialogue. No other performer joined him; Greenspan played his interlocutor—and all twenty-one other characters—himself. He also read the stage directions aloud—another instance of aggressive speech that, like the casting, pointed to another absence. The telling of an event renders the doing of it superfluous, just as the description of a scene obviates the need to show it. Both acts of omission spring from the conviction that what is staged is always an inadequate approximation of what has been written—

and that only by impoverishing the theater can one enrich the imagination. So strict is this belief, and so concentrated in himself is his play, that Greenspan didn't leave his chair until the end of each act—one last mark of his spectacular asceticism.

It may also have been a mark of self-preservation. At the Foundry, the upstage loading-dock door seemed capable of rising at any moment and sucking everything away, leaving behind an emptiness starker than the one we contemplated before the play began. For all the apparent hubris of Greenspan's solo performance, he entered on the knife-edge of oblivion, and his presence existed under threat of imminent evacuation. The chair was perhaps his only anchor. Longtime Greenspan spectators may recall that he set the first production of *Dead Mother* (1991) on a similar precipice—an unnaturally shallow stage directly in front of the theater's double exit doors.[1] The choice of site was a provocation—ostensibly innocuous or perhaps practically necessary, but still capable of stirring anxiety. There, as in *The Myopia,* steel seemed a thin membrane between the shaped, structured life onstage and the limbo of an untheatricalized world beyond.

A similar layout lent gravity to the otherwise lighthearted first production of *She Stoops to Comedy* (2003) at Playwrights Horizons. When actors entered through upstage doors, we could just glimpse the vanity tables and lightbulb-framed mirrors of the dressing rooms beyond. As a reminder that the stage-world had been manufactured, the view wasn't especially memorable—but as a warning that it could also be easily dismantled, it cast a pall. Not that there was much to dismantle: like Greenspan's other stages, this one was swept clean of all decor save a double bed—one that, in a joke nicely disappointing our expectations of dramatic action, was used for just about everything but sex. In conditions of such austerity, some spectators may have lingered over another surface, the theater's floor. It was the product of exquisite craftsmanship, long strips of wood forming a glossy, honey-colored field—the only promise of stability in a world of fluid identities and slippery allegiances.

Greenspan's most allusive form of economy was one of his earliest and least intentional. When *The HOME Show Pieces* (1988), written for the tiny HOME for Contemporary Theatre and Art in New York, was remounted at the Public Theater in 1992, it seemed to be a chamber work lost in an opera house. The last of the piece's four movements took place in a spartan kitchen that looked even barer in the Public's cavernous Martinson Hall. Light breaking through grimy windows high on the Martinson's upstage wall (designers of other productions usually cover them) dwarfed the cast further: the actors barely displaced the air weighing down on them. But the mise-en-scène drove home Greenspan's argument about his characters' less visible dislocations and less measurable estrangements.

In all these instances, Greenspan contests the meanings usually assigned to empty spaces in other theaters. Greenspan's stages aren't vessels to be filled with activity. The platform is never less prominent than the people on it. The walls never recede to the background. By extension (we might imagine), the blank page with which Greenspan begins—the surface of writing that is recalled by the surfaces of the stage—is never wholly effaced by his often ornate narratives. He makes sure we keep in mind the fragility and inevitable obsolescence of even the most outlandish actions; that we sense the outrageous statement's proximity to silence. Greenspan may be a practitioner of what Tony Kushner calls the "Theater of the Fabulous"—the "next step" after the Theater of the Ridiculous, composed of "irony, tragic history, defiance . . . glitter, drama . . . the magic of the grotesque [and] the carnivalesque"—but it would be wrong to assume that such a style, in Greenspan's case, is smug. In the truest "fabulous" theater, Kushner argues, "the illusion is always incomplete, inadequate." Behind the baroque edifice or under the glittering surface is a zone that style cannot reach. All "art is like that," Kushner concedes. "There may be nothing, but that nothing has power."[2]

Kushner's definition of nothingness is capacious enough to include social as well as formal absences. In particular, he has in mind the cycles of "irreparable loss" that structure recent gay history (ix). Greenspan acknowledges this void, nowhere more so than in *Jack* (1990), a play that recounts a young man's death from an unnamed disease—"one of the many" who "got sick . . . and many still to come."[3] But this elegy is just one variation on a theme of mortality, and of less definite threats to kinship, that runs throughout Greenspan's theater. "I'm tired of talking to the dead," says a character in *The HOME Show Pieces,* an actress chafing at the role assigned her by an uncannily Greenspanian playwright. "There's a lot of that . . . .in all his work." Her fatigue and annoyance are as important as the obsessive mourning. There's no sentimental effort at recovery here, no romantic hope that even the most emphatic "talking to" the dead will lend dignity to the embarrassing spectacle of being left alone. Embarrassment is, in Greenspan's world, a more productive emotion than grief. Surfacing along with pathos, it draws off the distorting glamour from the nobler feeling, allowing us to see desolation cold. Genuine feelings of any severity in Greenspan are usually accompanied by self-consciousness. His characters preemptively cite a clichéd pose so they won't unwittingly conform to it. They travesty sorrow to prevent self-seriousness: the latter attitude is all too common, Greenspan implies, among performers who treat death as something extraordinary. If the actress in *The HOME Show Pieces* is "tired" of talking to the dead, that's because loss, in this world, is routine.

For Greenspan, the dispersed family or torn social fabric is the norm. His theater's typical partners conduct their relationships through closed doors or on the telephone, or across unbridgeable temporal divides. Some can't forge bonds that are more than situational or utilitarian. Even when the separation isn't literal, they can "feel there is a wall up," as one character puts it. Craters open on every affective surface, requiring a leap of faith to achieve any union. The title character's suicide in *Dead Mother* has shaped a gap that only widens as her adult children try farcically and vindictively to deny her absence; they also end up forcing attention to long-ignored rifts among themselves. Another mother has died in *The HOME Show Pieces,* and with her has gone the domestic security promised in her play's title. The protagonist, Frank, hasn't spoken to his father in nine months or to his brother in almost five years; friends are present only as disembodied voices on his answering machine. Frank confirms his isolation in listless sessions of masturbation and in hapless, if earnest, attempts to sing "People Who Need People." Greenspan's little-known *Son of an Engineer* (1994) opens with a young man returning home to find that his parents have moved away (or so he thinks) without telling him. A short, early play, *Dig a Hole and Bury You Father* (1989), captures the arrested development of all Greenspan's surviving offspring. If only its protagonist could take action as definitive as the one named in this title! Instead, she visits her mother's grave for surprisingly feisty conversations. When Greenspan revisits this kind of generational agon in *The Myopia,* he treats it in a far more lyrical (if no less antic) mode. A writer hoping to finish his late father's musical about Warren G. Harding must first secure the borders separating them—"where [his] father leaves off and [he] begin[s]"—in both the manuscript and himself. Even in the rare Greenspan play without a death, such as *She Stoops to Comedy,* the action is haunted by the deaths-in-life imagined by other writers. The forced and self-willed banishments in *As You Like It,* the play Greenspan's actor-characters are rehearsing, help them make sense of their own less dire displacements.

All these empty spaces—shaped by mortality, animosity, or self-absorption—become platforms for drama. To see them as gaps to be filled or deficits to be erased would be to miss a theatrical opportunity. *The HOME Show Pieces* contains a telling exchange that summarizes Greenspan's dramaturgy: "Where do you want to take it from?" asks one actor-character, wanting to run a scene. "How about 'there's nothing else to say'?" says her scene partner, naming precisely the strategic disposal of substance and draining of energy that, for Greenspan, is the precondition of originality.

Alison, in *She Stoops to Comedy,* echoes that dialogue when she says, "I'm losing language" just before forging a connection with the disguised Alex. In many other plays, Greenspan's voluble characters reliably arrive at a blockage, abyss, or toe-stubbing flaw in speech's otherwise smooth landscape—one that threatens a full-scale breakdown of language. The breakdown never does occur. Inarticulateness is a departure point, not a last gasp. At many moments in several plays, Greenspan's characters stop in the middle of speeches and grind in place, repeating a trivial phrase until it's scrubbed clean of even minimal denotative value. The neutral fragment has ambiguous uses. Does it protect the speaker from the shame of more complete utterances? Or does it serve an opposite purpose—becoming an instrument with which the speaker can poke at his or her own repressions, shake off habits of evasion, and thereby plumb depths of thought below practiced speech, disclosing emotions unsusceptible to "psychological" drama? Much depends on how such scenes are played, of course, and even more, on the needs and expectations we bring to them.

A reading that values the stammer as a kind of exploratory speech—a signal sent by characters seeking reserves of untapped expressive power—will help explain why Greenspan favors characters who are actors and writers. They are present less to mark the equivocal border between illusion and reality—that Pirandellian commentary has long ago exhausted its potential for revelation—than to make a more compelling argument about the uses of frustration onstage or off, at or away from the desk. One might now hear a familiar Beckettian idea: "nothing with which to express, nothing from which to express . . . together with the obligation to express."[4] Greenspan acknowledges the kinship in *The HOME Show Pieces* ("I first met Beckett in 1988," says the play's protagonist, dishonestly), before he stops us from making too much of it in his later work *2 Samuel 11, Etc.* (1989). "Similar to the Beckettian equation," says this play's embattled dramatist, "yet in all relevant respects dissimilar."[5] Indeed, Greenspan asks complicating questions of Beckett's overquoted (and easily sentimentalized) description of the writer's bind. He does so, in part, by restoring the absent subject to Beckett's phrases—the I who does (or doesn't do) the "expressing"—before weighing (and resenting) the burden of such an articulate self. When Greenspan's actor-characters nearly collapse from the strain of upholding their roles—as Harold does in *Dead Mother,* retreating to a bathroom to vent the self-hatred he's been suppressing ("you disgraceful faggot!")—or when they struggle to get a purchase on an emotion (as in *She Stoops to Comedy* or in the "Too Much in the Sun" section of *The HOME Show Pieces*), they seem to be resisting two opposite but equally undesirable fates. At one extreme is helplessness—not having a scripted line to say or rehearsed action to complete. At the other is the no less vulnerable condition of competence—being exceedingly visible because virtuosic, or easily consumed because compactly packaged in their roles. They are embarrassed egotists, reclusive divas and hams. They suffer from stage fright but won't retreat entirely from the scene. Their desire for spectacular self-abasement is stronger than their instinct for self-preservation.

The same paradox is even more pronounced among Greenspan's writer-characters. In the midst of composition, they sputter and go silent, anxious about writer's block but also finding it a strangely stimulating and reassuring condition. (This is the fate of the obsessive-compulsive Febus in *The Myopia* and of the idling playwright in *2 Samuel 11, Etc.*) Even at its most agonizing, the block provides a kind of security or protective camouflage denied them when they compose new, revealing prose. Or such is the promise; the reality is more equivocal. The ellipsis may be less frightening than an explicit, too-candid word; an equivocal dash less risky than a name. A repeated phrase, stuck at a verb, happily delays the moment when the subject of a sentence (say) must commit to an object. Yet the relief is short-lived. Silence causes a deeper shame. These writers push back against muteness yet still worry that the long-impacted disclosure will betray them more. They want confessional release but postpone opening the taps for fear of being unable to control the flow.

It's in this context that Greenspan's minimalist stages make their strongest claim on us. Their invitation to metatheatrical thinking, while irresistible, takes us only so far; more penetrating is their challenge to orthodox ideas of this or any artist's persona. Naked themselves, the stages are naked-making, as merciless in their exposures as is Greenspan's writing. They swiftly, even roughly, accomplish what speech does gradually: dismantling the presentational composure of their occupants and submitting for our scrutiny the separate parts—masks, manners, motives—that no longer add up to a whole. In the end, we must reassess how we confer individuality on any figure—not just the no longer cohesive artist, dispersed among his utterances, or his fragmenting characters, but any self that claims uniqueness. One of Greenspan's unlikely kindred spirits—Charles Dickens—helps us grasp this procedure. The novelist anticipates the playwright in his so-called platform performances—readings that Dickens conducted on a spartan stage, during which he played all the parts. (Could these be what Greenspan has in mind when, in a note on the similarly structured *Myopia,* he places the play in "the story-telling tradition"?) In a letter to a friend, Dickens implicitly corrects those who would see his performances as an enlargement and glamorizing of his persona. On the contrary, he writes, "the platform absorbs my individuality, and I am very little troubled."[6] It's worth pausing over the last part of Dickens's sentence. What does he mean by "very little troubled"? What, more precisely, constitutes the burden of individuality? A prize that others regard as a reward for artistic labor—a consolidated personality—is here dismissed, even resented, as a straitjacket—a kind of importunate suitor "troubling" the writer for recognition. He implies he'd be more autonomous, paradoxically, if he could always have less of a self.

To pursue these associations is eventually to find oneself deep within contemporary debates over close-fitting definitions of identity. Greenspan preemptively raises this inevitable subject—and deflects it—when, in *The HOME Show Pieces,* his surrogate declares, "I really don't consider myself a gay playwright." A character in *She Stoops to Comedy* joins him in disdaining obvious categories. Simon Lanquish wearily asks, "who needs a play about a gay man who . . . ?" and finishes his question with a comically exhaustive list of possible plots. Indeed, as those who are already sensing the consonance between Greenspan's shape-shifting drama and queer theory will have realized, to call these "gay plays" is to miss their point and duck their challenge. A more accurate tag would reflect an approach to playwriting that, as David Savran puts it in a discussion of queer drama in general, "represents not a stabilization but a disarticulation of identity."[7] That phrasing should be especially attractive to Greenspan's readers. The playwright's anatomizing of speech is perhaps a more literal expression of "disarticulation" than Savran has in mind, but it makes the critic's conclusion irresistible. (It also resonates wittily with Michael Warner's discussion of the "dominant assumptions about what goes without saying, what can be said without a breach of decorum, who shares the onus of disclosure, and who will bear the consequences of speech and silence" in a culture that assigns supercharged and at times unbearable significance to the avowal of sexuality.)[8] Greenspan's fractured or repetitive utterances imply speakers whose own cohesiveness is in question. His characters continually divide and multiply—a mitosis that allows a son to play his mother in *Dead Mother;* a leading lady to also play a leading man (and her best friend to play her own partner) in *She Stoops to Comedy;* the lecturer in *The Argument* (2007) to assume the persona of both Aristotle and his twentieth-century exegete Gerald Else; the playwright-protagonist of *The HOME Show Pieces* to become his own admirers in a fantasy of fame; and the Author of *2 Samuel 11, Etc.* to play eleven different characters while taking a shower. All these self-replications and self-displacements reach their apotheosis in *The Myopia*'s kaleidoscopic proliferation of the solo performer.

By collapsing many stage figures into one actor, Greenspan purposefully undermines our faith in the distinctness and knowability of any single character. The move is enough to put Greenspan at odds with most theater, of course. In the context of canonical gay drama, he seems to take particular aim at the very complacencies so distasteful to Simon Lanquish in *She Stoops to Comedy.* Nowhere in Greenspan are there seamless narratives of guilt and self-acceptance, or persecution and transcendence, or pride declared in the face of external indifference. Narrative itself, as we've seen, is embattled and uncertain here. (It's telling that the protagonist of the first of *The HOME Show Pieces* can't concentrate on the novel he's reading.) Moreover, we don't encounter protagonists who appeal for our sympathy as they come to terms with forbidden desire, or as they manage it once it's been authorized, or as they recover from its eventual, inevitable disappointment. To do so—to make their claim on us by virtue of their affective lives alone—characters would have to be better at excluding all that interrupts the development of emotion: their distractedness, impatience, and even boredom with what should be transporting or agonizing sensation; their analytic self-consciousness; or simply their awareness that every apparently private response actually derives from an archive of feeling available to all.

Yet Greenspan is no closer to those artists who share his aversion to preciosity and breathless emoting. To be sure, Greenspan is irreverent, even outrageous—but his wit doesn't set the tone unopposed, and more often than not he resists camp. He cuts the ironist's knowingness with sincerity, and holds back from rancor in favor of less revealing drollery, even diffidence. There remain aspects of life impervious to archness. This satirist's memorable lines hit their target only after carefully simulated trial and error—something that the polished writer is supposed to deny needing. So, too, with his acting. When Greenspan plays a woman, he doesn't aim for a credible, or even incredible, illusion. More often than not, he wears just an allusion to femininity—a strand of pearls in *Dead Mother,* for instance—or eschews drag entirely, forcing us to look elsewhere for confirmation of his character's gender or, even better, to give up the need for confirmation altogether. (Just as his stage is shorn of any decor that would limit the imagination, so too the actor's own surface.) Bravura turns in Greenspan are painstakingly built up rather than launched; farcical narratives are foretold but not executed, or are interrupted early in their run, arrested just when the characters might rush headlong into chaos. There's never comic abandon in art this dubious of the unmonitored id. She *stoops* to comedy, as his title has it; she doesn't surrender to it, or confidently orchestrate it, or ride it deliriously.

Any definition of Greenspan's style—or more precisely, his relationship to style—has to come to terms with this seemingly impossible blend of extravagance and reserve. Is it too much to call it a marriage of vulgarity and tact? Not if one considers *The HOME Show Pieces,* where the protagonist becomes "meticulous," as a stage direction puts it, immediately after masturbating. (The same fastidiousness characterizes his way of wiping himself while using the toilet in a later scene.) One could also cite *The Myopia,* where Greenspan tempers the freakishness of certain characters by the formality of their representation. An elephantine woman known as Koreen "appears" in the form of Greenspan's right hand, its supposedly mammoth scale established alongside the actor's left-hand index and middle fingers, which stand in for Febus, Koreen's husband. The couple's appalling domestic scene holds to this side of monstrousness by the dexterity with which Greenspan manipulates his fingers. He literally gestures toward but does not embody the grotesque, and thus ensures a kind of antic *bienséance.*

When Greenspan crosses lines beyond which others won't go, he does so not with the radical's defiance but with a gesture back toward a code of manners he has no desire to forsake. He is at once the writer who composes sexually and scatologically frank prose (so many scenes set in bathrooms!) and the reader who turns for inspiration to such chaste-seeming writers as Ferenc Molnár, Thornton Wilder, George S. Kaufman and Edna Ferber, and Brandon Thomas, the author of *Charley's Aunt.*[9] Greenspan's dress-less transvestism honors both the pathetic Judy Garland "on twenty dexedrine" (as he writes in *The HOME Show Pieces*) and the wholesome Carol Channing (who makes an appearance in *The Myopia*). If *The Argument* and a 2010 lecture-performance based on Gertrude Stein's "Plays" are any indication, he is equally responsive to classical poise and modernist flux. Even his bawdier muses—Aretino (Greenspan adapted *Il Marescalco* as *A Horse's Ass*), Aristophanes (*Old Comedy,* a 2008 Greenspan play, is a version of *The Frogs*), and Oscar Wilde (the trials are the subject of *Only Beauty,* from 1997)—are transgressive within secure borders, if such a thing is possible. Theirs is antique or aestheticized sex.

Art reins in or cools down instinct even when there is no disciplining source-text. The explicit descriptions of sex in *2 Samuel 11, Etc.* and *The Horizontal and the Vertical* (1986) are just that—descriptions, his characters' ardor reserved for rendering scenes precisely. As speech, they become occasions for the deployment of style—one in which clarity of imagery, disdain for metaphor and abstraction, and control of rhythm become, rather than merely serve, his subject matter. D. A. Miller, in his meditation on what he calls "Absolute Style" in Jane Austen, captures well this quality of writerly attention. It is the "overwhelming urge to give correctness *a theatrical form.* To manifest grammatical correctness as spectacle."[10]

Private life in Greenspan does not enable the release of inhibition. Far from it. In his bedrooms and bathrooms, characters maintain an unwavering commitment to decorum. The figure who masturbates in *The HOME Show Pieces* does so no less deliberately than he reads a book; the same bed is the platform for both activities. As a result, we never presume, as we watch these closeted scenes, that we're gaining access to characters' inner, "real" selves. They screen themselves, and ultimately lose their selves, in the exquisite delicacy with which they complete the most indelicate acts.

The larger significance of these gestures will occur easily to those schooled in well-established arguments against an interior essence of gender or sexuality—or for that matter, the self in general—in a world governed by contingency.[11] Greenspan lodges his own objections to interiority in bracingly literal terms. At the start of *The Myopia*'s second half, the Narrator tells us he has cut the third and fourth acts—material that together comprises what he terms the "Inner Play."[12] It is a correlative, he adds, to one of the "two parts" of "each and every one of us." This act of dramaturgical hollowing out—of serving his play cored—is only the most extreme expression of Greenspan's habitual avoidance of the narrative middle. In all his metatheatrical plays, he pays most attention to preludes and aftermaths—the fluid period when his actor-characters are rehearsing, his surrogate playwrights are composing, or his onstage spectators are getting ready to go to the theater, and later, when the actors do a postmortem, the playwrights bask in praise, or the spectators debate the value of what they've seen. Putative centers—the mounted productions of *As You Like It* and of the play rehearsed in (and also called) "Too Much in the Sun"; a stage adaptation of *The Odyssey* alluded to in *Dead Mother;* the finished Harding musical; and even a speech about the theater that young Warren remembers after he delivered it—are embryonic or wholly speculative. Still other gaps open in *The Myopia.* The versions of Harding we meet are the greenhorn and the dying elder statesman; only fleetingly do we see anything from his presidency. One could make the case that *The Argument* and *Plays* also frame but do not intrude upon the space dedicated to presumably "central" dramatic action and character. Aristotle and Stein erect structures that will allow us to see a play that remains theoretical—one that is possible but not, on these stages, present. If, for now, we watch the theorists' labor, Greenspan implies, we'll enjoy dramas no less revelatory than the works that later artists have composed to their specifications.

Greenspan's preference, here and elsewhere, for potential rather than completed art hints at similar priorities in people. His purposefully tentative theater could be taken as a synonym for the ideal identity that Eve Sedgwick calls "constitute[d] . . . as to-be-constituted."[13] Theories being worked out, manuscripts being drafted, scenes being rehearsed, and stage sets described but not assembled stand in for equally speculative selves. They all contain more than they yet disclose. Leo Bersani helps Greenspan's readers name still more ways this theater resists interiority; he also, not incidentally, should give pause to those who would label it too prescriptively. "There is no 'homosexual psychology' here," Bersani writes, approvingly, of André Gide.[14] Neither is there in Greenspan, as we've seen, despite his preoccupation with such psychological conditions as shame, longing, and self-doubt. What *is* here is a series of actions that recall what Bersani, writing about unrelated subjects, calls "self-scattering," "self-shattering," "self-subtraction," and "self-dismissal," along with "ego-divesting" and "ego-annihilation." These terms, scattered throughout his work, comprise a lexicon of decomposition—six degrees of self-separation. This asceticism is so extravagant as to release drives otherwise constrained by character—a process Bersani names precisely as "self-impoverishing self-expansion."[15] The oxymoron could describe the simultaneous erasure of character and proliferation of performer that occurs whenever Greenspan disperses a single character among multiple speakers, or asks a single speaker to embody multiple characters. Bersani's language of loss, when applied to Greenspan, isn't only metaphorical—the deceased title character of *Jack* sits silently throughout his play's first half, haloed by three speakers whose intricately narrated memorial renders him wholly external, absent yet excessively present, disseminated among his mourners—nor is it limited to character. Explaining his motivation for realizing the elaborate stage milieus and actions of *Son of an Engineer* only in recited stage directions, Greenspan writes that the practice "permitted me opportunity to create in words worlds and environments and then, in words, erase them."[16]

Greenspan's most suggestive embodiment of this thinking merges character and environment. In *The Myopia,* Febus's son, Barclay, consists of only a single eye, scanning the world around him like a travesty of Emerson's "transparent eyeball." ("All mean egotism vanishes. . . . I am nothing; I see all.")[17] A hyperarticulate instrument for seeing out, Barclay rebuffs those who would look in. "Oh how my dramaturgy is like my life," he says. "Both inscrutable." Barclay is more prop than actor, more "it" than "he." His presence, uncertain at best, is fatally compromised between the play's two halves—a period in which (we're told) he breaks into many pieces. Greenspan's terms for his character's fate uncannily echo Bersani—"our scattered Author" has been "shattered"; both eye and I are reduced to just "a shard here and there."

Such a fate inverts a persistent, and unexamined, expectation about all plays that measure the wages of passion. Barclay's crack-up follows a moment of searing insight—one that offers none of the self-consolidating rewards to be gained from other epiphany narratives. "We see things—about ourselves—and we are shattered," says the Orator. In this world, figures who fearlessly confront their darkest or most atavistic impulses, who finally recover what repression has banned, aren't made whole but rather are irreparably broken; they don't clarify but blur. Characters who understand this calculus disappear preemptively, or at least camouflage themselves. In another reversal of precedent, Greenspan's angriest, randiest, or most ambitious protagonists don't gather themselves up and seize the stage, magnifying their stature as they magnify their desire. On the contrary, they take cover, even flee the scene. They disguise the source of emotion, using elaborate fronts—dummy selves—to launder the most forbidden passions, ensuring that no transgression, or even lapse in charm, can be traced to them.

There are many theatrical precedents for this strategy, of course, and Greenspan acknowledges two of them in *She Stoops to Comedy.* Its characters' own points of reference for their behavior are *As You Like It* and *The Guardsman;* these plots help to anchor Greenspan's figures amid unpredictable currents of lust and self-loathing. Following Shakespeare and Molnár, Greenspan absents his characters to make room for all the emotions that character obscures. He does the same in *Dead Mother,* where a son's swelling rage at his father bursts forth from behind his mother's mask. In both plays, we can study the structure of feeling without the distraction of characters insisting upon their sincerity. The same desire impels Greenspan to hand off his role to an actress for the final section of *The HOME Show Pieces:* she speaks candidly about the writing that her character attempted in earlier sections and about the diminishing pleasures of onanism—both forms of blockage relieved only when she (or he?) stands before a mirror and lip-synchs to Judy Garland, the act a double deflection of his presence. Greenspan demonstrates a similar sleight-of-hand in assigning roles to the play's remaining cast-member. This actor plays the protagonist's boyfriend (who is reduced to a voice heard through a bathroom door); the protagonist's aunt (who is visible, but who mostly speaks on the phone—another veil over character), and an actor struggling to impersonate a role (a father similar to but not identical to the protagonist's). In all three cases, presence is uncertain, unverifiable, hard to pin down to a single locale.

As these examples suggest, most Greenspan characters are compelled not simply to vent hostility, discharge lust, or burn with jealousy, but to render these emotions well—with a degree of flair that will invite lively attention in return. The details of their pathos don't say much about them—by design, these desires and resentments are commonplace—but the virtuosic technique with which they perform them does. Greenspan gives over the stage to this or that primal urge primarily so we can see the effort to harness and ride it—to make a drive form a pattern.

Nowhere is this clearer than in *2 Samuel 11, Etc.*, where a playwright struggling with a work in progress stops resisting the homoerotic fantasies that regularly break his concentration. Once he does so, his protagonist, embodied by an actress standing near his desk, speaks dialogue from those scenarios instead of her scripted lines. After one especially steamy reverie—"oh, mike it feels so good," etc.—the writer turns away from his surrogate and says, "I've got to find a way to get this down on paper" (1–9). The line, together with the geometry of the scene, is an elegant illustration of what D. A. Miller calls the "personal sourcelessness" of the most uncompromising styles.[18] This self is not in the pornographic scenes it supposedly yearns for; it sits apart, thinking about how to represent them. The more successfully the writer does so, the more completely he as their fantasized subject disappears. He recedes gradually, and finally irretrievably, behind the manifestations of taste. As his breathless phrases, modulations in narrative rhythm, and approximations of tone become more theatrical, more written, we become less intimate with their creator. This stylist dedicates himself to the outside of beckoning erotic scenes, hoping not so much to share in their sensations as to codify them, allowing them to be felt again and again—to translate experiences into images that can then be fetishized. To be successful, such a practice must be ascetic, self-denying. Like the ideal Diderotian actor, this kind of writer doesn't surrender to the scenes he hopes to write. Or as Miller puts it, a style this emphatic depends on "the stringency of its refusal to realize its author personally . . . , its commitment to absent [oneself] from . . . representation" (56). The "perfection" of this style is the perfection of "No One" (68).

Yet onstage, a space far less flexible than the novelist's page, *someone* is there, unequivocally. To adapt this notion of style to live performance, one must be willing to sacrifice privileges of access—to concede that we may not gain any special knowledge of the performers just because we share the same space, or can look at them without the more obvious mediation of print or film. We have at least to wonder what we're not seeing as we lay claim to the bodies standing before us. In *The Argument*, Greenspan helps us mark the transition from our false hope of intimacy to the more sober awareness of our separateness, and from our wish for a performer's transparency to our acknowledgment of his or her actual imperviousness. A close look at this one work may turn up principles of a dramaturgy informing all the plays in this volume. In the spirit of its main source-text, the play serves to articulate Greenspan's own poetics.

As first presented by Target Margin Theater in New York, *The Argument* begins casually. Greenspan saunters onstage without the houselights dimming, dressed in street clothes and still wearing his own watch and ring, both hands in his pockets. He lets his first line slide out experimentally, as if testing the waters, not wanting to impose on us, or not willing to risk self-importance by striking too declarative a tone. "The art of poetic composition in general / and its various species," he says, inserting an "uh" between the first and second words. Yet all these signs of insouciance are deceptive. The "uh" is carefully placed, repeated from performance to performance, and the hands are pocketed to show restraint—a deliberate, no less choreographed contrast to the emphatic gestures that will follow. In his seemingly aimless stroll onstage, Greenspan in fact heads toward a yellow-taped X on the floor. Nothing unusual about this bit of decor—many stages mark an object's or performer's placement this way—but this X seems as much for our benefit as for Greenspan's. Far larger than it needs to be, it is continuously visible to us from our vantage point above the stage. Throughout the performance, we can, if we wish, measure just how far Greenspan strays from home.

This ongoing negotiation between the systematic and the spontaneous—between analysis and impulse—will become Greenspan's subject, overtly and covertly, throughout *The Argument*—as it is in all his theater. Of course *The Argument,* as its title suggests, puts analysis front and center. Its text draws not only from Aristotle on tragedy but, as we've seen, from Gerald Else on Aristotle. Else (1908–1982), a longtime professor at the University of Michigan, himself combined patience and recklessness in one sensibility. His major work, *Aristotle's Poetics: The Argument* (1957), is a 670-page monument to obsession, marked by eccentric readings that remain controversial among present-day scholars. Its themes and tone are echoed in Greenspan's other source-texts, *Plato and Aristotle on Poetry* (1986, an elaboration of a manuscript left unfinished at Else's death) and the footnotes to Else's translation of the *Poetics* (1967).

One of those notes, discussing Aristotle's anti-romantic approach to theater, is especially pertinent to Greenspan's own work: "Thought does not exist in drama unless the characters express the thought in speech." In quoting the passage, Greenspan invites us to look critically at a number of assumptions about the imaginative and intellectual lives of stage figures. In part, Aristotle (as interpreted by Else) offers distinguished precedent for

Greenspan's own skepticism about innerness. A psyche's subterranean rumblings may exude meaningfulness, but to a writer as empirically disciplined as Greenspan, writing for an art dependent on manifested action, they are merely hypothetical, with no standing until they surface into audible words. The shared language that gives shape to thought—and thus ensures its intelligibility—also unavoidably shaves away idiosyncrasy. Here, too, the unsentimental artist will feel sharply the difficulty in finding a happy balance between private (but mute) feeling and public (but possibly impersonal) expression. A sentence from Aristotle's *Rhetoric* makes the point more prescriptively: "Avoid ambiguity, unless indeed the ambiguity is deliberately sought, as it is by those who pretend they have something to say when they have not."[19] Upon such convictions Greenspan builds his own argument for a theater that recognizes subjective feelings only after they've been translated into stark, palpable emblems. "Our emotions are not merely irrational as Plato has made them out to be," says Greenspan's Aristotle, appropriating a passage from Else. "They have also that rational side—or are at least amenable to reason." With reason comes clarity and coolness, shape and order—a transformation that Greenspan's speaker recommends when he admits into theater "emotion authorized and released by an intellectually constituted structure of an action." Like the form of speech he earlier elevated over thought, action is, or should be, resistant to the obfuscations of the subconscious.

Greenspan's choreographed performance in *The Argument*—reminiscent of the semaphores modeled by Delsarte—is a stringent realization of this principle, for here no plot gives the illusion of his protagonist's depth. His milieu is a classroom and his persona is that of lecturer. Just about every other aspect of biography recedes in deference to Aristotle's ideas; his passion is only for their clarity. Greenspan doesn't try to sell an overtly artificial manner as natural—no movement is left to chance—and doesn't open an aperture onto an unguarded interior. Rather, meaning stays in full view. Poses and gestures comprise a text that runs parallel to the lecture; we track its development as we track the argument it serves. Standing on his X, Greenspan shifts weight deliberately from one leg to another, leans forward as if fighting a strong headwind, twists his torso left or right, and tenses his arms as if preparing to shoot a cross-bow. He draws from a set repertoire of poses to ornament almost every phrase. Purposefully histrionic gestures further underscore and frame significant words. That these words all denote the extreme emotional states itemized in the *Poetics*—pity, fear, and their subtler gradations—is telling. The accompanying gestures limit the associations the words may provoke, replacing images of expressive license with telegraphic code. The more eruptive or lavish the passion, the more organized and concise the gesture. He renders "pity" by placing his hands on either side of his eyes—palms turned in, fingers curled shut—and then slowly pulling them down his cheeks. "Fear" inverts the sign. The palms face out, the fingers unfurl, the hands stay put at his temples. Whenever he says "pathos," he turns stage-right and pounds his fist upon the air. Is he stabbing his victim? "Catharsis" is earthy: Greenspan pulls both hands toward his chest and presses down the length of his torso, as if aiding the evacuation of waste. More decorous, but no less explicit, is the sign of "recognition." Greenspan's whole body rears back; one hand flies up to his brow; his eyes peer down the length of the other, extended arm, as its hand points to an invisible, surprising other—a pose pulled unrevised from any handbook for staging melodrama.

Even when Greenspan isn't captioning emotions this boldly, our eyes stay on the surface, kept from seeking explanatory motives and histories. He stresses the mathematician in Aristotle as much as the aesthetician—and the outline of his aesthetics as much as its substance. (For the same reason, he also, in a lighter moment, reminds us that Aristotle was a botanist—someone, in other words, who doesn't swoon over beauty but classifies it.) This Aristotle is most alive when he thrusts his arms forward and counts on his fingers the six parts of tragedy, or the four qualities that epic shares with drama, or the three "modes of imitation," or the two "operative causes" of each mode. As he does so, Greenspan implicitly asks us to approach his own work with the same structuralist sensibility—to arrest our attention at the borders of his scenarios, where their architecture is best viewed, and to note the meaning-making role played by pace, meter, number, and geometry—everything that controls the sequence and duration of separate acts of seeing. (This is why speakers in many plays are called Character 1, Character 2, and so on; why his most graphically sexual drama is called *The Horizontal and the Vertical;* and why one of his first plays, *Principia* [1988], its title alluding to Newton, compulsively tallies numbers and measures distances.)

This show of organizational competence may imply that no unpredictability, much less disorder, is possible in Greenspan's theater. Yet *The Argument* is wise enough about math to admit what math cannot account for. Gerald Else, surprisingly, models this humility. For all his ecstatic pedantry, the classicist regularly tempers obsession with prudence, and even wanders away from provable fact into more illuminating conjecture. The combination may be just what drew Greenspan to him. In a passage from *Plato and Aristotle on Poetry,* Else hears in Aristotle's emphasis on "probability" a concession that "human life at its best is not as tidy as mathematics. . . . Its native principle is not necessity but . . . 'the by-and-large, for-the-most-part.'"[20] Greenspan doesn't quote the passage, but he does uphold its spirit in his own stresses and withdrawals, his way of alternating between earnestness and winking ambiguity as he brings the *Poetics* to life. His Aristotle is a "by-and-large, for-the-most-part" theorist. He demystifies tragedy but doesn't forget that it is an art, and therefore is capable of eluding every aggressive attempt to turn it into mere knowledge. This mathematician is at his most dazzling when dealing with unprovable proofs. One might look again at that overlarge X taped to Greenspan's stage, seeing it now as the algebraic symbol of his theater—an open, as yet uncalculated, unnumbered variable in this most variable of arts.

The X remains unsolved as the play moves toward its conclusion. If anything, it begins to taunt us. The argument—and the *Argument*—it defaces flirt openly with speciousness. After cementing his case for a distinctly tragic dramatic structure, Greenspan's Aristotle begins prising loose a brick here and there. His "defense of poetry / . . . is itself / tragically flawed," he admits, and envisions a day when "someone" will "come along / to correct" his "mistakes." He also prepares his listeners for another unheard discourse—his theory of comedy, presumably no less fallible than his theory of tragedy. Of course Aristotle's sequel is lost to us, and this knowledge allows the absence of that fabled text to become a presence, yet another magnetic emptiness, in Greenspan's theater. A merely theoretical theory, it beckons as *The Argument* ends. Like the stage floor's unsolved X, it compels thinking. Perhaps, Greenspan suggests, comedy isn't that easily sequestered from other genres after all. Drawing again on Else's posthumously published work, Greenspan dwells on the ambivalence of Aristotle's teacher, Plato. The antitheatricalist's dialogues, he reminds us, are great theater, and one of them, *The Symposium,* concerns a tragedian who wrote a comedy "that will not stay in the comedic mode." This theory-spiting, taxonomy-snubbing play leads Greenspan's Aristotle to imagine a new form—"heretofore unknown . . . now comic, / now tragic"—that plays by genre's rules only until they forestall surprise, and inverts identities only until inversion itself becomes conventional. Even before Greenspan tells us that *The Symposium*'s remarkable flexibility about style (and anomalous sympathy for poets) dates from a period when Plato was in love with Dion (the Sicilian ruler's brother-in-law), we may have already concluded that this new, hybrid form of drama is tragedy queered.

"People . . . doing things," Aristotle writes in the *Poetics,* whittling down his definition of drama to its simplest form.[21] It is still maddeningly opaque for all that. Else renders the idea more heroically as "drama belongs to the doers."[22] How could it not? After the theatrical minimalists taught us to find valid dramatic action even in seemingly inert landscapes and bodies, it becomes hard to imagine *not* doing something onstage. Theater's sheer temporality ensures that, at the very least (as Clov puts it in *Endgame*) "something is taking its course." But if Beckett and others long ago animated stillness, there is still work to be done in animating action itself—in welcoming into drama an idea of "doing" that is heedless of purpose. The Aristotelian principle is so familiar it calls out for alienation.

By answering that call in *The Argument,* Greenspan nudges us toward the counterintuitive conclusion that all his plays are, in one sense, haunted by Aristotle. They don't, of course, obey his rules of narrative sequence, character construction, and audience manipulation: Greenspan violates those as unapologetically as do other experimentalists. But perhaps he achieves a more surprising experimentalism by attending to the primary theatrical condition—the actor submitting to time. We may have passed too quickly over the well-worn notion of plot as tragedy's "principle of motion." The radicalism of this deceptively basic idea becomes apparent only when we realize how unthinkingly we translate performances of continuous motion into static, linked pictures and self-contained vignettes—polished stones extracted from a production's perpetual current. How would our understanding of character, argument, and narrative have to change if we worked harder to retain our experience of a production's actual flux, its open-endedness, its ceaselessly mutating shape and irremediable instability?

Judith Butler's memorable appropriation of the language of the *Poetics*—"gender is always a doing"—is one sly way to demand a more flexible idea of action, and one with obvious pertinence to a reading of Greenspan's own subversive Aristotelianism (34). So, too, is Joseph Roach's embrace of "kinesis" as a more assertive alternative to mimesis, seized out of impatience with performance that contents itself with merely "imitated" action.[23] Roach has dance and dance-theater in mind as the forms most hospitable to this newly emboldened (rather than merely ornamental, illustrative, or otherwise dependent) kind of moving. But the seemingly more tradition-observant Gerald Else helps us see that it can flourish in drama, too, if we only look for it. Readers who delve deeper into his work will encounter, over and over, a kinetically inflected version of Aristotle and thus, by extension, of theater in general. "The important thing to remember," Else writes, is that the famous six elements are "stages in the art and process . . . of making tragedies rather than parts of *a* tragedy" itself.[24] When Aristotle refers to "plot," for example, he means the "drafting" of the plot; "character" refers to the "visualization" of character, and so on.[25] Here, in a move Greenspan would surely admire, Else shifts our attention from the lives onstage to the life seated at the desk—from the finished text to the uncertain labor of "making" it. If we assent to such a reading, we agree to forgo theater's special pleasure—immediacy—and instead see its action through the writer's obstructing presence. Such a play reverts from narrative and structural coherence, which is stable if perhaps inert, to incoherence, which is ungraspable but alive.

To spectators of Greenspan's adaptation of "Plays," this shift will recall no one more than Gertrude Stein. Indeed, the easiest way to make sense of Else's outlier version of the *Poetics* is to think of it as the work of a Steinian Aristotle. "My ultimate business as an artist was not with where the car goes," Stein once wrote, "but with the movement inside that is of the essence of its going."[26] Here and throughout her work, Stein insisted upon the same open-ended, unjustified idea of action—the writer's action, not the character's—that Else finds in Aristotle. All these ideas are more concrete, and more convincing, when applied in Greenspan's narratives. It's not only that, as we've seen, his many writer-characters prolong the agony of selecting words and fine-tuning sentences, fearing the end of revision more than its trials. (Only upon calling a work finished will they, like all artists, have to concede that it doesn't match their unrealistic aspirations for it.) A spectator can sense this same preference for the unknown over the known, and for insecurity over security, even when characters get up from the desk or have other outlets for their restlessness. It is the rare Greenspan play that doesn't claim as its own the principle of "people doing things" as the foundation of drama. Claim it—and insist on its most thorough fulfillment. In *The Myopia,* the Raconteur fondly recalls a production in which the stagehands were the only people "actually doing something." Whenever they changed the set, something was "actually" happening that was more expressive than the mere pretenses toward action in the "real" scenes. The Orator's doppelgänger matches this enthusiasm in her own tribute to Gertrude Stein's *What Happened,* a play comprised of the "happening" that mere stories fail to capture. After her speech, it seems that characters in every scene ring changes on the word "happen." (In this regard, it's telling that Greenspan's earliest, unpublished texts were written for choreographers.)

Greenspan declares his intentions most openly in the first exchange of *She Stoops to Comedy.* Composed of sentences that, in any other context, would be banal, its significance is easy to miss. "What're you doing?" Kay asks. "What am *I* doing?" her friend Alex answers from the privacy of her bathroom. "What're *you* doing?" Her next line, "I'm changing," tightens the link between doing and being—or, more precisely, between doing and becoming. Alex's later (and no less deceptively trivial) response to news that Kay has just arrived in New York from London—"how fast we move, the modern age"—confirms the high premium placed on flux, as do the rapid temporal shifts in this scene: one minute it's 1950, the next 1990, a moment later the characters are living in 1997. These jumps elaborate a concern of the play's prologue, spoken by Greenspan before he assumes the role of Alex. There he instructs us to think of the play's many synonyms for movement as metaphors for the artist's own productive restlessness. "The urge then to move across the words the page to paint a character on the stage. . . . This then to make through revision the stage a play of words moving its characters its plot its action." This rhapsody on theatrical kinesis is complete when, in a later scene, another character describes a playhouse whose purpose "keeps changing. It's been a million things."

These variations on the theme of motion will echo in a character's more intimate speech, when he or she trembles, aroused, with ambivalence even when capable of choice. In this world, choice doesn't signal action but ends it; the most animate characters keep their options open, entertaining more possibilities than they could ever execute. When, in *She Stoops to Comedy,* Simon and Alex find themselves alone in compromising circumstances, little happens but much is described. "How will it play out?" Simon asks, stepping out of the scene, and then sketches (but does not realize) the first of many scenarios. "That's one way it could go." Doing, here and elsewhere, is a telling. By refusing to choose a single path to follow, he succeeds in preserving the largest landscape of potential experience.

Enchanted by an open future, Simon is also reluctant to acknowledge the necessarily narrower dimensions of his past. Instead of telling Alex one authoritative story of how he met his partner, he floods the conversation with plots. "He goes to my gym, I met him online . . . he temps for my agent, we use the same laundry," and so on. Like many Greenspan characters, Simon is always aware that he is a manufactured being—that he is written, or being written, or even writing himself as the play unfolds. The same strategy, on a smaller scale, amplifies the presence of Kay Fein. Is she an archaeologist (as she was, we're told, in an earlier draft of the play) or a lighting designer (as she is at the final curtain)? Greenspan leaves the question unresolved until the last moment. It is another choice unmade as long as possible, preserving the writer's freedom against the less ample, more disappointing reality of embodied experience. Memorable as the characters unfailingly are, they won't let ordinary means of portraiture pull them into focus. They stand in the disheveling wind of contradictory emotions, allow obsessions to fracture them, smear under the pressure of time's passage. In this theater's grammar, the gerund contained within the notion of action—doing—greedily refuses to relinquish authority to the noun—the magnificent thing done.

Greenspan's equivocating also pushes back against a character's claims of self-knowledge, and by implication against an invasive spectator's desire to know everything about an onstage world and its inhabitants. "I'm not sure," Alex says when asked if Orlando knows that the cross-dressed Rosalind is a woman. "Or maybe he's not sure." Many scenes later, Alex cites another play where masquerade also loosens one's convictions. Did the wife in *The Guardsman* know her husband was in disguise? "There is this twinkle in her eye," says Alex. "But you're never quite sure what's behind that twinkle." The synonyms for uncertainty accumulate rapidly in *She Stoops to Comedy.* "I don't understand." "Don't ask me." "I can't remember." "I don't remember." "I'm bewildered." "I'm confused." "How the hell should I know?" In another kind of play, these confessions of ignorance would signal a crisis, but here they mark an opportunity—to be more engaged and alert; to sharpen the senses; to entertain unlikely, even outlandish, answers. (The passages recall *2 Samuel 11, Etc.,* which ends with the words "I don't know," and *Jack,* which includes a fugue on knowing "nothing.") These characters circle their own unsolved X. Their uncertainty, in this world, is a position of strength. When the questions stay open, there's more space for thinking. Lest we miss the point, Greenspan ends *She Stoops to Comedy* by gesturing to an invisible door and saying, "I'm going to leave it open . . . . [I]t's more interesting to leave it open."

"Leaving it open" as an approach to composition and performance—indeed, as a tenet of Greenspan's own poetics—is itself open to any number of interpretations, and the playwright nods to many of them as he moves from play to play, expanding the idea's usefulness as he does so. The earliest work collected here, *The HOME Show Pieces,* refers obliquely to it. Frank, someone as bewildered and unsure as the characters in *She Stoops to Comedy,* begins the last *HOME Show* piece by reading aloud from an unnamed book—one whose density may cause a spectator to tune out or, at best, to take Frank's effortful recitation as a sign of intellectual overreaching. If we realize (or discover) that Frank is reading Spinoza's *On The Improvement of Understanding,* the scene becomes startlingly resonant, attuning us to other scenes depicting the same process. Indeed, Frank's strain as he reads—stopping to parse a phrase or question a tautology, pushing and pulling at such sentences as "in order to know, there is no need to know that we know"—is very much the point. "Improvement" is the prize, distinct from and more valuable than mastery: it is ongoing, not over. To a playwright who treats intellectual impotence as fertile ground for theatrical creation, the process traced by Spinoza's title (and the equanimity tacitly recommended when "understanding" remains remote) will stand for all manner of development. Frank's attempt to sustain his concentration while reading, to carry on a phone conversation plagued by call-waiting, and to block out distraction while masturbating in the scene called "Doing the Beast" (a kind of "doing" Aristotle no doubt never imagined!)—along with his stop-and-start singing of "People Who Need People"—can be imagined now as savvy postponements of inevitably anticlimactic ends. The protagonist sinks into a comfortable continuous present and dedicates himself to pursuing a perpetually receding destination. He knows that arrival—and the catharsis it brings—will only prompt the questions "Now what? What do I do now?"

The desolation in those questions is something Greenspan addresses directly at the end of *The HOME Show Pieces* in a section called "The Big Tent." There, he finds further value in perpetual motion. After Frank quotes the Bible's merciless verdict on people who eat "that which is leavened"—they "shall be cut off from the congregation of Israel"—he sits down to dinner and accepts his boyfriend's offer of a piece of Italian bread; the lights go down as he bites into it. The two men breaking leavened bread together affirm one kinship even as they seemingly forfeit another. They voluntarily cut themselves off from a "congregation"—a network of cousins who "grew up near each other" and were "very, very close"—that may never have had a place for them after all. In the darkness following these last moments, we have unmarked space in which to realize that both biblical exile and present-day outsiderhood are as much opportunities as punishments. On the open landscape and in the constant movement of exile, those cast out are mercifully free from paralyzing norms. They can move gingerly toward new, still gestating, still usefully insecure modes of belonging. This play's ending—really a beginning—is among Greenspan's most beautifully calibrated.

If we're not already imagining other expressions of this dilating sensibility—the antidote to a mind that contracts around familiar prejudices—Greenspan's later plays nudge us toward them. After *The HOME Show Pieces* moves from the solitary man of the first piece to the domestic couple finally visible in the last, the process continues outward toward more broadly social and ultimately cosmological contexts. (It's only fitting that Greenspan's thinking about expansion itself expands.) *The Myopia* treats the political sphere as a Petri dish of darting schemers, oscillating enablers, and accelerating, colliding organisms of ambition. The insiders who run Harding for President "appear phantasmagorically, detected a moment, then, moving or stationary, quickly re-enveloped and invisible." Against such an inexorably moving machine no resistance is possible unless it, too, is kinetic: agile and mercurial. Harding is elected because he "didn't not want to be President enough"—the double negative proving that dissent requires as much motion as desire; that opting out demands engagement no less muscular than opting in. Without it, Harding spends his life "going nowhere." His destiny is foretold in one of his earliest scenes, when the young Warren can't get his mule to budge, and it is confirmed in his last, where he is "immobile, stymied in a painful wink." In Harding's case, it is as if the corruption he fostered while in office—and for which he set a standard still unrivaled—had encased and paralyzed him. (The marmoreal condition is matched by Koreen in her own last scene, when she turns "granitic.") The job of breaking apart this landscape, Greenspan implies, will fall to us. At the start of Act 4, he charges us to learn "moral mechanics" and "by changing ourselves, change this illusory world we temporarily inhabit."

In their acknowledgment of our ephemerality (and of the theater's, which helps us see it), these lines embrace a milieu larger than the political. It was envisioned first, and more fully, in *Dead Mother.* There, Greenspan valorized epic-scaled movement in fleeting references to the *Odyssey,* the metamorphoses of Thetis and Eurynome, and the journeys "in spiral fashion" through the *Inferno.* A deeper, secular consideration of the same principles begins to take shape when a dental hygienist in that play discourses on evolution while cleaning another character's teeth. Her lecture's rhythm models the irresistible momentum it describes. "Bacteria extending themselves promiscuously, recombining genes . . . regenerating quickly, replicating DNA—transforming its compositions . . . adjusting and expanding . . . either we'll evolve into another species, or we'll be extinguished. No thing is permanent . . . or fixed. It's shifting endlessly." When she interrupts her speech to say to her gaping, flagging patient, "don't close, stay open," we should easily hear the metaphorical implications of the dental request. And later, when a white whale swims onstage and says, "the dithyrambic goal of evolution's not refinement, darling, it's expansion," nothing should seem more natural.

Yet how far can this elastic universe expand without snapping? Or, more to the point, how far can Greenspan's stage do so? Can the playwright subscribe to the astronomer's faith in the universe's infinite dilation? Is theatrical space, despite its apparent borders, actually as unbounded as outer space? Is there a point where the Greenspanian ideal of openness, and of the churning, straining flux on which it depends, bumps up against common sense and must reconcile itself to the requirement of presence fundamental to theater? If one stops being able to see an ever-expanding mise-en-scène, or if one can't keep up with the blur of action, how (or at least how else) can performance reward our efforts of attention?

Greenspan might reply that all such worries are misdirected. His plays imply that we're *already* not seeing, or not seeing enough, even in theaters that obey convention. He addresses this deficit directly in *The Myopia,* of course. One character wears "thick bottle glasses." Another is "monoptic." A tower's only window is "like a single eye." We ourselves are enjoined to "look closely . . . now look again." In the play's obsession with visual impairment or mere laziness, one can sense a larger anxiety fully voiced at the end. If we agree with the Orator that "seeing [is] a way of learning," then we tacitly pledge ourselves to an Enlightenment cause, battling ignorance with ever more inclusive acts of attention. In Greenspan's utopian vision, our eyes should pursue the same "goal" of "expansion" that the hygienist in *Dead Mother* sees in evolution.

A similar moral, expressed in formalist terms, can be drawn from the many scenes in which Greenspan confines actors to chairs and beds, behind tables, or in bathrooms.[27] These varieties of Beckettian enclosure help focus a spectator's attention, to be sure, but they are more compelling for how they subvert it. The boxed-in performer casts into relief the surrounding space, helping us to perceive its vastness as if for the first time. No longer mere neutral territory, it is now charged with the allure of its inaccessibility. We can't look into Greenspan's rooms-within-rooms without wondering what they keep out. Even as the literal or figurative frames intensify our scrutiny of his all-but-immobilized performers, they refer us out to the frame around the stage. The water closets and armchairs cite the theater's own bordering walls. To the most restless of us, raking the stage with searchlight eyes, the entire building forms a boundary we yearn to transgress. We can never see enough.

This centrifugal mode of attention is implied in Greenspan's skepticism of a play's or character's interiority. Kept from probing a speaker's core, we are no more able to reach a spectacle's outermost banks. This is a theater of elsewhere, of secondary or referred spaces—a theater that thrives in zones perceived only with our peripheral vision. Look directly at the drama and it flees to edges further out. We've seen how actors in *The HOME Show Pieces* and *2 Samuel 11, Etc.* hand off their roles to others just when we may be getting possessive of them. A related logic determines narrative direction. The final stage direction in *Jack* tells us that "the speakers turn to their next page," but before they can say anything, the lights go out and the play is over.[28] Without a narrative ending, the story can unfold infinitely. Even simpler actions make the same point. Characters in *Principia, She Stoops to Comedy,* and *Go Back to Where You Are* (2011) step out of their personal dramas to look up—at birds, planes, the night sky, and the sun's transit. *Son of an Engineer* also fulfills Greenspan's dramaturgy of deflection. If it weren't enough that the action moves from "suburbia" in the first act to "Mars" in the second, the characters make sure we notice how inexorably Greenspan's theater is pushing toward, and then past, the borders of the tellable, actable, and showable. "There are a million worlds," a woman says to the play's protagonist, the so-called Killian Boy, perhaps meaning to jolt us out of our own myopic attention to the one onstage. Another woman, a scene later, sounds the same note. "We live under the stars," she says to the boy. "On a little ball rolling though space" (98). By the time Greenspan reaches the last scene, he trusts the sheer fact of time passing to swell up against the scene's inner walls, expanding the stage's volume and with it our awareness of how the characters themselves strain toward stages larger that the one we see. Now the Killian Boy seems finally to profit from the women's insight as, in the play's last minutes, he "looks out in all directions, surveys the horizons." It's as if Greenspan expects that a character who looks hard enough will be able to penetrate the theater's confining walls. "Time passes," writes Greenspan in a long stage direction, the scene's only text. "The vastness" (102). It presumably doesn't contract in deference to the blackout forcing an end to the performance.[29]

This recurrent tropism toward outer space and other horizons lends unexpected weight to otherwise fleeting allusions in Greenspan's theater. The reenactment of the *Inferno*'s descent in *Dead Mother* may bring to mind the famous last lines with which Dante marks his emergence from the poem's interior. "Through a round aperture I saw appear / Some of the beautiful things that Heaven bears, / Where we came forth, and once more saw the stars."[30] Can we think of the poem's "aperture" in terms of the theater's proscenium—both directing our attention past material lures toward worlds we'll never reach? Dante's upward trajectory anticipates the one that Gertrude Stein follows in the most beautiful passage in "Plays"—one that Greenspan slows down to savor in his performance of her lecture: "The light and air which any theater has, and a great deal of glitter in the light and a great deal of height in the air."[31] Both Dante and Stein return us to the third of Greenspan's three muses, Aristotle, whose decision to place "spectacle" last in his list of the six elements has always been hard to accept—the strongest challenge to spectatorial complacency. It makes more sense in the context of Greenspan's theater. The translation of "spectacle" used in *The Argument*—"visual adornment"—clarifies that what's really at stake are habits and priorities of seeing, targets also attractive to a contemporary playwright preoccupied by myopia. In staging the *Poetics* and, as we've seen, his other minimalist plays, Greenspan sides with the Aristotle who resists theatricality in order to save spectatorship. Spectacle, in this view, is a treacherously magnetic phenomenon, Medusa-like in its ability to transfix unsuspecting audiences, stopping us from looking anywhere else. (Like Harding in *The Myopia,* we too can be "immobile, stymied in a painful wink.") The spectacle detains us just when we should be most restless, jeopardizing the kinetics of attention (as important as the kinetics of dramatic action), limiting the eye's range instead of stimulating its appetite for as yet unstaged or even unimagined attractions.

This revaluing of spectacle brings us full circle, back to the Foundry Theatre production of *The Myopia,* where Greenspan's ambivalence over seeing is at its most pronounced. To be sure, he banishes spectacle as if to prove Aristotle right, but he also makes an exceedingly large claim upon us, magnifying his presence from his thronelike leather chair—a spectacle unto himself. The conflict over theatricality leads to one of Greenspan's most devious coups de théâtre—or rather, anti-coups, for its charge doesn't detonate until well after its threat seems to have passed. At the end of the production, he rushes from the stage as he speaks the last line, "E. O. P. End of piece. I thank you very much for your attendance"—an exit that, in its abruptness and haste, defeats the speech's efforts at a graceful conclusion. Sprung at last from the confining chair, he allows no gathering silence to put a period to his last moments onstage, to set him off against the ennobling background of a tour de force performance. Instead, he seems embarrassed, even harassed—performer turned prey. He showed the same flight-reflex after the first act. "He savors a moment his theatrical skills . . . satisfied with his craft," Greenspan said then about Henry Cabot Lodge, director of the back-room maneuvering we just witnessed—but soon afterward, as if to prevent his own "savoring," he rushed for the wings, announcing an intermission on the run. There as here, he could have chosen to exit in a blackout, but that convention would have lent unwonted ceremony to the scene, and thereby turned it into a picture—something static.

Even as Greenspan eludes us, he promises us other objects of desire. Like the many earlier modes of expansion in his theater, here, too, he gestures toward things not seen or spoken of, broadens his narrative and our sense of the world it represents, punctures the usually air-tight seal over the stage, and urges us to escape as well. That garage door upstage in the Foundry production doesn't lift, but its presence now seems less a threat than an opportunity. As Greenspan forcefully and elegantly leads the way up and out from the theater, he models that most implacable of performance styles: charismatic anti-charisma—a manner that compels more lasting interest by rejecting the tricks of the spellbinder.

NOTES

1. I am grateful to Michael Feingold for reminding me of this layout. See his "Editor's Note" to *Dead Mother* in *Grove New American Theater,* ed. Michael Feingold (New York: Grove Press, 1993), 300.

2. Tony Kushner, "Foreword: Notes Toward a Theater of the Fabulous," in *Staging Gay Lives: An Anthology of Contemporary Gay Theater,* ed. John M. Clum (Boulder, CO: Westview Press, 1996), vii–viii. Future page references appear parenthetically. Don Shewey, in "Tony Kushner's Sexy Ethics," writes that Kushner "proudly places himself and David Greenspan at the forefront of what he calls 'Theater of the Fabulous.'" *Village Voice,* April 20, 1993, 31–32.

3. David Greenspan, *Jack,* in *The Way We Live Now: American Plays and the AIDS Crisis,* ed. M. Elizabeth Osborn (New York: Theatre Communications Group, 1990), 159. Future page references appear parenthetically.

4. Samuel Beckett and Georges Duthuit, *Three Dialogues,* in *Samuel Beckett: A Collection of Critical Essays,* ed. Martin Esslin (Englewood Cliffs, NJ: Prentice-Hall, 1965), 17.

5. David Greenspan, *2 Samuel 11, Etc.* Plays in Process 11:5 (New York: Theatre Communications Group, 1990), 1–12. Future page references appear parenthetically.

6. Charles Dickens, letter to W. H. Wills, December 10–11, 1867, quoted in Malcolm Andrews, *Charles Dickens and His Performing Selves: Dickens and the Public Readings* (Oxford: Oxford University Press, 2006), 2.

7. David Savran, "Queer Theater and the Disarticulation of Identity," in *The Queerest Art: Essays on Lesbian and Gay Theater,* ed. Alisa Solomon and Framji Minwalla (New York: New York University Press, 2002), 161.

8. Michael Warner, *The Trouble with Normal: Sex, Politics, and the Ethics of Queer Life* (Cambridge: Harvard University Press, 2000), 180.

9. Molnár's *The Guardsman* inspired *She Stoops to Comedy.* Greenspan adapted Wilder's *The Bridge of San Luis Rey* as an as-yet-unproduced piece of music theater. Kaufman and Ferber's *Royal Family,* a play Greenspan acted in, is recalled in *Jonas* (2011). *Charley's Aunt,* according to Michael Feingold, is revived in *Dead Mother.*

10. D. A. Miller, *Jane Austen, or The Secret of Style* (Princeton: Princeton University Press, 2003), 84.

11. See, for example, Judith Butler's objections to "an interior 'truth' of dispositions" in *Gender Trouble: Feminism and the Subversion of Identity* (1990) (New York: Routledge, 2006), 46. Future page references appear parenthetically.

12. One may be tempted to read the phrase "inner play" as a deliberate echo of the subtitle to *Billy Budd*—"an inner narrative"—and therefore to wonder if Greenspan is taking distance from Melville's portrayal of wayward desire.

13. Eve Sedgwick, "Shame, Theatricality, and Queer Performativity: Henry James's *The Art of the Novel*" (1993), in *Gay Shame,* ed. David M. Halperin and Valerie Traub (Chicago: University of Chicago Press, 2009), 60.

14. Leo Bersani, *Homos* (Cambridge: Harvard University Press, 1995), 125.

15. See Leo Bersani, "Is the Rectum a Grave?" (1987) and "Aggression, Gay Shame, and Almodóvar's Art" (2002), in *Is the Rectum a Grave? and Other Essays*

(Chicago: University of Chicago Press, 2010), 30, 69; *Homos,* 94, 125; *A Future for Astyanax: Character and Desire in Literature* (Boston: Little, Brown, 1976), x; and *Intimacies* (with Adam Phillips) (Chicago: University of Chicago Press, 2008), 35. In *Intimacies,* Bersani recodes "ego-annihilation" as "ego-dissemination" (56).

16. David Greenspan, *Son of an Engineer* (Los Angeles: Sun and Moon Press, 1995), 6.

17. Ralph Waldo Emerson, "Nature" (1836), in *Selected Essays, Lectures and Poems,* ed. Robert D. Richardson, Jr. (New York: Bantam Books, 1990), 18.

18. Miller, *Jane Austen,* 59. Future page references appear parenthetically.

19. Aristotle, *Rhetoric,* in *On Poetry and Style,* ed. and trans. G. M. A. Grube (Indianapolis: Hackett, 1989), 77.

20. Gerald F. Else, *Plato and Aristotle on Poetry,* ed. Peter Burian (Chapel Hill: University of North Carolina Press, 1986), 111.

21. Aristotle, *Poetics,* ed. and trans. Gerald F. Else (Ann Arbor: University of Michigan Press, 1967), 19.

22. Else, *Plato and Aristotle on Poetry,* 85. In *Aristotle's Poetics: The Argument,* Else writes, "*we become what we do* . . . , our acts harden into character" (Cambridge: Harvard University Press, 1957), 70. Tellingly, Greenspan quotes only the first part of this sentence in *The Argument,* and thereby preserves the possibility of endless doing.

23. Joseph Roach, "Kinesis: The New Mimesis," *Theater* 40:1 (2010), 1–3.

24. Aristotle, *Poetics,* 89 n. 50.

25. Else, *Aristotle's Poetics,* 12, 280.

26. Gertrude Stein, "Portraits and Repetition," in *Lectures in America* (1935) (Boston: Beacon Press, 1985), 195. Also see Tom Sellar on "the process of change" in *The Myopia* and Marc Robinson on how "speaking itself . . . seem[s] kinetic" in Greenspan's early plays. Tom Sellar, "Near and Far: David Greenspan's Dramatic Vision," *Theater* 29:2 (1999), 57–59. Marc Robinson, *The Other American Drama* (New York: Cambridge University Press, 1994), 186–89.

27. Lee Edelman describes the innate theatricality of the doorless public bathroom stall—"a stage upon which the actor could always be subject to surveillance"—in *Homographesis: Essays in Gay Literary and Cultural History* (New York: Routledge, 1994), 265 n. 32. He also discusses the scenes of writing in a bathtub from the film *Laura*—an inevitable point of reference for the scenes of bathroom writing in Greenspan. See 205ff.

28. David Greenspan, *Jack,* 166. For a new edition of the play published by NoPassport Press (2011), Greenspan eliminated this stage direction.

29. Nick Salvato considers a related form of dilation—of time, not space—in his essay "A Horse's Husband: David Greenspan's Queer Temporalities and the Politics of Same-Sex Marriage," *Theatre Survey* 52:1 (2011), 7–28.

30. Dante Alighieri, *Inferno,* trans. Robert Pinsky (New York: Farrar, Straus and Giroux, 1994), 303.

31. Gertrude Stein, "Plays," in *Lectures in America,* 112.

The HOME Show Pieces

David Greenspan in "Portrait of the Artist" from *The HOME Show Pieces.* HOME for Contemporary Theatre and Art, New York, 1988. Photograph by Francisco Gonzalez.

The HOME Show Pieces

First produced by HOME for Contemporary Theatre and Art, New York City, from September 14 through October 1, 1988.

Doing the Beast

Character 1 David Greenspan

Too Much in the Sun

Character 3 Ron Bagden
Character 4 Kathleen Tolan

Portrait of the Artist

Character 1 David Greenspan
Character 2 Ron Bagden

The Big Tent

Character 1 Kathleen Tolan
Character 5 Ron Bagden
Character 2 Ron Bagden

Set Design by William Kennon
Lighting Design by David Bergstein
Directed by David Greenspan

The HOME Show Pieces was subsequently produced by Joseph Papp at the New York Shakespeare Festival / Public Theater, New York City, from January 1 through February 16, 1992.

The production credits were the same except for the following:

Tracey Ellis portrayed Character 4 in *Too Much in the Sun* and Character 1 in *The Big Tent.* Costumes were designed by Elsa Ward.

Synopsis

The HOME Show Pieces is a cycle of four short plays that chronicle a seven-year period in the history of their principal character. Each episode is located in a different area of "the house."

In the bedroom play, *Doing the Beast,* a man, masturbating in bed, is interrupted by a series of phone calls, all of which illuminate aspects of his puerile existence. The backyard play, *Too Much in the Sun,* is a satire in which two actors, preparing to appear in an "autobiographical work," deride and condemn the play's author for what they consider a disrespectful and unsympathetic portrait of his troubled family. In *Portrait of the Artist,* a little-known playwright sits on the toilet in the bathroom of his apartment, constructing fantasies of recognition and acclaim. The fourth play, *The Big Tent,* is located in the kitchen; in this episode, a phone conversation between the principal character and his elderly aunt links up three previously unrelated pieces, their events and characters.

Characters:

Character 1
Character 2, Character 1's lover
Character 3, an actor
Character 4, an actress
Character 5, Character 1's aunt

The same actor plays Character 1 in *Doing the Beast* and *Portrait of the Artist.* The actress playing Character 4 in *Too Much in the Sun* takes over the role of Character 1 in *The Big Tent.* A second actor plays Characters 2, 3, and 5.

Doing the Beast

[Light illuminates Character 1 getting into bed. His bed is a mattress and headboard on the floor. At the foot of his bed, right, a black rotary phone. Left of the bed, strewn on a chair, his day's clothing. He adjusts his pillows. He turns on a reading light. He picks up a book. He reads. He stops. Counts pages to end of chapter. Counts again. Reads again. Flips back one page—to refresh the memory. Turns page. Reads. He is having a difficult time concentrating—every time he readdresses himself to the book he drifts away from what he is reading. Again, counts pages to end of chapter. Drifts. Puts down book, turns over on his belly, and begins gently humping the mattress. After a while the phone rings. He stops humping, picks up.]

Character 1: Hello? Oh hi Aunt Ruth—how are you? No it's not too late. No, I go to bed late, you know, usually. No, I go to bed late. Yea. How are you? Yea. (?) I'm just doing some reading. A book. It's good. No, I've been fine—I've been—Oh no, I'm sorry, yea, I—no, I did get your call, yea, it was a busy weekend, and I had to work some—No, I worked an extra shift at the restaurant and then—it's fine, it's fine, it's fine . . . it's fine, you know, it's—you know. Right—In fact, I was planning on giving you a call today but—Right—I know. How are you? Oh you did, how are they? Un huh. Un huh. Oh really. Sounds good. No, I talked to them, when was it, last week, week before? I was—no, in fact it was, yes it was last week because they talked about—I was thinking of going out maybe this summer, you know, I have to see what work is like. Oh are you—when? Oh nice. Yea, weather will be nice out there then. Un huh. Un huh.

John? He's fine, he's fine. Yea, I saw him last night, in fact, we had dinner last night. He's fine, he's fine. Un huh. Un huh. Oh, I'll tell him. No, Lisa. Lisa. Her name is Lisa. Lisa, yea. He's been seeing her, I don't know, for—I don't know, a year now. I think they met—She's nice, you know, I mean, I haven't spent that much time with her. Right, John likes her. No, that was Kay. Kay. Kay. Kay, right, Kay. She lives in New Hampshire. Right. John was seeing her—well, they were seeing each other in college. Right, then Margie—Margie was his girlfriend before Lisa. Right. Kay then Margie then Lisa. Right, he mentioned her. I didn't really know her? I never knew her.

Un huh. Un huh. Sure, when is Passover? Oh really, it's soon. Yea. No, I'd love to come out. I'll ask him. Sure, I'm sure he'd love to if he can.

You know what I'll do is I'll give him a call sometime uh this week and see what's up for when is that? Un huh. Un huh. Un, I don't know. I can ask him—if she wants to come out too—sure. Yea, maybe the three of us will come out together. No, Lisa. Right, Lisa. Okay, maybe the three of us will come out—sounds good.

Yea—no—yea, I'd love to come out. Right. Well, I'll call you about—sometime later this week, how's that? Yea, let me talk to John first. Right, and Lisa. Okay. All right. Uh'm a little tired. All right. All right. All right, well thanks for calling. And I'll talk to you soon. Okay, give my love to them. Okay. Right. And thanks for calling. And I'll talk to you soon. Right. I won't. I will. Yep. Bye. Yep. Bye.

[He hangs up. Pause. He returns to humping the mattress. After a while the phone rings. He stops humping, picks up.]

Hello? Mary (!) hi hi hi hi. (*A Jewish accent.*) Darling, how are you? (*Accent off.*) I'm fine, how are you doing? (*Brings phone onto bed.*) Oh, yes? What's going on? Oh, right. Right. When do you leave? When do you—Yea. Yea. Are you excited? Are you excited? Yea. Yea. Yea, but I'm not—no, I'm not—I'm not sleeping. I'm not sleeping. I'm reading. Right. I like it, it's good. I was, then I put it down—this is like—this is like the third time I'm trying to get through it. Yea. I never get past the part where . . . you know where he reads his mother's letter? Right, near the beginning of the book. How are you? (*Moves himself and phone back toward headboard, ultimately leaning against headboard.*) I'm all right—I called because . . . yea, we had a big fight how do you know? How do . . . oh. No, it wasn't a big fight—it was just, you know, the usual thing. Maybe. In a way. We had dinner last night. We did see it first, we had dinner after. Horrible. It was horrible. Yes. Well, some of it was all right, it was just—I didn't like it, I never like his work anymore. Anyway, we had dinner after the movie and then, you know, we were supposed to spend the night together at my place. Right, this is last night. So we came back to my apartment and we went to bed and I wanted to make love and he just wasn't into it and I—no, I could sense that he like—it's like I'm doing everything and he's just like . . . limp and—right and so I said—I said—I said—I asked him if he, you know, if you—do you—are you tired and he said no but that we could make love in the morning and I said fine and then I—Yes, he's still seeing Lisa. I know. Margie? He hasn't seen Margie in—I don't know how long. She's in New Hampshire. No, that was Kay. Right, Kay. So, anyway, so I asked him—no, well I told him, you know, it was—it's very hard for me to—Yea, and then I asked if he'd rather be with Lisa tonight. No, this is last night, right. I asked him if he'd rather be with Lisa and—I don't know I just did 'cause I could sense that he didn't want to be there. He said yes. Naw, it didn't really bother me. I mean it made me angry, it hurt me, but, you know, because he really just wasn't there, you know. They see each other every—oh, I don't know, it varies—every other night, something like that. Well, we'll spend the night together once a week, twice a week at the most. So, I asked him if he'd rather get together tomorrow, you know, tomorrow night if he was tired and—but he and Lisa had tickets for some opera something tonight, so I said—I said how about—how about on Friday, we could get together on Friday night, and he's—no he's working on Friday night and—I don't know it just made me—no, so I told him we could see each other on Saturday or Sunday if—you know, it doesn't really matter to me, and that maybe it would be better if he just went home, that he didn't have to stay, you know, I mean I told him he didn't have to stay if he didn't want to, we could see each other on the weekend because—Yea, I mean I told him he might as well just go home since he didn't really want to be there. He didn't want to make love and I wasn't—I just—I mean it's very hard for me when he doesn't want to make love and so—so—(*Sudden laugh.*) so, anyway, so he said maybe that would be a good idea because he needed a good night's sleep, he had a big day today, today, and that he would call me tomorrow, today, and we could arrange some time for the weekend. Right, so he left, and then, you know, well, I started to get, you know, I mean I got angry because, you know, we were supposed to spend the night together, and this is what always happens and—what do you—what do you—what do you have another call? Do you have another call? Yea, I can hold. No, I can wait. Go ahead.

(*After holding.*) Hi. Yea, so I—Oh, really? Oh, hi to her. Hi, hi. Oh. All right, let me—let me—let me—let me—let me let you go. You have to go. You have to go. Okay, I'll hurry. Right. So, well, I was—right, I was angry and I called, and I told him I was angry, and he—well, he didn't say much, you know, he never says much—he said—well, he said he was tired, it was late, and I asked him if I could come over and spend the night, and he said—Well, he said he really wanted to get some sleep and I said, well, you know, we had agreed to spend the night together and—I—no, but he wasn't really there. Yea, so I—no, he said I could come over and that—but that he just wanted to sleep and he didn't want to make love. Right. So I asked if we could make love in the morning. Yea, go ahead, I can hold. I can hold.

(*After holding—longer.*) Oh come on. (*She's back.*) Hi. That's all right. I—right, I asked if we could make love in the morning and—He said he didn't know and that I shouldn't come over expecting that. I was, because we were supposed to spend the night together. I mean this always happens. I know. So, well, I didn't know if I should go over there or not, and he said it was up to me but that he felt we should just wait, you know, till the weekend. I know. So then—we—right, I mean I said—well, I didn't know if it's a good idea that we see each other anymore and he said—because—it's right and I said maybe we should think about not seeing each other anymore and—and we—well, we agreed to just wait—until the weekend—and we—we hung up and then I called him back a little while later, and I said I did want to come over, and that it didn't matter to me if we made love or not. That it didn't matter to me if we made love or not, and he said it was really late—I think it was like two in the morning at this point—and that he didn't want me to come over. He didn't want me to come over. He didn't. He didn't want me to come over, and that we should just get together on the weekend. Right. I know. But we had agreed to spend the night together! Yea. No, I went over anyway. Yea, I went over. No, we didn't 'cause he didn't—he didn't want to. Not in the morning either. I know and I—We didn't talk much in the morning. He got up—he was late, because—Yea, he got up—Late, and he was—Right, it was late. It was really—And then I said we could get together Saturday night maybe, and he said he'd call me today and talk about it. No, he didn't call. He wasn't home. No, I tried him at Lisa's but they already left for the opera. Yea, I can call there. She knows. She knows. Sure. So, that's how it stands. Oh, okay. Yea, I'm okay, I'm hanging in there. Okay, I won't keep you. Well, thanks for calling. Okay. Have a good time. I'll talk to you . . . you're getting back . . . when? Next week is—Fine, I want to see—Right, I really want to see that. Okay, good. Great. Have a wonderful time. And I'll talk to you then. Okay, thanks for calling. Okay, I love you too. Bye.

[He pushes down the button, the receiver still at his ear. Long pause, him staring blankly out. No. He hangs up. Replaces phone. He returns to humping the mattress. After a while the phone rings. He stops humping, picks up.]

Hello? This is he. Oh, right, hello. No, it's no problem. No. Right. Okay. Thursday is good. Okay. Two-thirty is good. And—right—and let me just grab my book, can—can you hold on a sec? (*He covers mouthpiece with his hand. Freeze. Uncovers mouthpiece. Speaks again to caller.*) Okay, go 'head; the address is . . . 413 West . . . right, and that's between . . . and . . . okay, great. 11th floor. 413 West. Yes. And you want to hear the same scene? The same scene. (?) The same scene. Okay. I'll see you then. Oh, thank you. No problem.

[He hangs up, returns to his humping. After a while the phone rings. He stops humping, picks up.]

Hello? (*A hang up.*) Oh, fuck you.

[He hangs up, returns to his humping. A moment later the phone rings. He stops humping, picks up.]

Hello? Hello? Uh, what number are you trying to call? I think you have the wrong number. No. No. That's all right. Bye.

[He hangs up, returns to his humping. Humps for a while. Hold. He is thinking. He rises. He gets out of bed. Moves to clothing. Fishes through his pants—careful. Retrieves scrap of paper. Looks at scrap. Gets back in bed. Straightens cover. Sets the phone in front of him, the book beside him. Meticulous. He ruminates. He dials.]

Hello, may I speak with Chris, please. Chris, this is Frank—we—we met the other day at—Right, how are you, did I wake you? Oh, I'm sorry—why don't I—can I call you tomorrow? Oh, how about—how about . . . how about on Thursday? Okay, or I'll try and get you in. Right, and you have my number? Un huh. Okay. No, it's okay, I can just—Right, I can just leave it on your machine if you're not home. I just called to say hi. And thank you for the other night. And to thank you for the other night. Okay, so I'll talk to you soon. Get a good night's sleep. Bye.

[He hangs up. Pause. He puts the scrap of paper in the book. Pause. He gets out of bed, fishes through his coat, retrieves a scrap of paper, returns to bed, picks up phone, dials.]

Hi, is this Rick? Rick, this is Frank—we met last week in front of—Right, with the bicycle. How are you doing? Did I wake you up? Oh, good. I'm fine, fine thanks. How about you? Oh, good. No, I got home fine, thanks. Yea, I enjoyed being with you. Un huh. Un huh. Un, yea, I just called to see, in fact, if you want to get together some time soon. I was thinking about seeing—Right, I mentioned that to you, right, it sounds interesting, doesn't it? Un huh. Un huh. I think it starts on Friday. Un huh. Un huh. Oh. Oh, that's great. Oh, really? No, I kind of had a suspicion. No problem. Well, maybe we can get together some time just to have dinner or something. Sure, I'd love to. Michael. Yea, or meet Michael, sure, I'd like to meet him. Okay, great. So why don't we just stay in touch. Okay. I'd love to. Oh, I will—one of these days. How long have you been seeing each other? I say how long have you two been seeing each other? Oh, really. That's great. That is so great. That is so great. Do you have another call? Do you have another call? Okay, so—Yea, I can hold.

[He places Rick's number in the book.]

Hi. Oh, okay then I won't keep you. Okay, talk to you soon. You have my number (?). Okay, you have a machine? Right. Okay, bye.

[He hangs up. Pause. He thinks. He considers the phone. No. He puts the phone to the left of the bed. He considers the book. He returns to humping. He humps. He orgasms. He lies there. Time passes. He rises. Checks himself. Pulls from behind the headboard a roll of toilet paper. Wipes himself. Wipes the bed. Returns toilet paper to behind the headboard. Sits down—feels the wet spot—pops up. Shifts himself and his pillows to the dry (left) side of the bed. Picks up book. Reads. Counts pages to end of chapter. Reads. Flips back one page—to refresh the memory. Turns the page. Reads. Suddenly.]

Yea, but if you didn't want to come over then why did we make plans? Yea, but we had agreed to spend the night together. Yea, but we had agreed to spend the night together. Yea, but we were supposed to spend the night together. Then why—yea, but you said you were tired and that we should get together on the weekend. But you said you were tired. But you said you were tired. But you said you were tired. Then why did you make plans to get together? But you said you were tired.

[Reads. Counts pages to end of chapter. Flips back one page. Turns to last page of book. Closes book, puts it down. Pause. Considers phone. Yes. Brings phone to him. Dials.]

Hi John, it's Frank—calling. It's about eleven-fifteen on Tuesday night. Hope you enjoyed the opera. Just called to say hi. I'll be up late tonight if you want to give me a call. Or I'll talk to you . . . I can talk to you tomorrow sometime, we can make plans for the weekend—we talked about that. Also, my Aunt Ruth called; I want to talk to you about going out for Passover. So, give me a call tonight or sometime tomorrow. Okay? Talk to you soon. Hope you enjoyed the opera. Bye.

[He hangs up. Pause. Puts phone off bed. Puts book off bed. Turns off reading light. Lies down on his back. Pause. Turns on his left side. Pause. Turns over on his belly. Pause. Adjusts his cover. He starts humping. Lights fade as he continues humping the mattress.]

Too Much in the Sun

[Light illuminates Character 3 and Character 4 sitting on lawn furniture. 3 in a chair, 4 on a lounge. Between them a low table. On the table, beverages, cigarettes, newspapers. 3 lights 4's cigarette. 3 does not smoke.]

Character 3: Now what were you saying?
Character 4: I was saying I don't like the piece that much.
Character 3: Which piece?
Character 4: This piece.
Character 3: This piece. (?) You don't like this piece. (?)
Character 4: No, I don't.
Character 3: Why not?
Character 4: It's very angry. It's a very angry piece.
Character 3: Yea.
Character 4: I mean, the way the author deals with his parents.
Character 3: Oh, yea.
Character 4: Not that there isn't, you know, cause—
Character 3: Right.
Character 4: For anger.
Character 3: Right.
Character 4: But there's no forgiveness.
Character 3: Right.
Character 4: I find no forgiveness.
Character 3: Well, there isn't any, none to find.
Character 4: So, I mean, I have a problem with the piece.
Character 3: Yea.
Character 4: I mean, I'm sure he had a difficult childhood and—
Character 3: Oh, so you think this is an autobiographical work?
Character 4: Oh yea.
Character 3: Oh, that's interesting.
Character 4: I mean, the whole way he depicts his mother.
Character 3: Oh yea.
Character 4: And I've worked on some of his other pieces.
Character 3: It's always the same. (?)
Character 4: Always. Very angry, dependent, violent mother figures.
Character 3: That's interesting.
Character 4: And I have a problem with that.
Character 3: Oh yea.
Character 4: I mean, as a woman I have a problem with that.
Character 3: See, this whole thing of forgiveness is interesting because—

Character 4: It's important to forgive.
Character 3: You've got to forgive.
Character 4: You've got to forgive and forget.
Character 3: Right.
Character 4: And not blame. You can't just blame somebody because you . . . well, you just can't.
Character 3: Sure.
Character 4: It's like the Jews who can't forget the Holocaust.
Character 3: Right.
Character 4: What's done is done.
Character 3: Sure.
Character 4: You've got to forget. (*Pause.*) And besides, I'm tired of playing angry, depressed women. I mean, those are the only parts he ever offers me.
Character 3: Oh, really?
Character 4: Yes! And I'm tired of talking to the dead.
Character 3: There's a lot of that in this play.
Character 4: There is in all of his work.
Character 3: Interesting.
Character 4: I mean, let the dead sleep.
Character 3: Sure.
Character 4: Let them rest.
Character 3: Sure, like my father.
Character 4: I'm tired of talking to the dead.
Character 3: I've had to learn to forgive my mother and father.
Character 4: You have to or you can't go on.
Character 3: Yea. I mean, A.A. has helped a lot with that.
Character 4: Oh, you're in A.A.
Character 3: Yea, I'll be sober two years a week from Tuesday.
Character 4: Oh, I didn't know that.
Character 3: Yea. But I really learned about forgiving my parents in Al Anon.
Character 4: Al Anon. What is Al Anon? I've heard of that.
Character 3: It's . . . it's a program . . . based on A.A. for people who become . . . inappropriately involved with alcoholics.
Character 4: You're like that.
Character 3: Yea, my boyfriend is an alcoholic.
Character 4: Oh, did you meet him at the A.A.?
Character 3: No, in S.A.
Character 4: S.A. (?)
Character 3: Sexaholics Anonymous.

Character 4: Sexaholic. And he's also an alcoholic?
Character 3: Recovering, recovering alcoholic, yea.
Character 4: Right. So you go the A.A., the S.A., and the . . .
Character 3: Al Anon. We both go to Al Anon.
Character 4: Al Anon, right. Wow.
Character 3: I also go to A.C.O.A., Adult Children of Alcoholics, I just started going to that.
Character 4: One of your parents was . . .
Character 3: My father and my mother.
Character 4: Oh, wow.
Character 3: Yea.
Character 4: Do your parents still drink?
Character 3: My mother is in A.A., my father is dead.
Character 4: Oh, that's good—your mother is in A.A.
Character 3: Oh yea, we go to meetings together.
Character 4: Oh, that must be nice.
Character 3: Oh yea, it's really great.
Character 4: That's wonderful.
Character 3: In fact, she's the one that suggested I check out Adult Children of Alcoholics.
Character 4: Really? Oh, wow.
Character 3: Yea, well she felt I must have a lot of anger—about my father and his drinking—and that I needed to get in touch with it.
Character 4: See, well that's the forgiveness I was talking about. I mean, do you think she's forgiven your father for his drinking?
Character 3: Oh sure. Well, it's hard to tell, you know, we really can't talk about him when she's around.
Character 4: (*With sympathy.*) Oh.
Character 3: She throws a fit.
Character 4: Sure. So you go to four of those . . . workshops.
Character 3: Unh . . . programs, yea. Actually, I go to five. Stuart and I go to Chapter Nine, Couples In Recovery.
Character 4: Couples In Recovery.
Character 3: Yea.
Character 4: Right. Yea, sometimes I worry about my pot smoking.
Character 3: You smoke pot?
Character 4: Unh . . . yea, sometimes—every once in a while—I like to smoke when I'm at home—alone—put on music, dance around the apartment. I mean, I can stop if I want to, I've stopped before. I like it.
Character 3: Maybe you need to check out a meeting.
Character 4: (*As she extinguishes her cigarette.*) I really don't have a problem

stopping. I mean, I do have a problem stopping, but, you know, it's not a problem.

[3 turns to the audience.]

Character 3: See, what happens in this piece—let me describe what goes on here because it's a little bit confusing. I mean—

[4 turns to the audience.]

Character 4: It's not that confusing, it's just not very interesting. I mean, what happens in this piece? Two characters sit in their backyard and . . . well . . . why don't . . . you were going to . . . why don't you tell them?
Character 3: Yea, all right, well, I mean, there's this man and this woman, and they're sitting out here in their backyard and—
Character 4: They're husband and wife.
Character 3: Right, they're husband and wife and—
Character 4: But—
Character 3: Yea, no, go ahead.
Character 4: I was just going to say, you learn in the course of the piece that the woman, that's me, is the man's second wife.
Character 3: And the man, that's me, is the woman's second husband.
Character 4: Right, the man's first wife died. And—
Character 3: And—
Character 4: Yea, go ahead.
Character 3: Yea, and the woman divorced her first husband.
Character 4: Right. Go ahead.
Character 3: So they're husband and wife and—
Character 4: And, oh, and before, before when we were talking, over here, a minute ago, that was us, not the characters, that was just us, him and me.
Character 3: Right.
Character 4: Didn't have anything to do with the play. So . . . Where were we?
Character 3: Unh . . . they're husband and wife.
Character 4: Right, and—
Character 3: And—
Character 4: And—and it's the man's birthday, he's turning seventy. Him, his character, he's turning seventy.
Character 3: Right. And they're sitting out here in their backyard, the man is reading the newspaper. They're both reading the newspaper.
Character 4: This is why we have all this newspaper out here.

Character 3: Right, props. And it's Thanksgiving—the man's birthday happens to fall on Thanksgiving.

Character 4: Right. And it takes place in California.

Character 3: In Los Angeles.

Character 4: That's why they can sit out in their backyard in November.

Character 3: You . . . What?

Character 4: What?

Character 3: You can sit out in your backyard? . . . in November? . . . in California?

Character 4: Sure.

Character 3: I didn't know that.

Character 4: Yea.

Character 3: Wow.

Character 4: And anyway, basically, the play just outlines the kind of dismal state of their marriage and the lives of their children.

Character 3: Not all the children. Well, they mention all the children. But the play focuses on the son from the man's first marriage who . . . well, he's in the Navy.

Character 4: He's in the Navy. And you learn that they're considering separating.

Character 3: The man and his wife are considering separating.

Character 4: Right.

Character 3: Right, they've been married about, what, fifteen years?

Character 4: Closer to twenty.

Character 3: Twenty, twenty years. And they're thinking of separating because, well, it's hard to tell what the problem is.

Character 4: They're just having problems.

Character 3: They can't agree.

Character 4: They're not communicating.

Character 3: And the husband, that's me, he says "Well I'm sorry it worked out this way."

Character 4: Can you believe that, that he'd say that, after fifteen years of marriage?!

Character 3: Twenty. Yea.

Character 4: I mean that's what he says. He's very detached. Isn't he?

Character 3: Oh yea.

Character 4: But the thrust, the resonant issue of this play, is about the son who is in the Navy.

Character 3: Right, the son, George. And you learn in the course of the piece that—supposedly—the way he was brought up by his parents, his mother, his father.

Character 4: The mother, the man's first wife who died.

Character 3: Right, that between her physically and emotionally abusing him—she completely rejected him—and his father treating him, I don't know, like an infant his entire life, that he just isn't able to cope with life like an adult.

Character 4: He's really fucked up!

Character 3: His girlfriend left him, he had a nervous breakdown, he went into a mental hospital—

Character 4: Right, well—

Character 3: But—

Character 4: What? Go on—

Character 3: Yea, I was just going to say an important point is that when George was born his mother first developed this—

Character 4: Right.

Character 3: What?

Character 4: No, I'm sorry, go on.

Character 3: Yea, I was saying that when George was born his mother was diagnosed with this, um, well, it's not specified in the text what exactly she was ill with.

Character 4: It was some—some life-threatening illness.

Character 3: Could be cancer, we don't know. But her diagnosis coincided with George's birth, and the woman—

Character 4: The first wife, not me.

Character 3: Right, always associated his birth with her getting sick.

Character 4: Right and—

Character 3: And blamed him for it. Blamed him for—

Character 4: Right, and—well, this is what the playwright is trying to say—basically—and this is—you know, this is where I have a real problem with the piece, because who knows, you know, why this son—

Character 3: George.

Character 4: Right, George—and this is based on the playwright's brother, by the way, you know—who knows why he turned out this way—he might have been born this way for all anyone knows. I mean, I've met the playwright's father—he's a lovely man.

Character 3: Is he?

Character 4: Oh yes. He fixed my car. When I was in California I spent a day out at their house, he spent the entire day under my car, looking at—

Character 3: Really?

Character 4: Yes. And the mother, the woman, the first wife that died, I mean that must have been, I mean, there's no sympathy—I don't think there's any sympathy for how much she must have suffered.

Character 3: Right.

Character 4: I mean her life was miserable—stuck in a marriage she never wanted—her parents pushed her into marriage—to a man she didn't care for who she ultimately became totally dependent on. Children she never wanted—she wanted girls, she got boys—denied an education—I mean—

Character 3: Right, he makes her out to be this monster.

Character 4: Right—

Character 3: Right, it's—

Character 4: And the father, where's some understanding about what he—

Character 3: Right—

Character 4: About what he must have gone through, this father, trying to raise children on his own, working all day, coming home, making dinner. Everything. This is what I was talking about earlier about the anger of the piece!

Character 3: And the attack, the way he attacks his father!

Character 4: He calls his father evil.

Character 3: Can you believe that, calling your own father evil?

Character 4: I would slit my throat before I called my father evil.

Character 3: Sure.

Character 4: And my father was a real son of a bitch.

Character 3: Me too.

Character 4: I can't even talk about my father. I mean yes, it's sad, the son turned out this way, unable to take care of himself, unable to . . . to . . . to function as an adult, but still to—

Character 3: Right.

Character 4: To attack your own . . . I mean whose parents were perfect? Were your parents perfect? My parents weren't . . . no one's parents were perfect.

Character 3: Right.

Character 4: It's something you have to accept.

Character 3: Right.

Character 4: And take responsibility for yourself.

Character 3: Responsibility for yourself—this is like, this is like Al Anon!

Character 4: Think about Chekhov! Think about Chekhov!

Character 3: Right.

Character 4: I mean, so understanding of . . . of . . . of—

Character 3: Exactly.

Character 4: Of whatever, you know. There are no monsters.

Character 3: Right.

Character 4: There are no monsters! There are none!

Character 3: You have a good point, it's true, I mean, who knows, is it that much of a science that anyone knows this is why someone turns out what . . . defected? I mean does anyone really know anything? I mean my mother was. . . . well, people said she was . . . you know, nervous . . . overprotective—but you know, it's hard to say.

Character 4: The same was true with my father. He was very abusive, spiteful, selfish, but, you know, you forgive.

Character 3: Right.

Character 4: And forget.

Character 3: Right.

Character 4: Like the Jews who can't forget the Holocaust.

Character 3: Exactly.

Character 4: Forget it already.

Character 3: Yea, you—

Character 4: Just let go.

Character 3: Right.

Character 4: It's over, forget it.

Character 3: "Let Go, let God!"

Character 4: Yea. (???)

Character 3: Anyway, so the play is kind of a history of this marriage and the two marriages that preceded it. Talks a bit about the man, the first man, the woman, you, was married to—he was—

Character 4: Very disturbed.

Character 3: Right.

Character 4: And also they make the point that the man, the man in the play, the part that you play, always got himself involved with women who were like fifteen years younger than himself. I don't know what that—

Character 3: Right, and about the woman's, the second wife, you, her mother, who's still in—she's like 96 years old in a convalescent home and how spiteful she is and bad-tempered.

Character 4: And how the woman, me, does not want to move away from her.

Character 3: The woman, the wife, you, right, doesn't want to move away from her 96-year-old mother. Even though she treats her horribly—the 96-year-old mother treats the woman horribly.

Character 4: Right, and her father we learn about the woman's, me, my father who was always giving into his wife.

Character 3: The 96-year-old woman.

Character 4: And how I, me, my character idolizes her father and . . . I don't know, it's all kind of cerebral stuff but very angry.

Character 3: So anyway they talk and talk and talk—it's kind of like *Virginia Woolf—Who's Afraid of Virginia Woolf?*—but without any of the drinking or yelling and—

Character 4: And the great language.

Character 3: Right.

Character 4: I mean I love that play. The language.

Character 3: Yea.

Character 4: I'd love to play that part some day.

Character 3: Right.

Character 4: Whatever. Doesn't have the poetry of *Who's Afraid of Virginia Woolf?* I mean that play is poetry. This is very, I don't know, pedestrian.

Character 3: And then at the end of the play the phone rings.

Character 4: No, first the wife, that's me, goes off to—you see they reach this . . . stalemate.

Character 3: An impasse.

Character 4: An impasse, yes, and there's nothing else to say—the woman has begged, she literally begs the husband, you, to see a—some kind of therapist with her, and—

Character 3: And—

Character 4: And he refuses.

Character 3: Right.

Character 4: So, the woman goes off to check the oven, she has a turkey in the oven because—

Character 3: It's Thanksgiving.

Character 4: (*Pause.*) Well, it's also the husband's birthday.

Character 3: That's right.

Character 4: And they're having guests over to celebrate her husband's birthday.

Character 3: Right. And Thanksgiving.

Character 4: (*Pause.*) Why do you keep saying that?

Character 3: What?

Character 4: That it's Thanksgiving.

Character 3: Because it is.

Character 4: Yea, but more importantly it's your character's birthday.

Character 3: Well, Thanksgiving is important too.

Character 4: (*Pause.*) Never mind.

Character 3: What?

Character 4: You keep doing that.

Character 3: What?

Character 4: Forget it. Where was I?

Character 3: You were going into the kitchen.

Character 4: Right. So she goes into the house to check on the turkey . . . You always have to say something to undermine me! You did this all throughout the rehearsals! And while she's in the house the phone rings.

Character 3: Right, and just as the phone rings—I'm sorry. (!) The man, that's me, I've already fallen asleep on . . . this—(*Kicks lounge.*) whatever this thing out here is—and—well—that is—I've fallen asleep before she goes in.

Character 4: Right, she tells him "Honey, I'm going in to . . ." Oh shit, what is it?

Character 3: What?

Character 4: "I'm going in to check the oven." Is that the line?

Character 3: Yea. Right. And I don't answer because I'm asleep. And she goes in.

Character 4: She's totally fed up.

Character 3: And then the phone rings.

Character 4: And then I answer and it's George, the son in the Navy whose life is totally fucked up. He's calling from overseas to wish his father a happy birthday, and I talk to him for a little bit, then I call out to my husband to come in to the phone because, I say "Honey, it's George on the phone. Honey." And . . . well . . . Why don't we just do this part for them. We'll do this part for you.

Character 3: And she comes back on stage and I go in and talk to George, my son.

Character 4: Yea, I mean it's kind of a weird ending. A weird piece.

Character 3: And a lot of the play is about the son in the Navy.

Character 4: That's why it's called *Too Much in the Sun.*

Character 3: It's a quote from *Hamlet.* "Not so my lord. I am too much in the sun." There's a pun on the word son, sun, son—something like that.

Character 4: Well, also because . . . well, whatever. So, I think we only have time for the end of the piece.

Character 3: It'll give you an idea what the piece is like. I mean, we've told you what happens.

Character 4: Nothing really happens.

Character 3: Nothing happens, it's just talk. Very talky, very talky play. So, we'll just do the end of the piece where I answer the phone.

Character 4: The rest is . . . You can just read it some time.

Character 3: Right. So we're going to need some lights for this in a minute. Okay, thank you.
Character 4: So, I'm—Where do you want to take it from?
Character 3: How about "There's nothing else to say."
Character 4: Yea, but then there's a long pause which we don't need to do. Let's take it from me going in to check the turkey.
Character 3: Okay.

[The actors clear the stage of their personal effects and get into position on the set.]

Character 4: Did you know that the playwright's brother—the person that George is based on—did you know he's getting married in September?
Character 3: He's getting married? I thought he was like really screwed up.
Character 4: He is.
Character 3: Where did he find someone to get married to?
Character 4: I don't know. I think she teaches parochial school. Something like that.
Character 3: Wow. Well, if it's meant to be, it's meant to be. I mean, it's hard to say, you know, marriage, being a father, might really snap him into shape.
Character 4: It might, it—
Character 3: I mean, I had a cousin, Harry, and when he was like six or seven, he was this complete terror, you know—he would get sent home from school—things like that—
Character 4: Right.
Character 3: And now he's married you know, and I mean, you should see him with his children, you couldn't find a better father.
Character 4: Really?
Character 3: So, I mean, it's hard to tell.
Character 4: Yea. (*Pause.*) Are you ready?
Character 3: Yea.

[Hold. Light changes. The actors perform the final moments of Too Much in the Sun. *Husband sleeps on lounge, wife sits in chair.]*

Character 4: Honey, I'm going in to check the oven, Honey. Honey. Honey. Oh, forget it.

[Wife exits. Husband lies like a corpse, sleeping in the sun. Time passes. A phone rings off stage.]

Hello? George! Hi, how are you? Where are you? Ooooh!! Is it nice? Is it nice? No, I can hear you fine. I can hear you. We're fine, honey, let me get your father. Honey, it's George. Honey, do you want to come in and talk to George? George hold on—how are you, honey? Yea, how is everything? Un huh. Un huh. George, I think your father fell asleep in the backyard—let me—yea, we were sitting in the backyard. Yea. Let me go get him for you. Okay. You're all right? Are you all right? Are you having a nice Thanksgiving? Good. Are you having turkey? Well, that's close enough. Let me get your father.

[Wife enters, wearing an apron, wielding a cooking fork.]

Honey, get up it's George on the phone.
Character 3: Oh. Right. Oh, yea.
Character 4: Hurry, he's long distance.

[Husband exits.]

Character 3: (*As he exits.*) Do you want to get on the other line?
Character 4: No, you talk to him—he called to wish you happy birthday.

[Wife straightens up papers and sits down in lawn chair, listening to the conversation. Like Niobe—she begins to cry during the following speech.]

Character 3: Hi, George, hi, how are you? Thank you, thank you very much, Happy Birthday, yea, it's my birthday. We're fine, fine, everything is fine. No—no, we're just sitting out there reading the paper. Yea, how are you? I say, we're just reading the paper. Yea, you're having Thanksgiving or something? Are you having Thanksgiving? Yea. (*Yawning.*) Yea. Yea. You having turkey? No, unh . . . the Nickelmans, we're having over. The Nickelmans are coming. Right. Martha and—Right. So how are you? What have you been up to? Oh, good. That sounds good. That sounds good.

[Lights begin to fade slowly.]

Very good. Very good. Very good. Very good. Very good.

[Lights are out.]

Portrait of the Artist

[From the dark, a man's voice.]

Character 1: Well, her early albums I liked quite a lot—I haven't cared for much of what she's done, last fifteen, twenty years. Yea.

[Light illuminates Character 1, left, seated on the toilet, his pants at his ankles, the Sunday paper spread at his feet. Left of the toilet, a window through which sunlight pours in. Up, slightly right of the toilet, a door—shut. A cat litter pan placed just right of the toilet, a plunger placed just left.]

Un huh. Un huh. Well, I think that's a question . . . Un huh, right. Well, I think that's a question . . . Un huh. Well, I think that's a question more for you than for me. I mean, why am I not better known. I mean, I've—for instance—I've sent you press releases and information about my work for—for years now—look how long it took you to come down and see my work. Un huh. Un huh. Well, I think it's—I think . . . Right, well, I think it's a complex . . . Right, well, I think it's complex, you know. Right, well . . . Right, well, I think it's complex, you know. Right, well, being . . . you know, being well known, you know, being famous, whatever, has never been that important to me. I mean—

[Knocks on the bathroom door. From the other side a man's voice, Character 2.]

Character 2: Good morning, sweetheart.
Character 1: Hi.
Character 2: Did (*yawn*)—did you feed the cats this morning?
Character 1: The cats? No, not yet.
Character 2: You want me to feed them?
Character 1: Unhhh yea, would you?
Character 2: What?
Character 1: Yea, feed them. Feed them. But don't give them too much okay? Just a spoonful or so. Okay?
Character 2: Okay.
Character 1: (*Pause.*) How'd you sleep last night?
Character 2: What?
Character 1: How did you sleep?
Character 2: Okay. (*Pause.*) Have you had breakfast yet?

Character 1: Unhhh no.
Character 2: Are you going to have breakfast?
Character 1: Yea.
Character 2: What do you want to eat?
Character 1: I don't know, cereal?
Character 2: Do we have enough milk?
Character 1: What?
Character 2: Do we have enough milk?
Character 1: I don't know, y'look in the fridge.

[Pause. He reads the paper. In all his reading, he never gets far enough to turn the page. Time passes. He speaks.]

Right, well, being famous has never been that important to me. I mean, I'm not trying to encourage . . . isolation and . . . I'm not trying . . . I mean I'm not trying to encourage obscurity or isolation but, but—

[Knocks on the door. 2's voice.]

Character 2: Sweetheart, I'm going to run out and get some milk.
Character 1: What?
Character 2: I'm going to go out and get some milk.
Character 1: We don't have any milk?
Character 2: I didn't see any.
Character 1: I thought we had some. (*Pause.*) What?
Character 2: I didn't say anything.
Character 1: Did you look carefully?
Character 2: What?
Character 1: Look behind the apple cider.
Character 2: All right, hold on.
Character 1: (*He holds.*) Un huh. Un huh. Well, I think all art is autobiographical—on one level or another—I mean, look at Paul Klee—I mean all those—

[From another room, 2's voice.]

Character 2: Sweetheart—there isn't any.
Character 1: What?
Character 2: There isn't any milk.
Character 1: Okay.

Character 2: I'm going to run to the store—I want to get some orange juice, anyway.
Character 1: What do you want to get? What do you want to get?
Character 2: Some orange juice, I want to get some orange juice.
Character 1: We don't need orange juice—we—why do we need—why do we need orange juice? We have apple cider.
Character 2: I don't like apple cider—it's too sweet.
Character 1: It's not too sweet.
Character 2: I don't like it. (*Pause.*) By the way, what are your plans for the day—did you want to do something?
Character 1: Unhhh yea. I want to get some work done today, but, yea—we can do something.
Character 2: It's such a nice day out—be great to spend it outdoors.
Character 1: Yea, okay. Do you want to go into the city?
Character 2: Unhhh, I don't know, we could do that.
Character 1: Okay. Well, let's think about it. We could see a movie in town.
Character 2: Un huh.
Character 1: What?
Character 2: I said un huh—we could do that. It's just such a nice day out, though, I hate to spend it indoors.
Character 1: All right, well, what do you want to do?
Character 2: I don't know—we could see a movie.
Character 1: Do you want to do that?
Character 2: I don't know—yea.
Character 1: Is there anything particular you want to see?
Character 2: Unhhh not really. How about you?
Character 1: Nnnno, not really.
Character 2: All right, well we can look in the paper.
Character 1: Okay. (*Pause.*) Or we could just go to the park, you—
Character 2: What?
Character 1: I say we could just go to park, you know, and just read. You know, whatever.
Character 2: All right, well let's look in the paper.
Character 1: It doesn't matter to me—whatever you want to do is fine.
Character 2: Okay.
Character 1: (*Pause.*) Oh, did you feed the cats?
Character 2: Yea.
Character 1: What?
Character 2: I can't hear you.

Character 1: Did you feed the cats?
Character 2: Yes.
Character 1: Oh, okay. You didn't give them too much, I hope. Did you? (*No answer.*) What? (*No answer.*)

[He looks down at the paper. Time passes. He looks up.]

Hello, hi. I loved it. I just loved it. Oh, well, thank you, thank you, thank you, thank you, thank you very much. I loved it. It was wonderful. I really, really loved it. Oh, well, thank you, thank you, thank you. Hi, how are you? It was incredible—I just . . . Well, thanks—I'm glad you enjoyed it. Hi, how are you? You were just incredible. Well, thank you, thank you—I'm glad you could make it. Thank you. Un huh. Un huh. (*Throws his head back in a silent triumphant laugh.*) I know. Yea. Un huh. Well, good—I'm glad you could ma—I'm glad you enjoyed it. This is my husband, David Mamet. Oh, hello, nice to meet you. Well, thank you. Thank you, thank you—thank you very much.

[He looks down at the paper, then right up.]

I've never really been that concerned with critics. I don't have time for critics. I've never really been that concerned with . . . I've never—I never concerned myself with critics. Un huh. Un huh. Well, look how long it took me to get a review. Well, look how long it took me—Well, look how long it took me to get a review. Well, it's interesting, and I think indicative, because years before he dismissed the very same work as arch and portentous. Right, well, it's—it's interesting, and I think . . . It's interesting, because . . . It's interesting . . . I think it's interesting, and I think indicative, and to a certain degree . . . It's interesting, because—because . . . It's interesting because years before . . . Years before he dismissed . . . It's interesting, because years before he dismissed the very same piece . . . He dismissed the very same work years before . . . It's interesting, because years before he dismissed the very same piece as I think . . . I think he used the word . . . I think he used the words . . . I think he described the work . . . I think he described the work as being arch and portentous. Well, I think—in fact, years before a particular critic—whose name I won't mention—Well, it's interesting, and I think indicative, because years before he dismissed the very same work as arch and portentous. It's interesting, and I think—

[He looks out the window. Speaks.]

Hi. Hi. (*Makes a little noise with his tongue.*) Hi. Where'd you get that nut? Where'd you get that nut? Yes, you—where'd you get that nut? (*Another little noise.*) Hi.

[Looks away from the window.]

Un huh. Un huh. Why do you ask? Yea, but why do you ask that question? Well, personally, I don't care for her as a critic—I never have. In fact, I think beneath that thin veneer of leftist, feminist politics, she's simply—she's terrible. I think she's worse than he is. In fact, I never bother reading either of them. (*Looks out the window.*) It's interesting, and I think indicative . . . It's interesting, and I think worth noting. I mean you ask—you ask me why I don't—It's interesting, and I think worth noting. I mean you ask me why I don't read reviews—the very same material . . . The very same critic . . . The very same material that he labeled—that he's labeled—that he referred to . . . It's interesting, and I think worth noting—

[Knocks. 2's voice.]

Character 2: Sweetheart I'm running out to get the milk now.
Character 1: Okay.
Character 2: Is there anything else we need?
Character 1: (*Looking at the cat litter pan.*) Unhhh . . . Oh, we could use some kitty litter.
Character 2: Okay. And—
Character 1: Oh—
Character 2: What?
Character 1: Can—
Character 2: What?
Character 1: Can—can you buy some bananas—for the cereal?
Character 2: Okay. Anything else?
Character 1: Unhhh . . . No, that's all I can think of?
Character 2: What?
Character 1: That's all I can think of.
Character 2: Okay. I'm going to get the paper too.
Character 1: No, don't, I already got it.
Character 2: You have the paper?
Character 1: Yea, I'm reading it—I have it in here with me.
Character 2: Did you go out this morning already?
Character 1: Yea.

Character 2: What time did you get up?
Character 1: I don't know, about seven-thirty.
Character 2: Sweetheart, you never get enough sleep!
Character 1: I'm fine.

[Phone rings.]

Character 2: Do you want me to get that?
Character 1: Yea, would you? (*Pause.*) I mean, I think it's interesting and worth noting . . . I mean I think . . .

[First offstage conversation begins.]*

I mean you ask me why I don't read reviews. This same critic that labeled . . . The same critic that labeled . . . This same critic that labels . . . that labeled . . . It's interesting, and I think worth noting that the same critic—this same critic labeled this same . . . Right, well the same material that he labeled . . . that he—Right, well the same material that he labeled significant and important writing, he dismissed years before—I mean, I think it's interesting—I think it's interesting—I think it's—I think it's worth noting—I think it's worth noting—you ask me why I don't read reviews—

[2's voice.]

Character 2: Sweetheart, it's Tom on the phone.
Character 1: Oh. Okay.
Character 2: Do you want me to have him call you back?
Character 1: Yea—or tell him—tell him I'll call him back in about ten, fifteen minutes. Okay?
Character 2: Okay.
Character 1: About fifteen, twenty minutes, okay? (*Pause.*) I think it's worth noting that the same critic . . . This same critic that—I think it's

*Character 2's conversation with Tom:

Hello. Hi Tom, how are you? Pretty well, pretty well, thanks. How about you? Un huh. Un huh. Right. Unhhh, yes he is; he is, yea—he's unh, hold on one second; he's in the bathroom; hold on, let me see . . . No, hold on a second.

Hi Tom, can he call you back in about fifteen minutes? Okay. All right, talk to you soon. Okay, bye.

worth noting that this same critic—See, it's interesting and I think worth . . . (*Calling to 2.*) What? What?

[Nothing. He looks out the window. Time passes. Knocks.]

Character 2: Sweetheart, I'll be right back.
Character 1: Okay.
Character 2: I told Tom you'd call him back in about fifteen minutes.
Character 1: Okay, thanks.
Character 2: By the way, what was that package you got the other day?
Character 1: What?
Character 2: The package you got yesterday. Didn't you—
Character 1: A package. Yea. Yesterday.
Character 2: Right.
Character 1: It was just a script being returned.
Character 2: What?
Character 1: A script. A script was returned.
Character 2: Oh. (*Pause.*) From where?
Character 1: (*As his bowel movement begins.*) Unhhh, a theater in Seattle.
Character 2: Oh. It was a rejection?
Character 1: (*As his bowels move.*) Yea.
Character 2: What?
Character 1: (*Still moving.*) Nothing. Yes, it was a rejection.
Character 2: Oh.
Character 1: (*Still moving.*) Second this week.
Character 2: What?
Character 1: (*Done moving.*) Second one this week.
Character 2: Oh.
Character 1: (*Pause.*) What?
Character 2: Nothing.
Character 1: Okay.
Character 2: All right, so I'll be back in a couple minutes.
Character 1: Okay.

[Time passes. Alone in the house.]

No, I don't. No I don't. No, I've never. No. You see, if I thought for a minute these organizations, these . . . You see, if I thought for a moment that these organizations were interested in my addressing the complexity of the given issue . . . No, I don't . . . No. I mean . . . I don't think a given organization requests my serving as a spokesman, or an honorary host—a figurehead—whatever, because of a belief or an interest in my addressing the complexity of the given issue—these requests are made because I'm a celebrity. In that sense—and in that sense it's slightly . . . and in that sense it's extremely exploitive. I've never . . . No, I've never. Well, I've never felt comfortable in that role.

Yes, but I don't aspire to that. I don't aspire to . . . Yes, but I don't aspire to that. Right, well he's always expressed his intention of maintaining a popular theater. I don't aspire to that kind of popularity. What do you mean? I mean, why, if I say I don't . . . I mean why . . . I mean, what about my saying I don't aspire to being popular suggests to you a desire on my part to be unpopular. I think there's an attitude in this—

[Phone rings. An answering machine picks up. 1's voice: "You've reached 471-2464. Please leave a message." A woman's voice is recorded: "Hi Guys, this is Janet calling. Just called to say hi. I'll talk to you later. Bye." Even before her message is complete, 1 speaks.]

Being famous has never really been that important to me. I mean, being famous has never really been that important to me.

Thank you, thank you very much—I'm glad you enjoyed it. Thank you. Thank you. I'm glad you enjoyed it. Well, thank you, I'm very flattered. I've been an admirer of yours for . . . Thank you—I've admired your work for some time.

I first met Beckett in 1988. He saw a work of mine that was . . . He saw a work of mine I was performing in London—I think he was there directing a revival of *Play*. Right. Well, he was very . . .

Thank you very much, I—Thank you very much.

So it was . . . I first met Beckett, this was in the Spring of '89—of 1990. I was performing a new work of mine in London. He was there directing a revival of *Play* at the National Theatre, and I think it was Harold Pinter who had heard from someone—I've forgotten who—about what I was doing, and he and Beckett came, and they were very complimentary, and . . . He was always very cordial. He was always very cordial. He was always very cordial. He was always very cordial . . .

I really don't consider myself a . . . Well, what do you mean by a gay playwright?

[2's voice.]

Character 2: Hi, I'm back.
Character 1: Okay.
Character 2: How much longer are you going to be in there?
Character 1: I'll be right out.
Character 2: Okay, 'cause I want to take a shower before breakfast.
Character 1: Okay, I'll be out in a minute. (*Pause.*) Thank you very much—I'm glad you enjoyed it. Well, when I was younger, being . . . Well, when I was younger, being celebrated, gaining some recognition—it was an attempt on my part . . . it was an attempt, I think—I think it was an attempt on my part . . . I think it was . . . When I was younger, being famous, being recognized—which I wasn't, by the way, very successful at—it was an attempt on my part—I think it was an attempt on my part to meet some inner need that was being . . . that hadn't been met. I mean the yearning I had, at that time, to be famous, to be a celebrity, to feel accepted . . . I think to the degree that I've accepted myself, I no longer crave or yearn for that kind of, you know, recognition. So, though I still have those pangs of . . . Oh sure. Sure. Sure. Oh, sure. I think—I thinkIthink I've always wanted to be famous. Oh sure, well I think I've always wanted to be famous. Well, I think I've always wanted to be famous. I've always wanted to be famous. I think there's a part of me that's always wanted to be famous. I think there's a part of me that's always wanted to be famous. I think the more I've been able to meet my needs in reality, however, the less fantasy . . . I don't have a great need to be famous. I've never had a great need to be famous. Being well known, being a celebrity has never been that important to me.

[Hold. 1 reaches behind, grabbing the roll of toilet paper at rest on top of the toilet, wipes himself, looks behind at the soiled paper, dropping it into the toilet. Hold. He begins to sing, in a delicate falsetto, imitating the voice of Barbra Streisand.]

"People, people who need people . . . People, people who need people, are the luckie . . . People, people who need people, are the luckiest people in the world. We're children, needing other children . . . "

[Knocks on the door. 2's voice.]

Character 2: Sweetheart.
Character 1: (*Pulling more toilet paper.*) Yea?
Character 2: Did someone call?
Character 1: Oh yea, Janet called.
Character 2: What did she want?
Character 1: I don't know, listen to the tape.

[As he wipes he begins to sing again, while in the room the tape of Janet's call is played.]

"People peo . . . People . . . (*Drops the paper in the toilet.*) We've travelled single-o; maybe we're lucky, but I don't know. With them just let one kid fall down and seven mothers faint. I guess we're both happy, but maybe we ain't. People, people who need people, are the luckiest people in the world. People—We're children, needing other children, and yet letting a grown-up pride hide all the need inside, acting more like children than children. Lovers . . . Lovers . . . Lov . . . Lovers are very special . . . Lovers are very special people. They're th—"

[Knocks. 2's voice.]

Character 2: Sweetheart.
Character 1: (*Pulling more paper, wiping, dropping paper in toilet when wiped.*) Yea, I'll be right—
Character 2: Would you—
Character 1: What?
Character 2: Would you—would you want to get together with Janet and Bruce tonight? I was thinking we could get together with Janet and Bruce tonight.
Character 1: With Janet and Bruce? Unhhh . . . yea, all right.
Character 2: I was thinking we maybe we could see a movie with them tonight. (*Pause.*) What?
Character 1: Okay.
Character 2: You said you'd wanted to see a movie.
Character 1: Un huh.
Character 2: Would that be okay with you? Or did you want to spend the evening alone together?
Character 1: No, that'd be good.

Character 2: Are you sure?
Character 1: Yea, that'd be fine. (*He drops paper in toilet.*)
Character 2: Okay. I mean, we don't have to get together with them.
Character 1: Un huh. Well—well, what do you want to do? Do you want to see them?
Character 2: Unhhh yea, I guess so.
Character 1: All right, so why don't we do that.
Character 2: Okay. Okay, then I'm going to give them a call now. Okay?
Character 1: Yea, okay. (*Pause.*) "Lovers are very special people; they're the luckiest people . . . they're . . .

[Second offstage conversation begins.]*

Lovers are very special people; they're the luckiest people in the world. With one person, one very special person; a feeling deep in your soul says you are half now you're whole. No more hunger and thirst, but first be a person who needs people. People who need . . . First be a person who needs people. People who need people are the—"

[2's voice.]

Character 2: Okay. Sweetheart—Sweetheart, that's good with them.
Character 1: (*Pulling more paper, wiping, dropping paper in the toilet when wiped.*) Okay. Did you talk to them?
Character 2: Yea, I talked to Janet; she's going to call us back in about a half hour so we can settle on where to meet and at what time.
Character 1: Did they want to see a movie?
Character 2: Yea.
Character 1: Okay.
Character 2: This is okay with you, getting together with them?
Character 1: Uh uh, yea.

---

*Character 2's conversation with Janet:

Hi Janet, it's . . . hi. No, I went out to the store for a minute. No, he's in the bathroom. Yea. I'm pretty well. Yea, a little bit. It's coming along. Yea. Yea. Listen, we were wondering if you—if you and Bruce would like to get together tonight. We were thinking of seeing a movie. Yea, we could have dinner—or we were thinking of seeing a movie. Right. Yea, or both—sure. Un huh. Un huh. Okay. Sure. We'll be here. Okay. Okay. All right, so—yea—you . . . all right, well we'll talk to you then. Okay. Okay, bye.

Character 2: (*Pause.*) Are you coming out soon? I need to take a shower.
Character 1: I'll be right out. (*Pause.*) "First be a person who needs people. People who need people are the luckiest—"

[Voice of 2.]

Character 2: You know, (*knocking*) maybe we can meet them downtown for Ethiopian food.
Character 1: What? (*He pulls more toilet paper.*)
Character 2: I'm saying, maybe we can meet them downtown—take them to that Ethiopian restaurant we went to.
Character 1: Ethiopian? Un huh, okay, that's a good idea. I'll be right out. (*Pause.*) "No more hunger and thirst. But first . . . No more hunger and thirst. But first be (*He stands as he continues singing, bending over slightly to wipe himself.*) a person who needs people. People who need people are the luckiest people in—"

[He drops soiled paper in toilet and flushes. Nothing happens. He flushes again. Again nothing.]

Oh shit. Shit. Sweetheart! Sweetheart!! What? Uhgch . . . Sweetheart did—
Character 2: What's the matter?
Character 1: Did you—what happened to the toilet?
Character 2: What's the matter?
Character 1: It's stopped up.
Character 2: I don't know. (*Pause.*) Is anything happening? (*Pause.*) Maybe it—
Character 1: Never mind. I'm sorry. Forget it . . . it's okay.
Character 2: Maybe you just need to pull that lever in the tank.
Character 1: Okay, thanks, all right, I'm all right—I'll figure it out. I'll be right out.

[He straightens himself out a bit, buttons his pants, etc. He takes the plunger from beside the toilet and plunges. Nothing. He lifts off the top of the toilet tank.]

Goddamn it.

[He jiggles a little the mechanism in the tank. Nothing. Again. He sings.]

"First be a person who needs people. People who need . . . First be a person who needs people. People who need . . . First be a person . . . First be a person who needs . . . First be a person who needs people. People who need people are the luckiest people in the world."

[Hold. Knocks. He turns to the door. Lights out.]

The Big Tent

[The Kitchen. Center, a table with four chairs. Right of table a stove top. Up right of table a sink. Left of table a refrigerator. On the stove, a large pot—a soup put on by Character 1—a kettle, a ladle, and wooden spoon for the soup, and two soup bowls warming near the pot. The vessels should not contain real liquid or food. The appliances need not be anything more than skeletal. Down left of the table, resting on a low table, the phone used by 1 in Doing the Beast. *Down right of table, at rest on a kitchen stool, a cordless phone. Light illuminates 1. He is played by the actress who played Character 4 in* Too Much in the Sun. *He is sitting at the table, a book open before him, a tea cup beside him. He reads aloud from the book.]*

Character 1: "A true idea—I shall take care not only to demonstrate what I have just advanced, but also that we have hitherto proceeded rightly, and other things needful to be known. A true idea (for we possess a true idea) is something different from its correlate; thus a circle is different from the idea of a circle . . . a circle is different from the idea of a circle. The idea of a circle is not something having a circumference and a center, as a circle has. Nor is the idea of a body that body itself. Now, as it is something different from its correlate, it is capable of being understood through itself. For instance, the man Peter is something real."

[1 looks up toward the pot, hold, then looks back to book.]

"The man Peter is something real. The true idea of Peter is the reality of Peter represented subjectively, and is in itself something real, and quite distinct from the actual Peter. (*Hold.*) For instance, the man Peter is something real. The true idea of Peter is the reality of Peter represented subjectively, and is in itself something real, and quite distinct from the actual Peter." Okay. "Now, as this true idea of Peter—

[Enter Character 5, played by the actor who played Character 3 in Too Much in the Sun *and Character 2 in* Portrait of the Artist. *She is carrying a tea cup, identical to the one beside 1. She moves to the stove—to stir the soup.]*

—is in itself something real, and has its own individual existence, it will also be capable of being understood—that is, of being the subject of another idea, which will contain by representation all that the idea of Peter contains actually. This is the same as saying that, in order to know, there is no need to know that we know, much less to know that we know that we know."

[5 halts.]

Character 5: You know, I think I'm gonna call Frank.
Character 1: (*Lifts his head.*) Wait. (*5 holds.*) " . . . all that the idea of Peter contains . . . "
Character 5: Should I call Frank? I'm gonna call Frank.
Character 1: Okay.

[5 moves to the stool, picks up the phone, pulls out its antenna, presses the buttons.]

Character 1: "Thus, as the truth needs no sign, it follows that the true method does not consist in seeking for the signs of truth after the acquisition of the idea, but that the true method teaches us the order in which we should seek for truth itself . . . , or the . . . "

[Phone rings.]

Oh, I get it. Kind of. Wait. " . . . but that the true method . . . " Wait.

[He picks up the phone stage left.]

Hello?
Character 5: Hi Frank.
Character 1: Oh hi—Aunt Ruth—how are you?
Character 5: Have I called at a good time?
Character 1: Unhhh shhhure, sure.
Character 5: You're sure.
Character 1: Yea.
Character 5: Yes?
Character 1: Yea, no—yea.
Character 5: Because I wouldn't want to disturb you.
Character 1: No, it's fine.
Character 5: I know you get very busy.
Character 1: No, no, no, no, no, no—no; it's a perfect time.

Well, the piece is too long. Of course it's too long.

[All ***bold*** *printing is spoken by 1, and is unheard by 5 or 2.]*

Character 5: You're sure?
Character 1: Yea, I'm just doing some reading.
Character 5: Oh . . . What are you reading?
Character 1: A book.
Character 5: Oh, are you enjoying it?
Character 1: It's good—yea, yea, yea—how are you doing?
Character 5: Happy Passover.
Character 1: Oh right, yea, thanks, same to you.
Character 5: So how are you?
Character 1: I'm pretty good, pretty good, pretty good.
Character 5: That's good. It's been such a long time since I've seen you.
Character 1: I know, right.
Character 5: You must be very busy.
Character 1: Ahhhh. . . . a little.
Character 5: (*Pause.*) Have you been—have you spoken with your parents lately?
Character 1: Unhh . . . no, not . . . No.
Character 5: Oh.
Character 1: (*Pause.*) How about you?
Character 5: Yes, I spoke with them on Sunday night—they called.
Character 1: Un huh.
Character 5: Wait, was it Sunday night? Saturday or (?)—Saturday or Sunday night. I tell you Frank, I think I'm getting old. But yes, yes—

Character 1:	Character 5:
Un huh. Yea?	I did talk to them.

Character 1: Good, good.
Character 5: Yes. So tell me what you've been doing—I know you're always keeping very busy.
Character 1: **So tell me, what have you . . . So tell me . . . . . . what have you been doing? So tell me, what have you been . . . So tell me what have you been doing? . . . what you've been doing. . . . what you've been doing. So tell me what you've been doing. So tell me what you've been doing—I know you're always keeping very busy. I know you're always keeping very busy. I know you're always keeping . . . I know you're always very busy. I know you're always keeping busy. I know you're always keeping so busy. So busy? Very**

busy. So busy. Very busy. Very busy. I know you're always keeping very busy.

Character 5: So tell me what you've been doing—I know you're always keeping very busy.

Character 1: Oh . . . I'm working on a new piece—some new writing, and . . . I'm doing—preparing some grant applications, working at the restaurant.

Character 5: The same place you were working at?

Character 1: **No, I haven't spoken with my father for months. I think—like I think it's been like nine months.**

Yea, place on 18th . . . at the restaurant. But unhh . . . Yea, that's about it.

Character 5: And you say you're working on some . . .

Character 1: Some writing, yea, right, for a new piece.

Character 5: This will be performed some place in the city?

Character 1: Unhh yea. Yea.

Character 5: Oh, I would love to see it. Frank, will there be any performances during the day? A matinee?

Character 1: Ummm . . . I don't think so. No.

Character 2: Oh. Because you know it's difficult for me to come into the city at night.

Character 1: Yea . . . Don't . . . You know . . . that's fine. (*Pause.*) But—

Character 5: Because you know I'd love to be there.

Character 1: Yea, yea. (*Pause.*) But anyway this . . . is a new piece—and . . . I'm enjoying writing it. Ummm . . . So—

Character 5: Oh, well very good.

Character 1: Yea.

Character 5: (*Pause.*) Frank, do you see John any more? Have—

<table>
<tr><td>Character 1:
John? What?</td><td>Character 5:
You—you</td></tr>
</table>

Character 1: I haven't—I haven't seen John forrr years—it's like four or—

Character 5: Oh.

<table>
<tr><td>Character 1:
Yea—or four or—What? Sorry?</td><td>Character 5:
Oh, I—thought maybe—No.
What were you—</td></tr>
</table>

Character 1: Yea. Five—maybe five . . . years. I've—I've run into him on the street a couple of times, but no, we don't—I don't—w—d'—IIII don't get together with him . . . at all.
Character 5: Oh.
Character 1: So . . .
Character 5: No, I was just wondering. I was thinking today about when you brought John out for Passover.
Character 1: Oh yea, right.
Character 5: It was Passover, wasn't it? Yom Kippur or Passover?

Character 1:	Character 5:
I thi—	Passover. It was Passover.

Character 1: Right.
Character 5: With John.
Character 1: Right. Right.
Character 5: Because Dottie is coming.
Character 1: Oh.
Character 5: You remember Dottie.
Character 1: Yea.
Character 5: From upstairs?
Character 1: Right.
Character 5: Dottie.
Character 1: Dottie, yea.
Character 5: Well, she's coming down for supper—
Character 1: Un huh—
Character 5: Oh and Frank—Frank you have to see this supper we're having—there's so much food! I wish you could be here. There's a chicken . . . and—by the way, are you still a vegetarian?
Character 1: Yes. Yes. Yes.
Character 5: (*With disappointment.*) Oh, because I'm making a beef brisket.
Character 1: (*With disappointment.*) Oh.
Character 5: Anyway, Dottie was asking about you.
Character 1: **Hi, John, this is Frank calling. It's 11:15.**
Character 5: Wasn't that sweet?
Character 1: Un huh.
Character 5: I told her you're keeping very busy.
Character 1: Right, right.
Character 5: Because she remembers you from when you came out with John.

Character 1: Un huh.
Character 5: I'm telling you Frank, people remember you.
Character 1: That's great.
Character 5: But you don't see John anymore (?).
Character 1: No. No. No. No.
Character 5: You remember Dottie, don't you?
Character 1: Oh yes, yes.
Character 5: Her husband is blind and deaf.

Character 1:	Character 5:
That's right. What? Oh yea.	Oscar. Oscar. Oscar.

Character 1: Right.
Character 5: She's such a nice lady.
Character 1: I remember that, yea.
Character 5: Her daughter is married to a man . . . they live in Italy—he's from Italy.
Character 1: Oh yea, that's right—I think I remember that.
Character 5: I can't remember what he does for a living, but they have two darling little daughters.
Character 1: I think—you—yea—right.
Character 5: What are their names . . . ?
Character 1: **Kay. Kay. Kay, right, Kay. No, that was Lisa. Margie. No, then Lisa. Yea. He's fine. He's fine. Yea, I saw him last night, in fact—we had dinner together last night.**
Character 5: You know, I can't remember their names.
Character 1: That's okay.
Character 5: They're—next time they come out for a visit from Italy you'll have to come out—they're so sweet.
Character 1: Un huh. Okay. (*Pause.*) So—
Character 5: Yes. And Andrew—how is Andrew doing?
Character 1: Andrew, he's fine.
Character 5: What was that?
Character 1: He's fine, he's fine—fine, yea.
Character 5: Is he working?
Character 1: Yea. Oh yea. He's working . . . today, in fact. In fact, he should be home pretty soon—I'm expecting him.
Character 5: I'm sorry you both couldn't make it out tonight.
Character 1: Yea, I know—we are too.
Character 5: Because it would have been so nice to see the two of you.
Character 1: I know.

I know—because—well—Aunt Ruth was our favorite—I mean we just . . . adored—adored Aunt Ruth. Whenever my mother was ill—well, she was always ill—but whenever she went into the hospital—for surgery or whatever—Aunt Ruth would come out to take care of us—help my father take care of us. She would take us Steven and I to Marineland . . . Disneyland—stuff like that. Ruth is my father's older sister.

And when my mother died in '68—she moved out to California to live near us—help my father take care of us. She was living with her mother, at the time, Grandma Anna, who I think she had moved back in with after her marriage to Lou, unhh, ended. And then my father took us away that summer—summer after my mother died—we drove across the country visiting relatives. And then when we returned, weeks later . . . Grandma Anna had died. Then Aunt Ruth moved back to New York and started living with my great Aunt Helen until . . . maybe until she married . . . Irv. Yea.

Yea, we would've loved to, but, you know, we'll get out soon—it's kind of—

Character 5: You're always welcome—you know that—whenever you two have the time I'd love to see you. I know you're both very busy.

Character 1: It's hard with schedules—I know we'd both love to. Andrew—

Character 5: Is Andrew working? Oh, I asked you that. Where is he working?

Character 1: He's working at a restaurant ummm in the garment district called—

Character 5: Oh right. He's working there for a while, isn't he?

Character 1: Unhh yea, for . . . I'm not sure how long—about—

Character 5: Wasn't he working at some other place for a little while?

Character 1: Yea, yea, oh yea—

Character 5: In . . . downtown someplace.

Character 1: Right, that was—

Character 5: Because—

Character 1: Right—

Character 5: A Mexican kind of—

Character 1: Well, it was really a . . . kind of a Tex-Mex kind of place.

Character 5: That's right.

Character 1: And he's really—he's painting a lot—doing some really—beautiful painting, really—which is . . . you know—

Character 5: That's so nice. Have you been in touch with your brother at all?

Character 1: Unhhh no, I haven't . . . No, unhhh . . .

Character 5: (*Pause.*) Because I think when I spoke with him last he said he had written you a letter.

Character 1: Yea, right. I really . . . no, I just haven't . . . unhh—

Character 5: Might be nice to write him a letter.

Character 1: Yea, well—

Character 5: Because, you know, I think Maggie is a little—I think—I don't think she understands why . . . well—I shouldn't get involved—you know, why you didn't come to the wedding.

Character 1: (*Pause.*) Right.

Character 5: (*Pause.*) I think she'd like to be acknowledged. (*Silence.*) Her family—her brother was there—I just—I think just a card to acknowledge—you know, the marriage.

Character 1: Yea.

Character 5: She's a lovely girl. She really—I think she's very good for Steven.

Character 1: Un huh.

Character 5: I think—did—didn't Steven send you a picture of the two of them? Of he and Maggie?

Character 1: Yes, he did. He did.

Character 5: She's a very attractive girl, isn't she?

Character 1: Oh yea, yes, very . . . In fact—in fact, she's reminds me of my mo—

Character 5: I think she's very good for Steven.

Character 1: Un huh.

Character 5: I think she's a little spoiled . . . but—

Character 1: What?

Character 5: I think—I say, I think she's a little spoiled, you know, but—

Character 1: **Dear Frank We've been thinking about you last June Anne said she tried to reach you about Joanna who spent five weeks in bed with us and then ended up with painful back surgery after all we assumed you were away sometimes it is hard to reach you probably with your various commitments you are just not at home we do hope all is well with you your life in acting is not easy I just hope when not working you get unemployment compensation. Being in the arts can be precarious. Your brother Steven got married but it seemed apart from us—we never—as we never knew him we feel a sadness about this—we remember the years we sent gifts and never heard a word from him you on the other hand—**

(you on the other hand) remained attentive I think you knew us better—we—well we are paying attention to the marriage with a gift and truly wish them happiness perhaps at a future time we will know him better. Please let us know how you are doing. Joanna—gets—goes to New York from time to time her address is 103 Inman Street, Cambridge, Mass. 02149, phone 617-547-5780. On March 30th Aaron has an opening at the David Beitzel Gallery in Soho we'll try to get an announcement to you we would certainly love to see you with much—

Character 5: She teaches at a parochial—at a parochial school of some kind. Did you know that?

Character 1: Yes—I think Steven, excuse me, Steven . . . I think Steven mentioned that.

Character 5: I think he's even been attending some of the services at her church—which is, you know . . . well.

Character 1: Yea.

Character 5: What can you do? (*Pause.*) Have you spoken with Alan and Barbara lately?

Character 1: No, not—no, not lately, not for a while.

Character 5: Because didn't—your parents, I think, mentioned something about . . . Joanna—had some kind of surgery.

Character 1: Oh right, yea.

Character 5: Back surgery.

Character 1: That's right.

Character 5: On her back.

Character 1: Yea, yea.

Character 5: You don't know how she is. (?)

Character 1: No, I really haven't been in contact with them for a while.

I haven't really been . . . I really haven't been . . . I haven't really been . . . I really haven't been . . .

I haven't—really haven't been in contact with them for a while.

Character 5: Oh, because, you used to speak with them quite regularly.

Character 1: What?

Character 5: I thought you spoke to them regularly.

Character 1: Nnnot really, no. Just a letter—letters every once in a while.

Character 5: For some reason I thought you were in touch with them.

Character 1: No.

Character 5: (*Pause.*) So what else?

Character 1: Unhhh . . . let's see, I guess that's about it. Ummm . . .
Character 5: Frank, can I ask you something?
Character 1: Sure.
Character 5: I know it's none of my business—so you'll excuse me for being nosy?
Character 1: Okay.
Character 5: Do you mind?
Character 1: No.
Character 5: Okay, because . . . Oh, by the way, how has your health been?
Character 1: My health? Uhhh fine, very good, very—
Character 5: You're feeling pretty healthy (?).
Character 1: Oh yea.
Character 5: Good.

[Pause. As this section proceeds, Ruth grows tearful.]

Frank, did something happen between you and your father?
Character 1: (*Pause.*) Um—
Character 5: Because . . .
Character 1: Yea?
Character 5: Well, Tobey mentioned there had been some kind of—misunderstanding between the two of you.

Character 1:	Character 5:
Un huh (*Pause.*) Well—	Did some—What?

Character 1: No, sorry, you were . . . what were you . . . what were you going to say?
Character 5: I was just wondering. I know your father is very upset about whatever happened.
Character 1: Right.
Character 5: (*Pause.*) You know, Frank,
Character 1: **I'm so tired of you trying to make me feel guilty. I say I'm tired of your trying to make me feel guilty. Oh, look Dad—**
Character 5: I probably shouldn't get involved, but I want to tell you something.
Character 1: **Yea, well I don't give a fuck what Albert Einstein said. I said I don't give a fuck what Albert Einstein said!**
Character 5: I want to tell you something. Do you mind?
Character 1: No.

No, Irv was Aunt Ruth's second husband. Her first husband was Lou. And Lou was a gambler. He liked to play the horses. This was the reason that—that was the reason that Ruth ultimately divorced—divorced him, you know. He was throwing all their money away at the track.

> **he was throwing all their money away—throwing their money away—throwing away their money throwing away all—all their money—all of their money**

He was throwing away all of their money at the track. She divorced Irv because . . .

Character 5: Do you think you could call him to try to work things out? I just hate—I tell you, Frank, I just hate to see this thing—

Character 1: **This thing—this kind of thing—this kind of a thing go on. Do you know what I mean? Yea. Everyone has misunderstandings.**

Character 5: Do you know what I mean?

Character 1: Yea.

Character 5: Everyone has misunderstandings.

Character 1: No, I know, I know. I just don't—I don't—

I don't think you trust us. The bedroom piece—everybody knew that piece was too long. We told you it was too long. We told you to cut it after the orgasm. I told you that twice. Tom Bradham said the same thing. Barry Kaplan, too, thought it was too long. I mean, how long does it take before you trust us? Other people come in here, and we feel we can respond to their work, that they'll—and that they'll consider our point of view. With you we feel there's a wall up. A what? A wall up. You know, which we don't understand. It isn't as though we have no experience. Sure. It goes back to what we said at the beginning of this discussion: how do you see us?

Character 5: Frank, okay, I think we have very different points of view about this kind of thing. For whatever it's worth, I think you should call your father and try to work things out with him.

Character 1: Yea, I—

Character 5: Try to—excuse me—try to help him understand, Frank. I don't—I don't think—I think he's frustrated—because you—

Character 1: Yea, well, I mean, I appreciate, you know, your . . . you know, your expressing your point of view, but I have . . . I don't have any interest in remaining—

Character 5: Also, you know, he fell off his bicycle, your father.

Character 1: What?

Character 5: He was riding his bicycle with Jasmine, and I think she stopped suddenly—or she pulled at the leash—something—and your father fell off the bike.

Character 1: Un huh.

Character 5: It's nothing serious. But I know he was hobbling around for a few days.

Character 1: Yea. How's the dog; is the dog all right?

Character 5: Jasmine? I think she—

Character 1: **" . . . demonstrates a supple and witty mind at work, but its resistance to making concessions for the audience can be more frustrating than gratifying, and it's difficult to locate—avoid locating the author's purest motive in his last line: 'Never forget me.' "**

Character 5: Have I upset you by what I've said.

Character 1: No. No. (*Pause.*) No.

Character 5: You're sure?

Character 1: Yea.

Character 5: Okay. So what else should I know?

Character 1: Well, let's see—

The worst, of course the worst—absolute—is that when after the eleventh, twelfth (maybe) time today I've masturbated, and nothing is coming out at all now of the dried-up penis my practically swollen it's sore or cut on occasion a small cut from rubbing so often I notice a small stain of blood in my shorts a scab when dried and gone through three or four maybe pairs of underpants by now changing after each decreasing cum until only an empty surge and what do you think after all this hump and bump to men I imagine I'm so distressed disgusted by now I put on Judy Garland at Carnegie Hall recorded live at Carnegie Hall 23rd of April in 1961 I was living growing up in California at the time where the desert meets the sea as the now polluted globe the then polluted globe goes rounding the home star in space that all of is moving the whole liquid mess is moving and Judy she's belting it out in those high heels Hal Gross told me she was on twenty dexedrine that night miracle she could stand at all night the fish in our aquarium hang placid and wide-eyed and watching me in front of the mirror I'm in front of the mirror now the cats are fighting or playing ripping up the couch either way you cut it out you guys come on get the fuck out of here Grey boy! go! or sleeping dreaming the lip

synching behavior to Judy's pumping it out the emotions swell they climax with the orchestra and ovation as my cum stained shorts settle serenely settling in in sticky slumber jostled rudely rudely jostled out when out at last the laundry bag they're jostled rudely out into the soon to be or not to be hot white bleached white water washed with bleach. (*As Mary Martin.*) "Er er, er er er, er er, er er er, er er, er er er er er errrrrrrrr!" "Oh Peter, you are clever!"

Character 5: And where was this?

Character 1: Museum of Broadcasting.

Character 5: Museum of . . .

Character 1: Broadcasting. Museum of Broadcasting.

Character 5: This is in Manhattan?

Character 1: Yea, on 53rd Street.

Character 5: Isn't that interesting. Is it open to the public?

Character 1: Oh, yea.

Character 5: This is the version with Mary Martin?

Character 1: Yea—how . . . how accurately, do you think, have I represented you in this piece?

Character 5: I think—

Character 1: I mean, is it . . . it isn't . . . I don't feel it's that accurate a portrait, at times. I mean, I think some of it is pretty . . . much on the mark.

Character 5: Yes, yes. (*Pause.*) I think you portray me as a bit more aggressive than I really am.

Character 1: That's possible, yea.

Character 5: That thing about your father falling off his bicycle—I didn't say that, try to make you feel guilty.

Character 1: No, actually, Tobey said that.

Character 5: Did she?

Character 1: (*Chuckling.*) Yea, about the bicycle.

Character 5: Un huh, hmmm . . . Some of it is clear.

Character 1: I mean, I do make you more assertive, I suppose, because you're the only other character . . . I mean, since I don't—I'm not making my father a character in this piece, and I have to have someone . . . but you know, actually, I didn't include some of the conversations we did have—we had when you tried to convince me to attend Steven's wedding.

Character 5: I don't think I was that assertive.

Character 1: No, but you were very unrelated—there were—

Character 5: What do you mean by unrelated?

Character 1: Well, I mean all the things you said about what a nice thing it was, and that it didn't matter how—if Steven was screwed up, that—

Character 5: I didn't say that.

Character 1: What?

Character 5: I don't think I said that Steven was screwed up.

Character 1: No, I said that.

Character 5: You said that.

Character 1: Yea. Right—yes, but—right—but you said it didn't matter what I thought about his getting married—I should just go to the wedding because he was my brother—didn't matter what I thought. I mean, considering the fact that Steven had been in a mental institution—that he had a history of beating up his girlfriends—

(*Out of nowhere.*) **Oh, come on, Frank, you make a big deal out of nothing, you—Hey! Dad, you are not in this play! Now fuck yourself and get out!**

Character 5: No, you're right—you're right, there.

Character 1: I mean, I agree—you're right—I . . . I think it's a fair represen—

Character 1:	Character 5:
—tation of	Yes, it's—I mean—

Character 5: I don't think I intended to imply it was an unfair representation.

Character 1: Un huh.

Character 5: I just don't know if it adequately addresses the complexities of—

Character 1: Right. Yea. Well, but actually, but—no, I do address certain complexities. Don't I? I mean, I would like to better be able to portray . . . You know, I realize . . . I don't know what I'm saying. Nowhere in—This piece catches me at a cert—particular point in my—It doesn't necessarily demonstrate some of the . . . Oh, fuck!

Character 5: What's the matter?

Character 1: Nothing, I'm just not . . . Never mind.

[1 goes to stove to stir the soup.]

Character 5: (*Pause.*) I think we've operated under the illusion of being closer.

Character 1: Yea—felt closer. We have a very long history together. I've a lot of . . . Your taking care of me when I was young . . . My mother being . . . There's a lot of . . . , I don't know, feelings—I'm still very—well, not very, but somewhat attached to you.

Character 5: Are you imagining a time when you won't feel that way?

Character 1: Envisioning a time? Unh—

Character 5: Imagining, envisioning . . .

Character 1: A time when I won't feel attached—as attached . . . ? Possibly.

Character 5: Un huh.

Character 1: Like I was saying before, was that I had to, in this piece, create a dramatic structure where there was a tension—

Character 5: You're changing the subject.

Character 1: What?

Character 5: You're changing the subject.

Character 1: Am I? What do you—

Character 5: Yes. We were talking about whether you conceive of a time, in the future, when you would feel less attached—I think involved, actually, involved would be a better word—less involved with me.

Character 1: I think so. I think so. I don't know. (*Pause.*) But do you think—let me ask you a question. Do you think you'd be . . . hurt by this piece if you saw it? I mean, I doubt you'll see it. I mean there are no matinees, and I know you're not going to come into the city at night. Do—

Character 5: Well, I might.

Character 1: What?

Character 5: I say I might.

Character 1: Might . . .

Character 5: Come into the city to see it.

Character 1: You would?

Character 5: Sure.

Character 1: At night?

Character 5: Yea.

Character 1: Oh yea?

Character 5: Yea. Now that I've had my surgery, and I'm feeling so much stronger—I could possibly arrange to stay in town with Frances over night, see the play.

Character 1: You would stay with Frances—with Aunt Frances?

Character 5: I could ask her.

Character 1: You think she's going to—

Character 5: She might.

Character 1: Un huh.

Character 5: Maybe I'll see it.

Character 1: Oh God, really?

Character 5: You don't want me to see it, do you?

Character 1: Well, no, you can see it if you want—I don't know.

Character 5: Would you change any of the lines if you knew I was coming?

Character 1: Would . . . What do you mean?

Character 5: I mean, if you knew I would attend a performance, would you change any of the text?

Character 1: No.

Character 5: Really?

Character 1: No, I wouldn't change anything. Are you really going to see it, try to see it?

Character 5: I'm not sure.

Character 1: Okay.

Character 5: See, this is not an accurate representation of our relationship. We would never be having a conversation like this.

Character 1: I know. I know that.

Character 5: This is obviously a conversation—sounds like a conversation you would be having with yourself.

Character 1: Yea. Right. That's right.

Character 5: Both voices sounds like you.

Character 1: That's right. (*Pause.*) Interesting. All right, well, let's get back to the—

Character 5: But I do think it's an interesting question. How would you feel if she saw this piece? How would it make her feel?

Character 1: Right, okay. Well, let's get back to the play. I'm glad we had this discussion.

Character 5: I am too. By the way, is there much more that's left? I think we should be conscious of how much the audience can sit through.

Character 1: Okay. Well, all we have is one more short scene, and then that's it. Then a little final section.

Character 5: Okay, well let's do it. (*A doorbell rings offstage.*) I'm coming, I'm coming. Frank can you hold on one second, it's the doorbell, it's probably—Dottie is that you? Dottie, come on in, it's open. Dottie? Hold on, Frank.

[Puts phone down on table.]

(*As she exits.*) I'm coming, just a minute. Dottie, hi!

[1 puts the phone down on the low table, sets the table with soup spoons, napkins, a small candle in a candle holder.]

Welcome, welcome—come on in—hi; I'm on the—oh, Oscar—doesn't Oscar look nice; I'm on the phone with Frank—let me take this from you. I'll just hang it up.

[From offstage the voice of 2.]

Character 2: Hi.
Character 1: Hi, sweetheart. Hi.

[The same actor playing 5 now enters as 2.]

Character 2: Hi. How are you?
Character 1: I'm okay. How're you doing?
Character 2: I'm okay. (*They kiss.*)
Character 1: Yea? How was work?
Character 2: Miserable.

[Pulling from his shoulder bag a paper sack containing a loaf of bread, setting it on table. Bread not visible.]

Character 1: Really?
Character 2: No, it was just stupid. No money.
Character 1: It was slow?
Character 2: No, it was busy—I was running around—I couldn't understand it.
Character 1: Oh. Oh well.
Character 2: How are you?
Character 1: I'm okay.
Character 2: What'd you do today?
Character 1: What did I do? Unhh I did my laundry, I made a soup . . .
Character 2: Oh yea, it smells good.
Character 1: Yea, I think it should be good.
Character 2: (*Tasting it.*) It's delicious.
Character 1: Yea, it's—is it good—you like it?
Character 2: Very good.
Character 1: Thanks, yea. I also worked on the new piece today.
Character 2: Oh yea, how's it going?
Character 1: Oh pretty good, pretty good, pretty good.
Character 2: Yea?
Character 1: Yea. I'm thinking of it taking place in one kitchen instead of two.

Character 2: Oh yea, how are you going to do that? (*As he exits.*) Wait, keep talking, I just have to use the bathroom.

Character 1: I mean, it will take place in two kitchens, but one set could represent both kitchens—the kitchen in our house and Aunt Judy's—Aunt Ruth's kitchen.

Character 2: (*From offstage.*) Aunt Ruth, that's Aunt Judy?

Character 1: Right.

Character 2: (*From offstage.*) That's interesting.

[1 exits. Stage empty.]

Character 1: (*From offstage.*) Yea, I'm also thinking of changing Frank's name to Sam.

Character 2: (*From offstage.*) Un huh.

Character 1: (*From offstage.*) I don't think Frank is a Jewish-sounding enough name.

Character 2: (*From offstage.*) Yea, no; it doesn't sound . . . Yea, that's good.

[Toilet flush. 2 re-enters, followed by 1. 2 goes to taste some more soup.]

Character 1: Then what I thought I'd do, is have the actress who plays the actress in the backyard piece—

Character 2: Right.

Character 1: I'll have her play me in the kitchen.

Character 2: Un huh. Why're you gonna do that?

Character 1: Because—

Character 2: Why don't you just play it yourself?

Character 1: It's going to be too hard, I think—I don't know, maybe not, to direct, I think. Oh, I don't know—maybe I should.

Character 2: Well, I mean, it could be kind of interesting . . . if you can find a good reason.

Character 1: You don't like it?

Character 2: I don't know.

Character 1: And I'm also thinking of having a man play Aunt Ruth.

Character 2: Hunh.

Character 1: Because—like the same actor will also play you. There's going to be—like I'm thinking at some point Aunt Ruth will go out to answer the door buzzer, for like when Dottie—you remember Dottie?

Character 2: Who?

Character 1: Dottie.

Character 2: Dottie?

Character 1: Dottie.
Character 2: No.
Character 1: From upstairs at Aunt Judy's.
Character 2: Oh right, with the daughter in Italy whose husband—
Character 1: Right, right.
Character 2: With the husband that's blind.
Character 1: And deaf.
Character 2: I mean deaf.
Character 1: No, and blind. Blind and deaf.
Character 2: Fine, fuck, whatever.
Character 1: Right. And . . . are you okay?
Character 2: I'm—yea, I'm all right.
Character 1: Are you angry about something?
Character 2: No, I'm just tired—it was a hard day. I'm angry at running around and making no money.
Character 1: Yea. And while she's helping Dottie off with her coat, you'll come out—but the same actor will play both parts.
Character 2: Aunt Judy and me?
Character 1: Right.
Character 2: I like that.
Character 1: Yea, I think it could be good.
Character 2: Is that's—is that how it's going to end?
Character 1: No. I'm not sure yet. But I think maybe what's going to happen is a phone—that a phone is going to ring offstage—

[A phone rings offstage.]

—and you will go off—that is I'll go to answer it, but you'll say—
Character 2: Wait, hold on it's probably for me. Janet was supposed to call. She and Bruce want to know if we want to get together with them for a movie or something later this week.

[2 exits.]

Character 1: And you go off, and then come back on again as Aunt Ruth.
Character 2: (*From offstage.*) Hello. Oh hi Janet—I was just—No, it's fine, I just walked in. Oh, kind of crazy. Yea. How are you doing?

[2 re-enters as 5, picks up cordless phone.]

Character 5: Hi, Sam? Sorry—Oscar, you know, Dottie's husband—I had to help her get him settled. Poor thing can't find his way.

Character 1: That's right.
Character 5: He's so sweet, though. (*Pause.*) So listen, I'm so glad we had a chance to talk, I wish you were here, and I hope I'll see you soon.
Character 1: Yea, okay—
Character 5: Whenever you have the time.
Character 1: Well, my time should be opening up a bit soon, so we'll try to find some time to come out.
Character 5: Yes, all right—wonderful. Give my love to Andrew, all right.
Character 1: Okay, I will.
Character 5: And I'll talk to you soon.
Character 1: Yes, let's do that.
Character 5: All right, take care. Bye now.
Character 1: Bye.
Character 5: Bye.

[They hang up their phones. 5 exits, with her phone. 1 goes to stove and begins ladling out a bowl of soup.]

Character 1: Aunt Judy used to tell this story, sweetheart, about when she was younger—

[From offstage 2 re-enters when he has completed his costume change.]

Character 2: You mean when your father was born and your grandfather gave her the check to pay the doctor and told her it was up to her—if she wanted to keep the baby she should give the doctor the check. And if not, she should tear up the check, and they'd send the baby back to that farm in Hicksville, and that it was up to her whether or not they'd keep the baby, but if she decided to keep the baby, your father, he would be her responsibility.
Character 1: No. (*Handing 2 a bowl of soup, seating himself at the table.*) This was when she was a young girl—
Character 5: (*Putting the bowl of soup before 1.*) And the family lived very close to one another at that time up in Harlem.
Character 1: —the family was living in Harlem on 103rd Street, 3rd Avenue.
Character 5: (*Ladling another bowl of soup.*) And all the cousins, you know, we all lived within a few houses from each other because our parents had come over from Europe and we all grew up near each other.
Character 1: (*Lighting the candle.*) Un huh.
Character 5: We'd all go to the park—

Character 1: I think it was—
Character 5: Central Park together, all the time. Everyone was very, very close.
Character 1: I think it was Central Park. But I guess bit by bit—
Character 5: Bit by bit the families started moving apart.
Character 1:—this one moved to Brooklyn—
Character 5: Cousin Mary moved out to Brooklyn—
Character 1:—so and so into the Bronx—
Character 5:—Arthur and Florence up into the Bronx—
Character 1: And eventually—
Character 5: Eventually everyone was all over the place.
Character 1: I forget all their names now—all over the place. And she used to think—
Character 5: I used to think I wished we could all live together under a big tent—the whole family together under a big tent, and nobody would ever be apart.

"Seven days shall ye eat unleavened bread; even the first day ye shall put away leaven out of your houses: for whosoever eateth leavened bread from the first day until the seventh day, that soul shall be cut off from Israel.

Seven days shall there be no leaven found in your houses: for whosoever eateth that which is leavened, even that soul shall be cut off from the congregation of Israel, whether he be a stranger, or born in the land.

Ye shall eat nothing leavened; in all your habitations shall ye eat unleavened bread."

[2 pulls out a long loaf of Italian bread from the paper sack.]

Character 2: Would you like a piece of bread, sweetheart?
Character 1: Bread? (*Hold.*) Oh yea, please. Definitely, definitely.

[2 breaks bread, gives a piece to 1.]

Thanks.

[The two eat the soup and bread, and light fades slowly. When light is extinguished, 1 blows out the candle.]

Dead Mother, or Shirley Not All in Vain

David Greenspan in *Dead Mother, or Shirley Not All in Vain.* New York Shakespeare Festival/Public Theater, New York, 1991. Photograph by Thomas McGovern.

Dead Mother, or Shirley Not All in Vain

First produced by Joseph Papp at the New York Shakespeare Festival / Public Theater, New York City, January 1991.

Harold	David Greenspan
Daniel	Ben Bodé
Sylvia	Terra Vandergaw
Maxine	Mary Shultz
Uncle Saul	Ron Bagden
Melvin	Steve Mellor

Set Design by William Kennon
Lighting Design by David Bergstein
Costume Design by Elsa Ward
Directed by David Greenspan

Characters:

Acts 1, 3, and 5

Harold
Daniel, Harold's brother
Sylvia, Harold's wife
Maxine, Daniel's fiancée
Uncle Saul, Maxine's great-great-uncle
Melvin, Harold and Daniel's father

Act 2

Harold plays Eris
Daniel plays Peleus and Paris
Sylvia plays Thetis
Maxine plays Aphrodite, Athena, and Hera
Uncle Saul plays Prometheus
Melvin plays Zeus

Act 4

Harold
Daniel plays the Narrator
Sylvia plays the Whale
Maxine
Uncle Saul plays Alice B. Toklas
Melvin plays the Ferryman

Notes:

Harold never dresses as a woman! As with the other characters in Act 2, fanciful Greek costuming may be used. Aside from that, he should remain in his own clothing throughout the entire escapade. A single strand of pearls is added when he assumes the character of Shirley. No more than that.

Aside from the few props indicated in the script, the only "set" is a couch. It should remain center until the moment in Sylvia's Epilogue when Sylvia pushes it (and the tea cart) to the side. Scene titles are for the reader only; they should not be announced or projected during performance. Scene changes are instantaneous. No change of set. No music.

Uncle Saul speaks with a thick East European (Yiddish) accent. He doesn't need to be played by an elderly actor.

No intermission is necessary. If one is taken, it should occur between Acts 3 and 4.

Act 1

INTRODUCTION

Maxine: I would just like to say that I've come to this theater now for many years—since the early seventies—I'm a subscriber. And I really—I'm a big supporter of the work that goes on here—I really love it—I love this theater. But lately, I've . . . I'm beginning to feel a little . . . alienated because . . . well, the last three—I think—plays we've seen here the leading characters have been . . . gay people, and I'm just beginning to feel a little on the outside—I don't know. Now I don't feel . . . my—you know my son is gay and I don't have a problem with that—I think it's great—it's important that that kind of thing is seen on stage, etc. It's just—and I say this with the greatest appreciation for what you do here—it's just that I'm feeling a little left out. I guess I would like to see a play . . . more plays—with heterosexual characters. And . . . well, that's all. I think that's all I wanted to say. (*Pause.*) I hope I haven't offended anybody.

[Light changes.]

SYLVIA REMEMBERS

Sylvia: Yes. Yes, I remember, Daniel, I remember that night you arranged for Harold to come to me you did. It was dark the night air rushed in about me I left open my window. I regard the moon out my window—it is there—full circle in the sky is the white blot beyond the open window it hangs there bright moon hanging there I look to the moon is there. The breeze gently blown I feel it on my legs it blows against my ankles I rub together from the chill of the breeze blown in through the open window out which I regard the distant white moon bright stop.

Heartbeat. Stop. Heart beating faster now heartbeat I hear sound of I here still gazing at the moon out the window I hear steps nearing below the wind oh! steps feet meaning some thing/one climbing up the—"Oh, the trellis!"—oh, legs quivering now heart stopping breath stop moon human silhouette climbing in the sky someone covering the moon as Daniel said it would it be it, "Harold?"—climbing up the trellis? blotting out the moon out the window I look out now against the sky standing there man's figure standing there I look out.

I there now. It there. Figure. The . . . the figure of . . . It climb out the sky into room standing there—long solid shadow it step aside and the moon is there.

Man in the room. It/he in the room. It/he move in my room towards my bed, I oh!, my ankles quivering. The breeze I—oh!, it speak—it say something—what, I can't remember—something it say. I just say, "Shhh," softly, "Shhh," my voice just say. I say "It so dark." Face dark. I cannot see face, it must be "Harold?"—as you said, Daniel, it would be "Harold?"—through the window would come to me to love it must be "Harold? I say, Harold, who is it?" It say, "It is I." I. I, I see eyes, green eyes that I see all I see that's all I see I see his . . . his . . . his eyes I see his . . . I whisper, "Why, Harold, is that you?" Voice say, "It is I." I. I. I then I look to the moon still white I look to the moon. And he bends down to me.

Hands on my legs reaching down grab my feet with palms of hands cold hands warm it tickles soles of my feet I giggle giggle he it I giggle we hands grab my ankles. Pressure feels oh God! against my cheek his cheek against my lips his hands travel traveling up my legs into my gown nightgown I oh my tongue to my my lips his tongue it tongues my tongue slips out two tongues together in my my my mouth I, "Oh, I—Harold, I love you, Harold—" pressing down him down hard against me it it it it tongues to that his mouth my mouth's lips wet bitten "Ouch, I—Harold! I—" I hand his he hands it's pulling at my "Oh!, my my my my" down my "Oh, my" his fingers pressing in my hair down there his hands palm of his near thumb of his hand it's . . . it's . . . "It's there, yes—press" I pressing him down—down his rump I hands on his rump, it it it it "It dark" I say "Harold," I say, "True Love—I've I've I I've always loved you" my voice saying "Shhh, shhh, shhh, shhh, shhh, shhh, shhh, shhh."

[Light changes.]

DANIEL REMINDS HAROLD

Daniel: You do owe me one, Harold. Harold, you owe me one. You owe me a favor. Harold, you owe me a favor. You owe me a favor, Harold, I'm your brother.

Harold: Daniel—

Daniel: Harold, if it wasn't for me Sylvia would never be your wife. If it wasn't for me.

Harold: Daniel, I know and I'm—I'll—

Daniel: Harold—

Harold: I know, Daniel. In her room. You in her room that night with the moon shining white bright. You for me. You did for me. You said for me you would woo and you, you did. You for me did for me woo my wife Sylvia in my place.

Daniel: Yes I did for you woo for you I did for you were less than confident, Harold.

Harold: It's true, Daniel, I was less than confident. And you—

Daniel: What's more, and this I think a sign of true brotherly devotion I display for you I did at that time display my brotherly devotion to you whose i—whose ideas—idea was it to you—for you—to dress up as Mommy to convince—to fool Daddy—to convince Daddy to let you marry Sylvia? My idea. I told you that you could masquerade as Mommy and fool Daddy that you were Mommy. And as Mommy you convinced Daddy to let you marry Sylvia. That was my idea. I convinced you you could do it and you did do it. And you did marry Sylvia, didn't you?

Harold: Yes, yes, it's true. I . . . I had no id—

Daniel: Yes. I knew you could pull it off. If anyone knew, I knew if anyone you knew Mommy. It was you look like her, Harold—

Harold: But—

Daniel: Harold—

Harold: Daniel—

Daniel: If anyone, you could.

Harold: But it was dark. And I was there was only a moment I was there in the dark with Daddy was sleeping when—as I woke him you kept Mommy downstairs talking I crept into their bedroom as you kept Mommy occupied downstairs I crept into their bedroom dressed in one of Mommy's old muumuus I sprayed with her perfume on my neck and arms—I rolled into bed and wrapped my arms around Daddy's back and stirred him out of his sleep and whispered, "Melvin, wake up, I wanna talk to you a second, darling." "What," he said? I said, "Melvin." He said, "It's—Shirley—it's late." I said, "I know it's—" (and all this time you kept Mommy occupied downstairs with some—what was the story you were going to tell about a problem you were having with—what was the problem you made up to keep Mommy downstairs with you she was I'm surprised in hindsight she took time to listen to your problems—for that matter when did she ever have time for anyone's problems but her own she did have) "Melvin, I know it's late and this'll—but this'll only take a minute, so wake up and listen, I want to talk to you about Harold and this girl." And Daddy said, "Shirley, I don't want to talk about it now, I don't like the girl has no family, she wants Harold for his money, and Shirley," "For Christ sake will you listen to me, Melvin, listen to me when," I interrupted. And I spoke like Mommy. And I badgered him and I kept him awake the way Mommy would do when she wanted something really bad she'd just keep him awake until he was too weak and tired to refuse that time in the night with my arms around his paunch, stroking his face and chest I said, "Melvin," I said, "he's going to marry Sylvia whether we like it or not and if he doesn't get your—our—blessing, he'll leave us for that girl—Melvin, who are you—who are you going to leave the business to run the business to Melvin, for Christ sake, Danny is an idiot in business." I said you were an idiot.

Daniel: You—

Harold: That sounded like Mommy would say something like that.

Daniel: Yes it does, she would.

Harold: "You worked your entire life," I said like Mommy, "to leave this business that you worked your entire life for to a son of a bitch like that with no brains for business. And I swear" (I swore like Mommy) "he'll never speak with you again, Melvin, he'll never speak with you. Harold won't speak with you—with us—if you don't give permission. This I know because he said" as much as I thought this was stretching it as Mommy I was in the mood to stretch it. And with the hour late and my hands stroking him he agreed—he was so tired. And he fell off to sleep. And as he fell off to sleep, I fell out of the bed and as quickly moved out of the room I saw Mommy's shadow coming up the stair—the clump, clump of her white feet in fuzzy slippers she clumped up the carpeted stairs, burping the last bits of whatever it was she'd eaten while talking to you about a problem that never existed. And I ran to my room, ripped off the old muumuu, I washed off the fragrance. I leapt into bed and I fell to sleep.

Daniel: And whose idea was that, Harold? Whose idea was it my idea? Can't you help me out for just this once, Harold, do something for me for once be a brother to me for once. Brothers are supposed to help each other.

Harold: But Daniel, what you ask me!

Daniel: Harold, after all I've done for you, this small—

Harold: Small?!

Daniel: —favor I ask of you.

Harold: You're asking me to dress up as my dead mother.
Daniel: Our dead mother, Harold. After all I've done for you.
Harold: But Daniel—
Maxine: Daniel, I can't—I can't marry you without Uncle Saul's permission. And I'm telling you, Uncle Saul refuses to even consider our marriage until he's met your mother. After all I've told him that you've told me about—
Sylvia: Your mother? What did you tell her about your mother?
Daniel: I—
Maxine: It's such a small—
Harold: Small?

Maxine:	
—thing I'm	Daniel:
asking for—	Maxine, I—I—
Danny, I don't under—	No, you don't understand, it's
Danny. Danny, she's your mother—	
	Right, but Max—
She's your—	Max—
	All right, wait.
Sweetheart, she's your mother—	Wait.
Danny, how is it—tell me how is it possible she can't make the time to—make the—your own	It's not a question of time. It's—
How is it possible your own mother can't make the—	This has nothing to do with—
So, if it's not a question of time—	with—It's just that—
	Maxine, darling—
If it's not a question of time—	Baby, listen—Baby—
No. I want to meet your mother.	

Harold: So you told her . . .
Daniel: I told her that . . . Well, I really didn't tell her that . . . I just—
Sylvia: You told her your mother was alive?
Daniel: I—yes. I—no, Sylvia, no, I didn't—didn't tell her . . . I just . . . Yes, I told her . . . I told her that . . . that Mommy was—
Harold: Alive? Why?
Maxine: Because. I can't. I cannot—I will not. I will not marry you until I meet your mother. After—
Daniel: Maxine—

Maxine: After all you've told me about her. And besides—
Sylvia: Have you talked to Harold about any of this?
Daniel: No.
Maxine: Daniel, I can't. I can't marry you without Uncle Saul's permission. And Uncle Saul, I'm telling you, refuses to even consider our marriage until he's met your mother. After all that I've told him that you've told me about her—
Daniel: So Maxine thinks that Mommy is—
Sylvia: Maxine thinks your mother is—
Daniel: Sylvia thought I should speak with you, Harold. You see—

	Maxine:
Sylvia: But Daniel—	Well, frankly Danny I don't see why your— why your mother—
Daniel: Sylvia, what am I going—	your own mother can't
Sylvia: Why did you . . . Why didn't you just tell her the truth. Your—	attend—can't—

Harold: Mommy's dead.
Sylvia: What?
Harold: She swallowed a bottle of muscle relaxers. Half a bottle of muscle relaxers.
Sylvia: Oh, my God.
Harold: My father just called from the hospital.
Sylvia: A suicide. Oh, my God.
Daniel: I couldn't tell her that, Harold. I don't know, I just couldn't tell Maxine that Mommy had swallowed—
Sylvia: Daniel—
Harold: But Daniel—
Maxine: Danny—
Daniel: Sylvia—
Harold: So . . . so who is this Uncle Saul?
Daniel: What am I going to do?
Sylvia: Just . . . tell her your mother is out of town.
Maxine: I don't believe you.
Harold: See; this is getting so complicated I can barely follow it.

Daniel: Oh, Harold, come on—
Harold: Yea, but what about—
Sylvia: Your father—
Maxine: Your father—
Harold: What about Daddy? Does Daddy—
Daniel: No, I haven't mentioned anything to—
Maxine: Your father. What about your father? Will he be able to—
Daniel: No, Uncle Saul is staying in a hotel in Westwood. Daddy doesn't know anything.
Harold: You're promising me, Daniel, Daddy doesn't know a thing about—
Daniel: Harold, I promise you, Daddy won't be there. Come on, as soon as Sylvia and I . . . and I mean Maxine and I are married, Harold, I'm going to tell Maxine the truth. I'm going to tell her everything. Believe me, Harold. Harold, please believe me. I love Maxine like you love Sylvia. I love her, Harold. (*Gently.*) Harold?
Sylvia: I don't know. Maybe you should talk to Harold.
Maxine: Well, after my parents were killed—in the hijacking—I was placed in the care of my great-great-uncle—Uncle Saul.
Daniel: That's what I'll do. I'll talk to Harold.

ARRIVING AT THE HOTEL

[Harold puts on a string of pearls.]

Daniel: Sweetheart, we're here. Maxine?
Maxine: I'm coming, I'm coming—hi! come in, come in, come on in.
Daniel: Hi.
Maxine: Hi.
Harold: Hello, is this her? Maxine?
Daniel: Oh, yea, Max, this is my mother. Ma, this is—
Harold: What do you call her? What does he call you—Max? Like a man? What do you . . . She's a girl. Maxine.
Daniel: I know, Ma.
Harold: Never mind. Hello.
Maxine: Hi.
Harold: I'm Danny's mother.
Maxine: Of course you are. It's so nice to meet you. Come in, come in, make yourself comfortable.
Harold: Right—listen, darling, you'll excuse me I can only stay a minute. I'm sick with a cold, and—

Maxine: I know. Danny told me you're not feeling well. I want you to sit right down and be a good girl. I'm going to pour you a nice hot cup of tea. We have lemon and honey . . .

[Maxine rolls on a tea cart.]

Harold: Oh, I love her. Oh God, I love her, is she a doll or what? Oh, look at this, that's great. You're great. Let me look at you. Let me look at you look great. (*Hold.*) I love her. I love you. You do I love you in that dress you look swell really swell I'll always love her. (*Hold.*) How are you—excited—getting married to my . . . ?—come on, we'll sit and where's your uncle—what's his name—Saul, I'd love to meet him.

Maxine: Oh, right, let me—yes, he's in the other room. I think he fell asleep in the other—

Harold:	Maxine:
(*Sotto voce.*) How'm I doing?	(*Exiting.*)—room I'll—(*Stops.*) What?

Daniel: (*Hold.*) Nothing, sweetheart, nothing. Why don't you go on, get Uncle Saul.

[Maxine exits.]

(*Sotto voce.*) You're fine, you're fine. Just relax, don't talk so much, calm down.

Harold: (*Sotto voce.*) What?

Daniel: Yea.

Maxine: (*Offstage.*) Here we come.

Harold: Oh, my God.

Maxine: (*Offstage.*) What?

Daniel: Nothing, honey, nothing. Mommy's just a little—you know, nervous . . . meeting Uncle Saul.

Maxine: (*Offstage.*) Oh, don't be silly.

Harold: I'm not—what are you talking about—like—nervous. It's just that I can't stay long I'd love to stay but I'm sick with cold and my friend, Dorothy—I'm a friend of Dorothy—I've got to visit is crazy in the hospital. She's—

Daniel: (*Aghast.*) What?

Harold: It's true. I'm a friend of Dorothy—what can I do?

Maxine: (*Offstage.*) Oh, no.

Harold: It breaks your heart, I know—she lost her mind—so sad to say—I hate to say it's true—they locked her up.

Maxine: (*Offstage.*) That's terrible.

Daniel: (*Sotto voce.*) Harold, are you crazy?!

Harold: Crazy? I'm not crazy. She's crazy, but not dangerous. Or at least not as dangerous as—

Maxine: Okay, here we come.

[Maxine rolls Uncle Saul out in a wheelchair. He's as old as the hills—older.]

Daniel: Hey, here they are.

Harold: Oh look, look! here's the—here's your uncle—what's his name, Paul? is he in pain? that he's with that—I don't—didn't know you were a cripple—hello—I would have brought something for you if I knew my name is Shirley; hello; I'm Danny's mother of course I am in pain aren't you with that chair is he's deaf isn't he? can't hear me the poor thing he must be blind. Can he read lips? If I bend down to him close could he hear or read lips?

Uncle Saul: What?

Harold: Och, he's all right. I'm sorry, I thought you were deaf. I didn't know you could see I'm sorry how are you? Is he in pain? Is he lying to be nice? Is he comfortable?

Maxine: He's fine.

Harold: Tell me with uncle here do you have to change the bedpan? Does he have he use the bedpan? My mother—does he have a bedpan for God rest her soul—a lovely person she suffered everybody loved her—bedridden—my mother for so long I'd change her bedpan almost daily when I was a little boy—a little girl—coming home from school I'd stop by her room on the way to my room I'd stop by her she was sleeping or awake with the TV on watching her programs I'd take her bedpan and dump it I hated it! Cancer! Cancer! It was cancer! I hated washing out the doody and the pee from the pan in the sink or in the toilet I would do it. But always rinse—shit—out—what's the difference? I hated the scraping the doodys is such a mess it was sticking to the pan I'd have to scrape it. And spray with disinfectant or something spray. I loved her to death but I hated doing that. She—never mind—do you do that for your uncle?

Maxine: No. I—

Harold: Oh, forgive me, I've gotten personal.

Daniel: Mother (!!).

Harold: (*With sudden vehement impatience.*) What?! (*then honeyed*) darling?

Daniel: (*Stunned. Then calmly.*) Do you want to go freshen up? You know you don't have much time before I take you to the . . . bus to get to . . . "Dorothy," so maybe—

Harold: Yes, that's a good idea. You'll excuse me?

Maxine: Oh, sure.

Harold: (*To Uncle Saul.*) Have I made a good impression on you? I hope I have—because your daughter loves my son. I mean you—niece—here—whatever loves my son—he tells me he loves her and Danny's an honest one if there's one thing he wouldn't lie so tell me I hope you like my Danny too and give your blessing for Christ sake because these two I see should be together to have children. God wonders if I'll ever get—not that that's what I'm concerned with here—grandchildren—from my other boy, Harold—who knows what's the matter there—if it's his wife, Sylvia—I never liked her that Harold? who knows, he always was a strange boy. I don't know what he like—likes—like, I don't know, maybe he's a (?) . . . (*To Maxine.*) To carry on the name, it's important. (*To Uncle Saul.*) By the way, I'm sorry my husband couldn't be here he's got business—you—I know you understand. (*To Maxine.*) Oh, are you is she a doll! I'll be right out, darling.

[Harold and Daniel exit. Light changes.]

HAROLD IN THE BATHROOM

[From the dark the sound of a toilet flushing. Light illuminates Harold and Daniel. Daniel knocks on the door.]

Daniel: (*Knocking.*) Ma? Ma? It's almost time to go. (*Whispering.*) Harold, are you all all right in there, Harold?

Harold: Daniel, I'll be right out.

Daniel: Just a few more minutes and I'll get you out of here.

Harold: Okay, that's great.

Daniel: And listen—

Harold: What?

Daniel: Listen, Harold, calm down out there.

Harold: Yea.

Daniel: I mean what's going on out there?

Harold: I don't know, I don't know. Every time I open my mouth it's like . . . it's—

Daniel: All right—okay—forget it. Just—

Harold: Okay.

Daniel: Yea. (*After a pause.*) Why did you—

Harold: What?

Daniel: You—

Harold: What?

Daniel: You.

Harold: Who, me?

Daniel: Yea, you.

Harold: What?

Daniel: Why did you mention the hospital where—where who's Dorothy?

Harold: Who?

Daniel: Dorothy.

Harold: Dorothy?

Daniel: Yea—you—

Harold: I just made that up.

Daniel: Yea, but you . . .

Harold: What?

Daniel: Harold, you made it sound like Mommy. Like Mommy when—

Harold: Like Mommy, yea. I don't know—I—I—maybe I was thinking—

Daniel: That's where she took the pills.

Harold: The pills, that's right.

Daniel: When Daddy—God, Harold, I can't forget how she screamed down the hall when they wheeled her away strapped in. You weren't there. Where were you? You were at home. Or on your honeymoon with Sylvia. Which was it? Why can't I remember? You didn't hear how she screamed his name as we walked away down the hall. She screamed out his name. Screamed out his name. Screamed out his name, Melvin. Melvin, Melvin, come back, they're going to kill me. They're killing me here. They're going to kill me.

Harold: I know.

Daniel: I heard her call out his name not to leave me—don't leave me here, I'll kill myself, Melvin, please, I'll kill myself you son of a bitch—you—you son of a bitch she said. You—

Harold: Daniel—

Daniel: Poor Dad. (*After a pause.*) We shouldn't talk about it, Harold.

Harold: Right.

Daniel: (*After a pause.*) Right. And Harold, a few nice words to Uncle Saul, you know, if you could.

Harold: What?

Daniel: Before you leave.

Harold: Okay.

Daniel: Be a nice-like Mommy.

Harold: Okay.

Daniel: I mean—

Harold: What do you mean?

Daniel: I mean just say a few nice things to him. Ask him how he enjoyed traveling—that you hope to see him at the wedding, about his business. He's in the junkyard business—in Chicago. He sells scrap metal. Scrap.

Harold: What? I didn't hear you.

Daniel: Right. Okay, listen, I better get out there.

Harold: Wait. I—

Daniel: Just act nice a little. And then I'll drive you to your car.

Harold: What?

Daniel: I'm going to go out and talk to them now, Harold. I'll be in the other room.

Harold: Okay. (*Pause. Then as if into the mirror.*) I just don't remember you being very nice. ***What do you mean, darling?*** I mean you were ne***ver speak to me like that, Harold.*** I mean you were never ***Harold, don't you dare*** to me you were—***Harold***—you were always so frightening ***me with that kind of talk, darling. I don't l***ike the thought that I never felt at ease or peace with ***you would say that to a sick woman like*** Mommy, I ***could die for all*** your ranting or raving at ***me, a sick woman*** like this, right now—***you'd speak to me like this your own*** Mommy, you were ***Harold,*** I could I please, could I ***hope you burn in Hell for that kind of*** Hell? What the hell are you always talking about Hell ***for Christ sake the*** Mother, the Jews don't believe in ***hell if they*** don't give me what the ***Jews—they—yes they*** don't! they don't—***I don't give a crap, Harold, what the goddamn Jews believe in they***—don't tell me then what the Jews ***believe me, Harold, I can't take any more of*** what?! What am I doing to you when—when I want an ***answer me for Christ sake, Harold!*** you won't give me a chance will ***you wanna kill me, is that what you're—is that what you're*** just trying to see you more clearly for ***once I wish I never gave birth to you—you disgraceful faggot! Faggot!!*** (*After a pause.*) What? What?

What do ***you heard me.*** I don't know what ***you know what I'm talking about.*** No, I don't know ***Bullshit. I'm tired of pretending your*** Mother ***your*** Mother ***your marriage to*** don't start in on ***Sylvia didn't fool me one bit; so tell me how's your sex life with*** Sylvia is satisfied with ***no one could be satisfied with*** you are just out of your—***out every night looking for***—what are you talking about? You're ***a fag, a fag.*** I don't—***Why don't you just go home at night after work in-***

stead of Stop! ***stopping at that place—that park—that park that you***—No. ***It's three times now you're*** all right, wait! ***You're sleeping with men.*** No! ***aren't you?*** No!! ***Oh come on, Harold, you've been sleeping with***—All right! Don't!! Stop!!!

[Seven knocks from Daniel.]

Daniel: (*Timidly.*) Ma? Hey, Ma?
Harold: (*Into mirror.*) No. No more.
Daniel: What? Harold? Are you . . . ?
Harold: (*Whispered in his own voice.*) Okay, I'm coming out. I'll be right out.
Daniel: (*Whispered.*) Harold. Harold.

[Light fades to black, then illuminates Maxine, Uncle Saul, and Melvin.]

MELVIN ARRIVES

Maxine: Please come in, make yourself comfortable. What a wonderful surprise. Uncle Saul, this is Daniel's father.
Uncle Saul: What?
Maxine: Isn't this nice? I'm so glad you were able to make it. Danny is going to be thrilled I'm sure to see you here. He told us you were away on business, I was so disappointed.
Melvin: No, I was . . . yea—I was—yesterday—I had to . . . but, gee—no, if I had . . . sure for cryin' out loud . . . I mean—
Uncle Saul: What?
Maxine: Oh, excuse me. Uncle Saul, are you tired? Do you need to rest? Do you want to take a nap? Are you hungry? Are you sure? Good. I'm sorry.
Melvin: No, no, no. (*After a pause.*) This is your uncle?
Maxine: My great-great-uncle. My father's father's mother's brother.
Melvin: How do you like that.
Maxine: (*After a pause.*) Can I get you something to drink?
Melvin: Oh, sure. You got a—what do you got there?
Maxine: Oh, just about everything.
Melvin: Yea, how do you like that. You got a soda—maybe an orange or something lo-cal?
Maxine: Oh, sure. How's—
Melvin: (*Pointing to a soda.*) This is good.
Maxine: Oh, here—here's a diet.

Melvin: Oh, that's good, that's good. I like that.
Maxine: Danny should be right with us.
Melvin: Oh, okay.
Maxine: How did you find us by the way?
Melvin: I spoke with my son Harold's wife, Sylvia. She told me the boys had gone to meet with you and your family. Is Harold still here?
Maxine: No, just Danny and his mother. She stepped into the bathroom. I'm sure she'll be right out in a—oh—Oh, here's Danny.

[Daniel enters.]

Danny, is your mother all right?
Daniel: Oh, she's fine—Dad(?)! hi—hey, Dad, what are you . . . get my message—to meet us here—is that how you found us? I'm so glad you could be here.
Melvin: Yea—no Sylvia—Sylvia. I—where's Harold?
Daniel: Who?
Melvin: Harold.
Daniel: Harold?
Melvin: Your brother.
Daniel: Oh, Harold. Yea.
Melvin: Yea, where is he?
Daniel: What do you mean?
Melvin: What do you mean what do I mean?
Daniel: I don't know.
Melvin: Sylvia said he came up here with you.
Daniel: Who—Sylvia said that—Harold? No, he just dropped me off at the—here at the . . . hotel, then went back to—
Melvin: Sylvia didn't tell me that.
Daniel: She didn't?
Melvin: No.
Daniel: Well, of course not, how could—she didn't know.
Melvin: What do you mean?
Daniel: (*To himself.*) What *do* I mean? (*To Melvin.*) I mean she didn't . . . know . . . it was . . . a surprise.
Maxine: A what?
Daniel: A surprise.
Melvin: What's the surprise?
Daniel: You mean you didn't—no, I guess Harold didn't have time to let you don't know about the surprise that Harold is planning a surprise—for Sylvia.

Maxine: Sylvia is your sister-in-law?

Daniel: Right. And Harold wanted to . . . well, I guess it's safe to say now about this, Dad. Harold is surprising Sylvia with . . . with a trip to Las Vegas.

Maxine: Las Vegas! Oh, that's so sweet.

Daniel: (*To Maxine.*) Sure. (*To Melvin.*) What time did you call Sylvia?

Maxine: That's great.

Melvin: What?

Daniel: What time did you speak with Sylvia?

Melvin: Around nine, I don't know.

Daniel: Okay, see Harold was going to pick up Sylvia after he dropped me off here and surprise her with the trip.

Maxine: I love that. And I really mean that, I love that.

Daniel: So around ten he must have gotten back to their place—they're probably gone by now.

Melvin: That's great. (*After a pause.*) So who's in the bathroom?

Daniel: I don't know, who?

Maxine: Don't be silly, Danny, your mother is in the bathroom. Does she know?

Melvin: That's impossible.

Daniel: What?

Maxine: About going to Las Vegas. What does he mean that's impossible?

Daniel: I don't know.

Melvin: I mean it's impossible.

Maxine: Is that what he means, Danny?

Melvin: Your mother can't be in the bathroom.

Daniel: That's right.

Maxine: Why not?

Melvin: Because.

Maxine: Because?

Daniel: Because . . .

Melvin: Because she's . . . She's—

Daniel: Maxine, my mother is not in the bathroom.

Maxine: Why?

Daniel: Because she's . . . She's—

[Harold enters.]

Harold: Because she's right here is why I—(*Seeing Melvin.*) Da, Da, Da, darling!, Melvin, sweetheart. (*With terror.*) What are you doing h—

Maxine: (*Before Harold can finish the word "here."*) Here she is! Here she is!

We were getting worried about you—but look who showed up, your husband is here. Oh, look at them, Danny, speechless, like they haven't seen each other for years. Oh, look, there are tears in your mother's eyes and your father is having a difficult time breathing. That's so sweet. And I really mean that, it's very sweet. Danny, I want us to feel that way when we've been married.

Harold: I've got to be going.

Maxine: Nonsense, you stay right there, you're not going anywhere, I want to talk to you. This is a very special occasion—Danny why don't you loosen your father's tie. Two families getting together—and . . . well, Harold is not the only one around here who has surprises. You know, I was thinking that—well, that . . . that Danny, that you know, that I wanted us to do something special—like . . . I don't know, I couldn't think of anything—something, you know, nice—really special that we could all do together and then come back here for some nice coffee and cake or something, sit and talk.

And then I remembered I'm a subscriber to a very nice little small theater—the Iliad Theater in West Hollywood. They do a lot of nice little small little plays—very intimate that, you know, you wouldn't see in some of the big houses like the Shubert or the Ahmanson at the Music Center or the Shrine Auditorium—you know, nice—in fact, my friend Fritzy, of Fritzy and Howard—you know them Danny—she works at the day care center with me—she and Howie divorced about a year-and-a-half ago—he was having an affair with—if you can believe it—his brother Donald's wife, Sonya—who I never liked—anyway, Fritzy and I—we know each other from when I was doing my nurse's training back in Chicago—which I never finished because I thought I was getting married to Jack—who Danny knows about—but Jack had a nervous breakdown—he could never get away from his mother, Ethel—who I always thought was very sweet, but evidently was driving or had driven Jack out of his mind—so when I came out West I re-contacted Fritzy—she had married a really sweet, nice man, Peter—who I never met—he was Roman Catholic—he got killed in—I forgotten how in some kind of horrible auto accident—anyway—his head was chopped off—ended up rolling down the La Cienega off-ramp going east on the Santa Monica Freeway—it was terrible—I know it sounds funny—but it was—anyway—so when I got out here just after Peter was, you know, killed, Fritzy and I became subscribers to this nice little small theater in West Hollywood I was telling you about about a paragraph-and-a-half ago—and they're doing—they often do really nice plays—sometimes I don't understand the plays they do—sometimes they do things that are just a little too way out—even for me—but you know you take your chances—you know, you get exposed to different kinds of things—it's nice—it's like taking your medicine—anyway—they are doing something now which is supposed to be—it sounds very interesting—Fritzy saw it—she didn't like it—but she said go see it—see for yourself—that actress we like—there's an actress who we love—she occasionally you'll see her on TV or in a film—I spotted her once in a film with that—who's that actor I like—used to be so handsome—he acted on Broadway, I think, years ago, then had his own series on CBS or NBC—he played a private investigator on Wednesday or Thursday nights—divorced his wife—also an actress—not very good but very pretty—she was having an affair with—if you can believe it—this guy's—this actor's accountant—I know because my friend Jeannie that—Danny you know Jeannie—Jeannie is a friend of mine—also from Chicago—nurse's training—she just had a heart attack—she's young but she weighs about three hundred pounds—anyway—Jeannie works for another accountant—Phil something—he has a gorgeous office in Century City—just went through a messy divorce himself—he was married to a woman from the Philippines—in fact, one of his kids—Phil's kids, I hear—I think his son, Joey, is heavy into drugs—you know, they have money—too much money—and there's not a lot of supervision for these kids—my friend Fern—you know, with the brain tumor—their kids—her and Seymour—Seymour's in the Peace Corps—but she has money from her father, Milton, who was a big macher in the jewelry business—their kids go to school in Beverly Hills—they go to Beverly High—and she tells me a lot of these kids—with money they get from they parents—and cars—one of them—a friend of Robbie—Fern's oldest—his friend, Madeline—actually, they're boyfriend and girlfriend—but they're not serious—there's another girl, Valerie, I think he's more serious about—Valerie's father is a producer—produces documentaries—and Robbie, you know, who wants to be an actor—I think he sees this as a contact—anyway Madeline has an apartment on the grounds of her father's estate in Beverly Hills—can you believe this—and there are some real drug problems—Valerie, for instance, I think is heavily into pot—anyway—this actress—I think her name is Misty something or other—oh, you would love her—actually, we saw her do *Carousel*—the musical—at that place in the Valley—you remember, Danny—she sings—what a voice some of these people have—I'm telling you, you're going to love her—she works out of this theater—The Iliad—and I guess in the play she plays three different roles—she's suppose to be wonderful—Fritzy said she's worth the price of admission—so I got us—that is I got—well, I got four tickets—for the matinee today—because I didn't see—and I'm sorry I didn't know that you'd be showing up, so—but please, don't—can't—can't you leave your friend, Dorothy—who I would love to meet sometime—leave her for today and join us please for the play—Uncle Saul, you see, is exhausted from all the excitement—I'm sure he'll want to rest here at the hotel—and then we should all—come on—all of us—go out to the theater and have a good time. Okay? Good.

[Hold. Then quick light shift. All exit but Harold. No break between acts.]

Act 2

ERIS

Eris: I am Eris, spirit of strife
and discord, despised by all
mortal and immortal
excepting my brother Ares
for whom I always will
stir up occasion for war
by spread of rumor and jealousy.

Either way indignant
have I climbed the height of Mount Pelion,
the one divinity not invited to this
the wedding feast of Peleus and Thetis.

What god was it then
brought these two together
into matrimony? Zeus!
whose passion for Thetis was
discouraged by a prophecy that
any son born to Thetis
would be greater than his father.

Thus afeard his power
would be threatened did Zeus

arrange this marriage,
inviting all the gods except myself
to celebrate. But I have come despite,
determined to strike division
among the Olympians.

Silent I am
invisible. Here comes
the bride and groom.

[Eris steps aside. Enter Peleus and Thetis.]

PELEUS AND THETIS

Thetis: No, Peleus, it was Hera
chose you as my husband.
She knew Zeus would sleep with me,
but I rejected his advances.
Peleus: And I, advised that you,
immortal, would resent a marriage to me,
a mortal—
Thetis: Hid yourself (I know it now)
behind a bush of myrtle berries
on the tiny island near the shores
of Thessaly.
Peleus: For to that islet's shore
would you Thetis daily ride
naked on the back of a dolphin,
there to take a mid-day sleep
in the recess of a secret cave.
Thetis: You grabbed me as I slept
and dreamt. I quickly metamorphosed.
Peleus: But I had been prepared you would resist
my embrace. And as you fiercely changed
first into fire, next into water,
then into a leopard—
Thetis: A lion.
Peleus: What?
Thetis: A lion! not—
Peleus: A lion—fine—whatever! And finally a serpent.
But I held onto you.

Thetis: You would not let me go.
And in the end you lay upon me,
and we were locked into a passionate embrace.
Peleus: Now we should take our place at the banquet table
beside the deities.

[Exit Peleus and Thetis grimly. Eris takes out the Golden Apple, lobs it after them, then exits. Enter Prometheus.]

PROMETHEUS

Prometheus: I am Prometheus.
I once tricked Zeus.
He told me manage a dispute
which sacrificial portion
should be offered to the gods
and which reserved for humans.
The all nutritious flesh
I wrapped up in the undesirable stomach;
the useless bones
concealed within the tempting fat:
I fooled the gods
and left the meat for men.

He punished me, withholding fire
from my beloved mankind.
But I stole it from behind his back
and gave it them—and he
spiteful as he is
chained me to Mount Caucasus
until I threatened him with prophecy of Thetis.
Now unbound I'm free and able once again
to aid the struggling homo
sapiens.

[Exit Prometheus. Enter Zeus.]

ZEUS

Zeus: I am lord of all heaven, Zeus.
My father was Kronos,

my mother Rhea—
both children of Terra
and her son Uranus.

There are those say Eurynome
(The Mother of Us All)
rose naked out of chaos, dividing sea from sky, dancing south on the water, breaking wind behind her.
She took this fetid wind between her hands and rubbed, fashioning the serpent Ophion, who turning lustful penetrated her.
And she, become a chicken, laid an egg from which the universe sprang—including Terra the earth, who as she slept bore Uranus and he took the sky and reigned over her.

Then Terra is angry and persuades her sons attack Uranus.
And Kronos led them lopping off his father's genitals with a sickle and ruling the sky until I when I was grown to manhood waged war with Kronos my father because he would devour me.
I threw the goddamned bastard into Hell and he has never since troubled me.

That aside, this wedding progressed perfect
until Eris in rage neglected
lobbed a golden apple inscribed
"For the Fairest" onto our dining table.
The fruit is claimed by Hera, Aphrodite, and Athena,
demanding I determine which of them receive it.

But I won't be embroiled in their dispute.
Rather to Mount Ida I sent the three goddesses.
There a handsome shepherd, Paris,
judges which of them is fairest.

Paris is unknown
a son of Hecuba and Priam, king of Troy.
Prior to his birth
a prophecy identified him as Troy's destruction.
He was exposed in helpless infancy on
the mountainside but lived
and is grown a charming youth.

[Exit Zeus. Paris enters carrying a sheep and the Golden Apple]

PARIS AND THE GODDESSES

Paris: It was this morning Hermes
the gods' messenger and son
of Zeus appeared to me and said
Athena, Hera, and Aphrodite approach—
that I am to select the one
who's fairest.

[Paris unfastens his garment, releasing a gigantic (fabricated) penis. He begins fucking the sheep.]

But how can I
simple shepherd be
an arbiter of divine
beauty?

I think I will divide the golden fruit
three ways, rewarding each
an equal segment that none
feel slighted. It would be terrible
to offend a goddess.

No, no, I cannot disobey the word of God.
He commands a choice be made;
to contradict would be a sin—
what can I do? If I choose one
I offend the others. If I don't
I encourage Zeus' wrath. Either way
I'm fucked.

[The sheep bleats.]

I see them. Yes, three figures,
female arm in arm walking in the sky
in our direction. Let's stop
for now.

[Paris pulls himself out of the sheep. The sheep bleats loudly.]

(*To sheep.*) Sorry.

[Paris tucks himself back in his clothes. From offstage the voices of the goddesses.]

Hera: Paris, you know why
we come.
Paris: I do
divine Hera—though I think
I'm ill-equipped to—
Athena: We are confident you'll stand
and make the right selection.
Paris: As you say
wise Athena. Still
I beg the two I cannot choose
not to be fierce with me. I
am human—and thus fallible.
Aphrodite: We promise to abide by your decision.
Paris: Thanks, Aphrodite. I wonder
will it be enough
to judge you as you are, or can
you be naked?
Hera: What?!
Athena: Naked?!
Aphrodite: All of us?!
Athena: Oh, for Christ sake!
Paris: Please, do as I ask.
I'll judge you each
one at a time. The others
kindly wait in silence by that tree.
Hera first.

[Enter Hera wearing a kitchen apron.]

Hera: Paris, here am I Hera, wife
of Zeus—reduced to ruthless intrigue most
of my married life because of Zeus'
infidelities. Examine my magnificent figure
conscientiously.
Paris: I will.

Hera: Paris, you should judge me fairest—
I can offer power and wealth to you beyond
your wildest dreams. I'll make you king
of oily Asia Minor, richest man alive.
Paris: No;
you shouldn't try to bribe me. I have seen
enough. Enough.

[Hera exits.]

Athena, your turn.

[Athena enters, with huge shield covering most of her body and a long spear. She wears a helmet.]

Athena: Okay, I know I am not much to look at.

Metis my mother was raped
by Zeus. An oracle declared
I'd be a girl, but if my mother had
a second child it would be
a boy fated to depose Zeus as Kronos
was by Zeus, and Uranus was
by Kronos. So Zeus opened wide
his mouth and swallowed Metis
and that was the end of my mother.

By the way, if I'm the chosen one I will
endow your mind with wisdom unsurpassed. You will
be always victorious in battle.
In all affairs—
Paris: No, do not offer like the other
insubstantial gifts. Wealth
and wisdom—power—are nothing to me.
I am a shepherd on a mountainside;
I do not need these . . . whatever these . . .
Please, go away.

[Athena exits off right.]

And now I'll call the last contestant—

[But before he can finish that sentence, Aphrodite enters. She wears sunglasses and open-toed high-heeled shoes.]

Aphrodite: Hi. You saved the best for last
didn't you? I'm Aphrodite—
"foam born" from the scrotum of Uranus. (*Pronounced "your anus."*)
I want that apple. Now listen Paris.

As we rode the winds of Pelion here to Ida
I couldn't help but notice your attachment
to these . . . animals. No, no,
I think it's sweet—really—but
Paris, you don't want to waste your life
fucking the flock. Do you?
Paris: (*Overwhelmed by her.*) Unh . . .
Aphrodite: Most singles can tell you what they want in a mate
but few can tell you what they need—too bad!
Because having a mate who can fulfill your needs
is the secret to a lifetime of love.

I happen to be an expert at identifying
personal needs. In fact,
helping successful singles like yourself
understand what they need in a mate
is my divine duty. Meeting someone is easy,
finding the right one—(*She's got hold of his penis.*) that's hard.

(*As she masturbates him.*) I do this through unique screening procedures—
there's nothing like it anywhere.
It's the secret of my success.
Paris: Un huh.
Aphrodite: There are no computers,
no embarrassing videos,
no awkward introductions to make you feel
uncomfortable. For instance,
Helen of Sparta.
Paris: Who?
Aphrodite: You've heard of Helen, haven't you?
Paris: No.
Aphrodite: She's the most

beautiful woman in the world
and passionate.
Paris: Really?
Aphrodite: Oh, yes. Currently she is married
to Menelaus, Agamemnon's brother. But . . .
I would give her to you if you like.
Paris: But you say she's married.
Aphrodite: Tough shit.
Paris, go to Helen with my son,
Cupid, by your side. Once
you've docked your tug in Sparta
we'll see she falls for you.
Paris: You think?
Aphrodite: I think that once you've met
all you two will want to do
is fuck, fuck, fuck, fuck, fuck, fuck, fuck, fuck, fuck.
A lot.

[Paris gives Aphrodite the Golden Apple. Then quick light shift. No break between acts.]

Act 3

LYNN'S SAGA

[Light illuminates Uncle Saul in his wheelchair. Harold stands visible in the shadows, unseen by Saul.]

Uncle Saul: So when I'll go with the dentist they'll have the girl clean my teeth—what's her name? Lisa something. She's a very nice girl—what is it? Lisa . . . Lynn! Lynn! That's what the name—she's a colored girl—she says to me—she says—she tells me, Mr. Goodman, you'll have to floss your teeth and I said, what do you mean? And she says—she puts the floss—the thread—in my mouth and she scrapes with it—she scrapes and she says to me put the thread between the teeth to scrape with the microbes—you gotta scrape because you gonna have the microbes off the teeth. You gotta break up the colonies from the microbes that are on the teeth. And she looks at me and I said, I said, All right, I'm gonna do that. She's a very sweet girl. She takes with the toothbrush—she takes it—and she shows me—she asks me what do I brush my teeth? So I show with her what I do and she says that's no good. And she takes it—she says—she takes the toothbrush—she takes—she takes it and she says—she takes it and she shows me what she wants I should be doing with it—and she does it. And I said, All right, I'm gonna do that. And then what does she takes the toothbrush and she turns it around with the rubber tip, and she puts the rubber tip in my mouth and she rubs it between the teeth and the gum and she says to me I want you should do this when you wash the teeth. So I said, What am I—I'm not gonna argue with her—I thought I'll do it because . . . she knows.

So she scrapes and she rubs and she says to me I want you should stimulate the gum when you brush the teeth. And I said to her what am I gonna want to do this for? And she says to me no, you gotta stimulate the gum with the pressure because it's good for you. And I don't know what she means. And she says you gotta put the pressure with the gum because what's gotta happen is you gonna put on the pressure—and what's gonna happen is the blood supply—you gonna cut it off for awhile while you have on the pressure with the gum. And this is gonna be good for you because the blood—you see—she shows me—she takes with the finger—and she puts her finger in my mouth and she puts on the pressure with the gum, and it gets a little bit white and she says you see what happened? We cut off the blood supply—and I said all right, so what? And she says now look what happened when I take off the finger and I stop the pressure from the gum. And the gum gets red because she says the blood comes back. And I said, that's good. And she says that's right that's good because the blood comes back is gonna flow into the gum strong and it's gonna be clean fresh blood. And I ask her is that good? And she says yes because the blood is full of nutrients and oxygen. She says the blood contains oxygen because when you breathe, the oxygen comes in with the lungs, it gets exchanged for the carbon dioxide—which you breathe out—and the oxygen gets in with the blood. And I ask her so what do I want with the oxygen? And she says you want to have the oxygen because the oxygen is gonna kill the microbes.

And this is what she tells me. She says to me

[Without interruption of the text, Uncle Saul's voice takes on the character of a young woman.]

Oxygen burns—it oxidizes. (Open wide. Thank you.) You see for over half its four point five billion year history—over half—the Earth's (A little wider.) atmosphere contains practically no oxygen. (Turn towards me. Thank you.)

There was life, of course, life was thriving on the Earth from almost its inception—altering the planet's surface and atmosphere—maintaining itself against the permutations of the world.

The first three billion years of life on Earth were microbial—anaerobic bacteria extending themselves promiscuously, recombining genes. They reproduced by doubling their size, replicating their single strand of DNA, then dividing. (You can close a little. Thanks.)

These non-nucleated cells—cells without a nucleus—invented the essential chemical reactions and metabolisms—not the least of which was photosynthesis—that's right, bacteria developed photosynthesis—not plants. There were no plants back then. No plants, no animals. Animals! We're an afterthought—and probably just for fertilizing plants. (Please rinse.)

So bacteria invented photosynthesis—which is the process of getting food from light and air. Photo—synthesis.

Now you know that life (Turn towards me.) needs hydrogen, because when added to carbon dioxide (Open. Good.) you can make organic foods—like sugar. Hydrogen gas was plentiful on the early Earth—

but it's light—it floats—it floats right into space. Did you ever see a hydrogen balloon? What happened? (*Uncle Saul speaks as himself, muffled.*) It floats. (*As Lynn.*) That's right, it floats—it floats away in space.

So hydrogen was getting scarce. But then bacteria tapped the most abundant source of hydrogen on Earth. Water—dihydrogen oxide—H_2O.

The strong bonds between hydrogen and oxygen in water were previously unbreakable until a kind of blue green bacteria developed a second photosynthetic reaction center utilizing higher energy light capable of splitting water molecules into their constituents of hydrogen and oxygen.

These frantic microbes grabbed the hydrogen, releasing oxygen into the atmosphere, setting off the most intense pollution crisis the world has ever known. Bar none. (Please rinse.)

Oxygen is toxic—especially when combined with light. You get a cut, what do you do? (N—open wide. Whoops. Sorry. Did I hurt you? I'm sorry. Turn towards me. Turn towards me. Thank you.)

Oxygen grabs electrons, producing chemicals that wreak havoc on the basic elements of life. Remember, I said oxygen burns—it oxidizes. That's right,

it's toxic. When you get a cut—if it's not too bad—leave it uncovered—let it breathe: exposed to light and air, infecting anaerobic microbes die—they're killed—their tissues are exploded.

Well, that's what happened on the Earth—and hopefully in your mouth—as oxygen was released it wiped out species left and right, exterminating the vast majority of living organisms on the Earth—more than any plague or nuclear holocaust ever could.

Yet life ascended and survived—it rallied symbiotically—fusing once again with a sex so fluid—recombining genes, regenerating quickly, replicating DNA—transforming its compositions—duplicating—developing aerobic respiration.

This essay into symbiosis led to new cells—cells with nucleus—and later plants and animals. Bacteria cooperatively merged—collectively forming new life that could exploit the new combustible environment.

What if there *was* a devastating ecological disaster—one that swept away all animals and plants? What *if* humans suicide with war or waste, plague, pestilence or famine? Life's longest living, ancient microorganisms are more than capable of adjusting and expanding once again, networking through genetic transfer and mutation, symbiosis, cohabitation—altering the environment and themselves contingently as they've done before and will again, no matter.

This lucky life is too secure to be derailed by human beings. (Un huh, don't close, stay open.) We are temporary vessels—repositories of one hundred quadrillion prokaryotic bacterial cells and ten quadrillion eukaryotic animal cells—our presence is so far one thirtieth of a percent on the timeline of the planet.

And even if we don't expire in violence—though it may be unavoidable—our time will come. And like the ninety-nine point ninety-nine percent of life forms that have lived on Earth, either we'll evolve into another species, or we'll be extinguished.

(*Uncle Saul speaks as himself.*) No thing is permanent, she said, (*As Lynn.*) or fixed. It's shifting endlessly. (Please rinse.)

[Uncle Saul inhales quickly, turns head towards Harold, exhaling a steady stream of breath. As he does, light dims on him, holding momentarily on Harold who inhales the breath of God. Then light out.]

Act 4

BACK FROM THE PLAY

[Light illuminates Harold standing beside and intensely focused on Uncle Saul. Time passes. Maxine enters with two bakery boxes.]

Maxine: (*As she enters.*) I'm sorry you had to wait at the—Oh, was—what?—was . . .

Harold: The door was open.

Maxine: Oh, I thought I locked it—I'm so glad. I felt terrible leaving you here—I had to run down to the desk to get—Uncle Saul—hi—we're back, we're back from the theater—hi—you were sleeping—did you take a nap or did you stay up? He's so sweet, isn't he. I'll tell you, growing up with Uncle Saul, it wasn't easy—he never talks—I had no one to talk with. Oh, he talks to himself, sure, or he'll talk in his sleep when he's dreaming because . . . gee, I hope I dropped the key in Danny's car and didn't lose it at the theater or—

Daniel: (*Calling from offstage.*) Sweetheart?

Maxine: Hi, we're—

Daniel: (*Entering, holding the hotel room key.*) Sweetheart, you left the key in my—

Maxine: Oh, good—I was—yes—I was—you know, I had to leave your mother standing there by the door. It was in the car, wasn't it—see, I'm not such a dummy—for ten minutes while—there was no one at the desk—and I—but who's ready for some cake? We have delicious cookies and there's a half-cake. I was going to get a whole cake, but then I thought . . . Danny, where's your father?

Harold: I'll have cake and cookies.

Maxine: Good. Good for you.

Daniel: He's moving the car.

Maxine: Why, what's the matter?

Daniel: Nothing. He didn't like where it was parked. There were some kids playing nearby. He was afraid they'd knock a ball or something through his windshield.

Maxine: You know, I got worried because your husband seemed upset during the play.

Daniel: What do you mean?

Maxine: Well, you know, right near the end of the play when that character that—that what's his name, who couldn't get home for years and years and finally did and had to leave again—and wandered again—around again—and then finally got home but ended up getting killed by his son who he never knew—your father jumped up and ran out of the theater.

Harold: That's right.

Daniel: I didn't notice.

Maxine: Oh. (*After a pause. Whispering.*) Excuse me, I have to use the bathroom. I'll be right back.

[Maxine exits.]

Daniel: Harold. (*After Harold does not reply.*) Harold. (*After Harold does not reply.*) Harold!

Harold: What?

Daniel: What's going on?

Harold: What do you mean?

Daniel: What do you mean what do I mean is what's going on—with you—with Daddy?! He hasn't said a word about . . . about. . . . you know—about . . .

Harold: Oh, yea. I told him I was a ghost.

Daniel: Oh. (*After a brief pause.*) What?

Harold: I convinced him I was a ghost.

Daniel: A what?!

Harold: A ghost.
Daniel: A ghost?! You convinced him you were a ghost?
Harold: Yes.
Daniel: Of Mommy.
Harold: Oh, yes.
Daniel: And he believed you?
Harold: Oh, yes.
Daniel: I don't believe this.
Harold: I told him I was a back from the grave for twenty-four hours to walk the Earth.
Daniel: And he believed this?
Harold: He did.
Daniel: I don't believe this. I don't believe this! This is . . . this is unbelievable! This is totally unbelievable! What kind of person would be fooled by this?
Harold: I don't know.
Daniel: Jesus Christ.
Harold: It's the best I could come up with.
Daniel: Oh, brother. I mean if I saw this on the stage I wouldn't believe it.
Harold: Well—
Daniel: Nobody would.
Harold: You think so?
Daniel: Come on Harold, if you saw this on stage would you believe it?
Harold: Probably not.
Daniel: You'd say, I'm sorry, I don't believe it.

[Maxine enters.]

I just don't believe it. I simply don't believe it.
Maxine: Well, I didn't believe it either—that makes two of us. (*Hold. Harold and Daniel sweat.*) In fact, I never believed a word of it—not for a moment. (*Hold. Harold and Daniel sweat.*) You're talking about the play, aren't you?
Daniel: (*Relieved.*) Oh, yea.
Maxine: It was so contrived, wasn't it?
Daniel: It was.
Maxine: And totally improbable. The things you're asked to believe. What kind of person would believe that?
Daniel: Don't look at me.
Maxine: Oh, and God, was it long.
Daniel: It was.

Maxine: It was too long, wasn't it?
Daniel: Much too long.
Maxine: Who ever heard of a seven-act play?
Daniel: That's right.
Maxine: I thought, I gotta get out of here.
Harold: That's just what I was thinking.
Maxine: I didn't get it, did you? I mean, how did the Greek stuff fit into the rest of the play?
Daniel: You got me.
Maxine: And then the old man breaking out into that monologue about . . . what was *that* about? Too devicey. And that dream business—Fritzy was right: talk, talk, talk. But then, this is the problem with his work.
Harold: Oh, really?
Maxine: Oh, yes. That incessant stream of words.
Daniel: I hear that.
Maxine: But—well, who knows? Maybe he'll get over it some day.
Harold: I sure hope so.
Maxine: Yes. (*After a pause.*) But that actress!!! Didn't you love that actress!!
Daniel: She was good.
Harold: She was very good.
Maxine: I think she's got it. (*After a pause.*) So, not really a good play, we think. But it was nice—we enjoyed ourselves—we're glad we went—we had a good time—we supported the arts—it got us out of the house—and now we're back! We're going to have some delicious cake and we'll have a nice talk. Who wants delicious cake?
Harold: I'll have—
Maxine: Oh, right, you asked before. See I remember.

[Maxine holds up a silver platter.]

By the way, isn't this a beautiful platter.
Harold: (*Regarding the platter.*) Oh, look at that.

[Uncle Saul rises, begins moving towards the bathroom.]

Maxine: Oh, wait a minute—excuse me. Uncle Saul, do you need to make a B.M.? Do you wanna make a B.M.? Okay, I'm gonna help you.
Uncle Saul: (*Without turning to her.*) What?
Maxine: Or do you want to do it on your own? I'm gonna let him take care of himself—he'll be all right. So, the platter. I got this the other day in

an antique shop on Wilshire Boulevard, right near San Vicente.

Harold: Oh, yea.

Maxine: I wanted to have something nice, for to serve the cake today.

Harold: It's beautiful.

Maxine: Do you love antiques? 'Cause I love antiques. I want to do the whole house in antiques.

Harold: Oh, really? What period?

Maxine: Mmm, I don't know. Country. Country style. You know, real warm and cozy, old-fashioned kind of. Anyway, Maxine continues talking but becomes inaudible. Her lips move, but there is no sound. Likewise, Danny, when he speaks no sound from him.

Harold is aware of the conversion—he notes they go on like this.

Daniel: Enter from right, the Whale.

[Enter the Whale.]

Only Harold sees it. The other two continue as before.

The Whale is a massive sperm whale—white—a huge harpoon fixed in its flank. It beckons Harold follow.

Harold: Where will you lead me—

Daniel: Harold wonders. "Into some sulphurous, tormenting flames?" No matter, Harold must have sperm. Sperm! Sperm! Sperm! Rich, warm sperm. "Eat me. Eat me. Eat me, baby, drink me." Harold must have sperm, and so he follows.

[Harold exits left following the Whale.]

Maxine: What a curious feeling, Maxine is thinking. "I bet it was that chili I ate at the theater." She exits quickly to the bathroom.

[Maxine exits right. Daniel undresses to his underwear as the Ferryman enters with a change of clothing for him—handsome dark clothing: he is now the Narrator. The Ferryman exits, then returns (after the necessary number of trips) with four music stands and four tall stools. Alice B. Toklas enters (no drag!!—attired in attractive black men's clothing), sits on the third stool from the left. The Ferryman sits on the far left stool. When the Narrator is dressed and is seated on the far right stool, Harold enters, with four black volumes—simply bound. He gives a volume to each character and sits on the remaining stool. Texts are opened and off we go.]

The Narrator: Enter from left, the Whale, with Harold in lascivious pursuit. The Whale sets itself on the floor of the stage, and, flukes up, sounds, disappearing from sight. Harold swoons. He wakes to find himself, dressed in his business suit, standing center in a vast darkness.

Harold: Oh shit,
I'm in the cruising park. I swore
I wouldn't come here anymore.

The Narrator: At that, a female presence gathers out of shadow, perched on a tree limb upstage right. It is the actor playing Uncle Saul—he is dressed in a simple blouse, plain skirt and low heels—all circa 1920.

Harold: Have pity on me, please,
whoever you may be. It seems
you come from some time past
the present.

Alice B. Toklas: In life I was companion to
that woman who when asked, "Why don't
you write the way you talk?" replied,
"Why don't you read the way I write?"

Harold: You're Alice Toklas, then.

Alice B. Toklas: I'm Alice Toklas, yes. It's—hi,
it's nice to meet you.

Harold: Oh hi, Miss Toklas, can
you—listen, can you help me?
I've gone astray from that straight road
and find myself within the dark wood
of this familiar park.

Alice B. Toklas: Familiar? Then you've made this round before.

Harold: It's three times that I've come here to
this place, this park, and circled like
the other men to look for sex.

First time I came nine months ago I met a man
who took me to his home. The second man
who took me home got very rough. The last time,
just a week ago, I met a man
who after we had sex here in the park
asked me for money.

Alice B. Toklas: Each time you come sounds worse and worse. And worse,

the worse it gets the more you'll come. Allowed
you'd season here in Hell.
Harold: Where will it end?
Alice B. Toklas: This dirt path has no end—it winds around itself
and suffocates the ones who run it. I know
a different route—a way within.
A lady there unwittingly would help you.
But you must use your wits and ask of her the past
before you can resurface as yourself.

I propose you come with me. I'll lead you into Heaven.
The Narrator: At that, that Alice slow descends to Harold's level.
Harold: But if to Heaven, shouldn't we ascend?
Alice B. Toklas: Oh no. Heaven is within
the Earth—not up in the sky.
It's a returning—
the most moving on there is.
Harold: Miss Toklas, where is Hell?
Alice B. Toklas: Hell? Bubeleh—
your life is hell. Why dream a Hell
that's after life? Come on.

And like the poet led by Virgil—
though your dream aspires to less
than his Commedia—take note.
Once in we'll right
then left beside the freeway wait
until a ferry comes to take you to the dead.
Your mother's there—
from her you could procure some useful info.
There's the gate ahead.
The Narrator: And so they go in silence till they settle near the entrance, upstage left.
Harold: Miss Toklas, please, that sign inscribed
ephemeral on the clouds above the gate—
its writing's strange and unlike any I have seen before.
What does it say?
Alice B. Toklas: ABANDON HERE ALL HOPE
WHO ENTER OF DIRECT PARALLELS AND PRECISE CORRELATIONS.

WHAT YOU SEE IS AN AMORPHOUS WASH;
THE MYSTERY WON'T BE SATISFACTORILY
RECONSTRUCTED.

MOST MYTHOLOGY AND SCIENCE IS
CORRUPT RE-PRESENTATION.

Harold: I puzzle over that.

Alice B. Toklas: That's the idea. Let's move on in.

The Narrator: At that a trapdoor in the stage floor opens, trumpeting a cleansing gush of steam. Alice Toklas dives directly in; the geyser reverses, and she's sucked right down the tube. Harold, hesitant, places his left foot timid near the blow hole. Instantly he's swallowed too. Down, down, down they go in cyclone-style until they reach the bottom and set out again. Light changes.

Alice B. Toklas: We've still a way to go.
To help us pass the time we walk
let's talk—sympose with me—
I'll be your Diotima.

Harold: What should we talk about?

Alice B. Toklas: That's up to you. But please
excuse me, Harold, if at times
referring to the past or to the future
I use the present tense;
in this your dream all time
will issue as an indistinguished moment.

The Narrator: And so it goes, they travel. Ideally, this Act takes years to play. The actors move about the stage in spiral fashion—two steps forward, one step back, two steps forward, one step back, thus describing ever smaller circles.

Patient, that considerating Alice Toklas, guiding that, at times reluctant and resistant Harold by the path of this own self-described direction. For even after certain truths are well-established in his mind, some long discarded doubt's rekindled, plaguing his—

Harold: But Alice, what about Leviticus?
"Thou shall not lie with mankind as with womankind:
. . . abomination—" I think of it, and I feel guilty.

Alice B. Toklas: Then Harold—boychikel—screw
your Levitical guilt to the shticking place—
that's all it is, besides, shtickdreck—

writ down by some alter kockers schmoozing in the desert
three thousand years ago.
Harold: Oy Gott.
Alice B. Toklas: But good that you remind me of the Jews—there are
illuminating similarities
and differences between the history of Jews
and gays.
Harold: Oh yea?
Alice B. Toklas: Oh, yes.
societies that do not tolerate
religious diversity are generally
intolerant of those whose sexuality
is nonconformant.

From early Christianity to concentration camps
both Jews and gays have been subjected to
harassment simultaneously—
portrayed as beasts bent on destroying
the children of the majority.

But Jews don't you know have Judaism—
ethics passed to child from parent—wisdom culled
from generations of oppression.

Gay people are not born into gay families
and taught the history of their kind or how they might
conduct themselves amidst the defamation
and affliction of the majority.
We suffer individually, alone,
without support of our relations. In this sense, Harold,
only gays are born into the home of the oppressor.

So much of what our kind experienced
has been deleted. Though worse than deletion
is alteration—twisted truths—
our lives, love, poetry, and art transvestited
by sadistic, unjust incorrectors.

This wasn't always true.
There have been periods we lived in peace

and prospered elevated in the state.
But little testament or gospel of accomplishment 's extant;
the record is corrupted and infertilized.
The truth has been molested by those justless buggers
who concurring with the justless whites,
white out the natural colors of history.
Harold: But history aside,
I've often heard the urge to couple with one's gender 's like—
it's like some conflict—some
conflicting something—like
the *distant father and*
the what is it—*the over-protective mother who—*
Alice B. Toklas: When you seek a counselor, Harold,
careful who you choose to help you navigate your ship;
many 's the quack out there who'd drag you through
the unproven straights of Oedipus.

Even in the more forgiving future
will there be those asses who maintain that
"gays have no reality awareness
of their partners or their feelings—"
the contact's "simply epidermal, mucous, anatomic."
"The homosexual act," they grind,
"is purely egocentric,"
"and any tender reciprocity is pretense."
They prate that all the homosexuals they treat
are masochistic.
Harold: Is it true?
Alice B. Toklas: I wouldn't be surprised—
clearly they're sadists; who but masochists
would choose them for shrinks.
Harold: How will we classify these Unnecessary Losses?
Alice B. Toklas: Circle Eight. Cantos twenty-nine and thirty—they're Falsifiers:
For they engage in fruitless Alchemy;
They Impersonate healers;
Their findings are Counterfeit (based on prejudicial research);
And so they bear False Witness.

Let them waste eternity away in Hell,
slaving unsuccessfully to change

each other into "homosexuals."
The Narrator: Light intensifies.
Harold: And are there others I should know about
who've checked themselves in unenlightened limbo?
Alice B. Toklas: The list goes on forever, Harold.
Even that Divine Comedian threw us into Hell.
He canto'd us as criminals of nature.
(*À la Bette Davis.*) What a dump!

The Narrator: Their pace accelerates, the spiral tightens. Alice Toklas prophesies to Harold of a Horrible Infecting Virus that will assault the coming decades—and how at first infection 's high among gay men. At that, the stage is showered from the flies with reams of made-for-TV movies that depict sweet little children and straight adults who have contracted AIDS from blood transfusions. The actors' path is thus made more difficult. Still, they manage to kick their way through all this garbage.

Alice B. Toklas: Among the many flushed away
will be your nephew yet unborn—
oh, yes that theater-going-Maxine's son
and Danny's—Kenny.
Harold: Wait—
Alice B. Toklas: There's no more time,
Don Juan—the ferry is approaching.
When on board ask the driver for his story.
He'll refuse, you'll see; so tell him that you know
he wrote insulting words upon his dead wife's stone—
he won't want that repeated. What's writ
I cannot say; but trick him; he is easily duped.
His dead wife's name was Faith—that's all you need to know.
Once landed on the other shore you'll find your mother.
Ask of her the past. Each time she strains the mem'ry,
pluck from out her purse a cigarette.
But do not let her see you do it. She does,
then all is lost. Then when they're yours
you wake yourself and wrap things up and say good-bye.
Harold: Good-bye? What happens if I—
Alice B. Toklas: Just—

The Narrator: Too late. Alice Toklas vanishes in light then darkness. Smog descends. From everywhere, the sound of heavy traffic. A '69 Mustang convertible pulls up from offstage left. Behind the wheel is the Ferryman.

The Ferryman: Hey!
Harold: What? Who?
The Ferryman: You.
Harold: Me?
The Ferryman: Yea, you. You need a ride across?
Harold: I do.
The Ferryman: Come on.
The Narrator: Okay, so Harold jumps inside the car. Light changes. Daybreak. A fiery sun rises on a scrim, upstage center. The Ferryman shifts into high gear and the car goes zooming over the heads of the audience.
Harold: Now Ferryman, my guide—
that guide that brought me to this freeway—said
you'd have a story I should hear.
The Ferryman: No way, no story.
Harold: Well,
she said if you won't tell that I repeat what you
insensitively chiseled on your dead wife's grave.
A phrase that's read insulting to the memory—
insinuating that her life was waste.
Her name was Faith.
The Narrator: The Ferryman shifts to a lower gear.
The Ferryman: Okay. I'll tell you, sure.

I had a brother, Meyer;
"Meyer the Flyer" I would call him 'cause
he'd fly away and do just what I told him.

Meyer—he did things for me—
but when he'd done them
I told him I did them for he.
And he, schlemiel, believed.

I sent him on a real hard journey once
to get me back our mother dead who died.
I heard that if she walked once more—
if only for a day—
I'd get some secret of eternal life from her—
I couldn't pass it up.

So Meyer dropped himself into the Earth
and brought our mother's shadow into light.

My mother taught me nothing—
the story I had heard was false.
But Meyer clear it was to me gained something.
"What something," I asked him—and he said
he "learned within"; but what, he didn't say.
And what he also didn't say—and this—
I don't know who it was who told to Meyer—
Meyer didn't say—
that if the guy who drives you 'cross in Heaven asks
you take the wheel a second of his car—
he didn't tell me to refuse this guy's request.
And so I made the journey Meyer made,
and took the wheel when I was asked.
The man jumped out
and I've been saddled with the driving ever since.

Harold: That's int'resting.

The Ferryman: You wanna take the wheel a sec?

Harold: No thanks.

The Narrator: The car sets ground again stage right.

The Ferryman: Then here we are—and look
some lady's coming up the ramp.

The Narrator: As Harold deposits himself down right, the Ferryman roars recklessly off left. Enter from right Harold's most sincerely dead mother, Shirley, swinging a large black bag. Her face is ashen—she supposes that her Sonny wants the moon. Music. Harold swoons. He wakes to find himself beside his mother in a small white space furnished only with a television set. Harold flips on the tube; immediately his mother is engrossed in her program—for preference, *The Hollywood Squares.* Harold asks Shirley three questions. And as she absent-minded answers him, he manages each time to pluck from out her bag a cigarette. The television on through all this, drowning out the dialogue from the stage. The questioning concluded, a contestant on the game show says, "I'll take Paul Lynde to win." Then Peter Marshall asks Paul Lynde, "Paul, what does it mean if you are anally retentive?" Paul Lynde responds, "It means you're full of shit." Shirley smiles. At that Harold bursts into fire, and flaming surges toward the surface. Curtain, Act 4.

[The actors close their texts as light shifts. No break between acts.]

Act 5

ALL THAT SPRAWL

[Enter from right, the Whale. From left, Melvin in his car.]

The Whale: One more song for all that sprawl—the songless city—it's the city of the angels—Los Angelés.

One last song—the song of Melvin driving madly through L.A.—perturbèd by the ghost he's seen—the grave has op'd—and up we go into the everlasting sunny 85—the one unending season—*Paradiso*—it's the city of the angelahs. From Tower Road to Baring Cross, from Springvale Drive to August Street—oh, what a fling through all that sprawl.

Let's find him now—let's find Melvinalah spun like a dreidelah through all that gross L.A.alah. He's run the road from Commerce all the way to L.A.X.

Melvin: Get back.

The Whale: He's coming out of Hillside now where Jolson's great erection to himself's cascading down past lesser lights like Mammy—

Melvin: Shirley's—

The Whale: —buried there. And Swannee Melvin—

Melvin: —surely not—she's dead—but walking—

The Whale: —driving

Melvin: —once again for one long day.

The Whale: —in all that sprawl.

Melvin: L.A.

The Whale: It's the city of the angels.

Melvin: I gotta find a place to park.

The Whale: So Melvin, sweetheart, why'd you visit Shirley's grave out here at Hillside?

Melvin: Why the hell I schlep out here to Hillside? Surely Shirley's dead, she's—

The Whale: Now at last the great grand theme. At last the dithyrambic goal of evolution's not refinement, darling, it's expansion—all that's—

Melvin: Left.

The Whale: On Centinella.

Melvin: Shit! I should go right. Why the hell 'm I—

The Whale: What's he doing?

Melvin: Left.

The Whale: Onto La Brea.

Melvin: No.

The Whale: Is it all without purpose—the unplanned city? inching east to Maywood, Vernon, South Gate, Lynwood, Downey, Rosemead. You wanna know the way this play works, listen up—this is the song of the smoggy road—this tells the whole unstructured story.

Melvin: Where 'm I going?

The Whale: Hell if we know, Melvin. All we know the meter's running, clipping long toward Glendale, Pasadena, Burbank.

Melvin: Look at that, the mirror 's filthy.

The Whale: Yes; and as he grime wipes south he sees it's Inglewood and Hawthorne, El Segundo, Santa Ana, Torrance, Anaheim.

Melvin: What a fucking city!

The Whale: Chaos.

Melvin: Right.

The Whale: On Exposition Boulevard.

Melvin: Oh, shit!

The Whale: The mishegoss. And that's the point—the point we'd make.

Melvin: Goddamn!

The Whale: He's east again—he leaves behind him Santa Monica, Culver City, and Beverly Hills, God love you.

Melvin: I can't believe—I shoulda stayed La Brea—their hotel is in Westwood on Wiltshire. Where 'm I going?

The Whale: That's the question, Melvin, baby. Why ya flying blind through all that sprawl? Your author knows, but she's as lost as you. She takes poetic license plates we're swerving out of Melvin's way he's—

Melvin: Jesus!

The Whale: Melvin—easy Melvin watch out Melvin honey watch the road—for Christ sake, Melvin, that's a red light—

Melvin: Stop!

The Whale: He's freaked out now—he's driving like a crazy—

Melvin: Fuck!

The Whale: Oh, but look at this; he's turned around—he's seen a vision of his dead wife—what's her name—who's excavated now—that saber toothy spouse of his ris' out the pit.

Melvin: Get back.

The Whale: (*Coming forward, addressing the audience.*) Come on now, let's be honest—our time is coming to an end. I'll speak to you as I've not spoke before. I've loos't off limits and imagination's lines—we're back on the open freeway now—'cause Melvin doubled back to 405, left-laning quick to Westwood. (I let him—what the hell.) This comedy is cockamamie from the moment go. I've tried—I've Troy'd—to masque up every little hole. I fantasized a theme would be erected to transcend the sticky glue of dramaturgy; but you've seen through all my disguises. You know, for one, that Harold could not dream a dream of Hell the way he dreamed of Hell—no way! This play 's the song of inconsistency—you're soaking in it—Madge-ination!

The Whale and Melvin: Harold'd never dream that shit.
How could he have thought of it?
No way nothing one small bit.
He don't got the brains for it.

Melvin: Harold ain't read Gertrude Stein.

The Whale: Dante neither.

Melvin: Shakespeare nein.

The Whale: But for play's sake that we pine,

Melvin and The Whale: We'll pretend the plot works fine.

Melvin: I gotta find a space—

The Whale: This maven author's looking for a path to wind around before she winds things up—

Melvin: —a spot to park with no damn kids around.

The Whale: —a little local color.

Melvin: Shirley. Left.

The Whale: And now no more poetic opportunity—'cause Melvy doubled back on us—but wait—just wait—the showdown's coming up at sundown: Melvin, Harold, Shirley—the father and the son, the holy ghost. Oooh, what a reserector set!

SHIRLEY TALKS BUSINESS TO SAUL

Harold: (*Opening the cake box.*) So Saul, my son, Danny, tells me you're in the . . . What—what kind of business are you in?

Uncle Saul: (*Sounds like "crap."*) Scrap.

Harold: What?

Uncle Saul: (*Again, like "crap."*) Scrap.

Harold: Oh, crap. Well, how do you like that.

[Harold takes out the half-cake. A rich chocolate cake. Looks like shit.]

We manufacture toilet paper and you sell crap: this is a marriage made in Heaven. I'll bet there's good money in crap.

Uncle Saul: It's a living.

Harold: (*Slicing a piece of cake.*) It's more than a living, Saul. It's a way of life. People don't have an appreciation. Listen, I lived twenty-three years of my life with Melvin; believe me, I know about waste. (*Eats a piece of cake.*) We inherited the business from my father, Morry. It was a shit business. (*Eats a piece of cake.*) My father pissed away all the profits at the track. Christ, what a family. They pushed me into my marriage. I didn't want to get married—to what, to Melvin? I didn't want to get married to Melvin. But my mother was pushing, my father . . . my mother was pushing. Marriage? (*Eats a piece of cake.*) I had my whole life before me. I was twenty-two years old. I was interested in music. But then I thought, What the hell am I gonna do with the rest of my life. So . . . I got married . . . I had children . . . and then I got sick. (*Eats a piece of cake. On the verge of tears. After a pause.*) Oooh, the cake is good, isn't it? It's so light. It floats. It floats right into space.

So where was I with the . . . oh, yea; so when my father, Morry—may he rest in peace that son of a bitch finally kicked the can, we inherited his crappy business. But I'll tell you something, Saul; that Melvin, he made the business from nothing, from the bottom up, from scratch. And look at him now—he's scraped his way to the top: a big macher in toilet paper. (*Takes out a cigarette from his shirt pocket, sets it on the tea cart.*) We don't manufacture for the home. Nothing fancy. The competition's tight and stiff. (*Takes out a second cigarette.*) For industry we do—gas stations, cafeterias, public schools. (*Takes out the third and final cigarette.*) That's where you'll find our paper. Sometimes cheap hotels. Wherever the business is looser.

THE FAMILY HAS A DISCUSSION

[Melvin enters.]

Harold: So, Melvin, there you are. You're gone for hours.

[Harold lights the first cigarette.]

Melvin: I was parking the car. Where's Danny?

Harold: He went with Maxine downstairs to the pharmacy.

Melvin: What's 'a matter?

Harold: Something she ate—I don't know.

Melvin: (*After a pause.*) So, why'd you come back?

Harold: For Danny.

Melvin: What do you mean?

Harold: What do you mean, what do I mean? He needed me. He needed his mother's appearance.

Melvin: Oh, yea?

Harold: You heard Maxine; no mother, no marriage. Besides, I wanted to see the family just one more time.

Melvin: One more time, and then that's it, you don't come back again?

Harold: Never.

Melvin: You gonna see Harold?

Harold: I don't need to see Harold.

Melvin: Just us?

Harold: Just you, just me.

[Enter Maxine and Danny.]

Maxine: Okay, we're back.

Daniel: Hey Dad, you're back. You un . . . find a safe spot?

Melvin: I think so.

Maxine: I'm sorry about all that commotion.

Daniel: Don't be sorry.

Maxine: It's terrible when you don't have control of yourself.

Harold: There's nothing worse.

Maxine: I sure hope this medication keeps me quiet.

Harold: I hope so too.

Maxine: You know, I feel like I'm already becoming a part of the family—it's such a nice feeling. Don't you feel that way, Danny?

Daniel: I feel . . . yea . . . good—yea.

Maxine: I can't wait to meet your brother, Harold, and his wife.

Daniel: Yea.

Maxine: What's he like? I mean, just give me a hint—a little something.

Daniel: Harold? Ummm . . . I don't know, he's uhh . . . I don't know—what's he like?

Melvin: He's a lot like his mother.

Maxine: He takes after you, that's so sweet. And when do they—I'm so nosy—but anyway, when do they get back from Las Vegas?

Daniel: When do they get back? Unhh . . . I'm not sure. Soon, I hope.

Melvin: They better get back soon. I'll tell you Harold's got a lot of nerve not telling me he's going away. He has a business to run. What do you think, a business runs itself?

Harold: Oh, listen to you—Simon Le Greed. Harold takes a vacation once every five years. He slips away for a weekend and Melvin's—

Melvin: Harold makes plenty of time for himself lately. He takes a course in the evening—some kind of farchadat something.

Harold: Ethics. He's taking a course in basic ethics. Leave it to Melvin to refer to ethics as farchadat.

Melvin: Why? What does that mean?

Harold: It means you wouldn't know an ethic if it hit you over the head.

Melvin: This is what I mean—Harold takes after his mother. A lot of talk that she doesn't know what she's talking about.

Harold: Right, but you know what you're talking about. You put Harold to work in that goddamn office of yours when he was fifteen years old.

Melvin: Oh, come on, Shirley.

Harold: And when it was time for college—Business Administration—Accounting. Harold had no choice.

Melvin: What are you talking about?

Harold: You think Harold wanted to study business—that he'd want to spend the rest of his life wrapped up in toilet paper?

Melvin: Harold could have studied whatever he wanted.

Harold: Oh sure, but you wouldn't pay for it.

Melvin: What?

Harold: Melvin—I'll never forget this—Melvin refused to pay for Harold's education unless he studied—

Harold:	Melvin:
	Shirley—
—yes—what Melvin	get off it.
wanted him to study.	
He wouldn't pay unless	
Harold majored in Business.	
"You want me to pay for	You see—Shirley likes to
college, you take what	She likes—
I want you to take. I'm	
not throwing away good	
money on	You know, you're talking
	ancient history, baby. These
	things happened a long
—good money on—"	time ago.

Melvin: Well, I was paying for it.

Harold: You see. And he still had Harold working at the plant on weekends in the office. Like a serf.

Melvin: Come on, Shirley, save it for your autobiography.

Harold: (*Extinguishing the first cigarette.*) It's the God's truth.

Melvin: No, no.

Harold: And listen to him, "He better get back here." He begrudges him a lousy weekend in Vegas. I hope they stay a month, both of them—they should have some pleasure. God knows they don't enjoy their lives.

Maxine: Oh, really?

Harold: They're not happy people.

Maxine: Oh, that's terrible.

Melvin: What are you talking about?

Harold: Just what I said. Harold and Sylvia—they're not happy. They don't make each other happy.

Maxine: Is one of them having an affair?

Melvin: Shirley, don't start rumors.

Harold: It's not a rumor—what am I starting? (*Lighting the second cigarette.*) Danny knows.

Daniel: What do I know?

Melvin: Maxine, you want to know—they're very happy, Harold and Sylvia.

Harold: No, they're not.

Melvin: Oh, what do you know?

Harold: I know.

Melvin: You see—you know what? Shirley doesn't like Sylvia. She'd love it if—

Harold: What do you mean I don't like Sylvia? I like Sylvia.

Melvin: You?! I could take you on a roller coaster ride with what Shirley thinks of Sylvia.

Harold: Oh, come on, Melvin.

Melvin: No, you come on, Shirley. You know that—

Harold: What do you know about Harold?

Melvin: What do you mean what do I—

Harold: You don't know anything about Harold. You never had—

Melvin: You see—this is what she's like.

Harold: It's true.

	Melvin:
Harold:	What do you know
I know—	about Harold and

believe me, I know abou— Sylvia? You don't—
If anyone, I know Harold.

Melvin: You don't know anything but yourself, Shirley. You're simple-minded and you're self-involved.

Harold: Oh, fuck you. (*To Maxine, politely.*) Would you hand me a napkin, honey?

Maxine: (*Handing Harold a paper napkin.*) Oh, sure.

Melvin: You hear that—fuck you? You see what she's like? Listen, Harold works in the business, he has a very nice life with his wife—who, to be honest with you I didn't like at first—

Harold: That's right.

Melvin: And neither did Shirley for that matter. You thought she was dumb. She said, "She's dumb." That's how Shirley talks about people. She calls them dumb. And then one night—very late—she rolls me over in bed—she's changed her mind. "We have to let Harold and Sylvia marry." You remember that?

Harold: Ah yes, I remember it well.

Melvin: But then you changed your mind again. And you see, that what she's like—she's moody. Two days later I'm telling her about I'm making arrangements—she says, "What do you mean you're making arrangements? I never said—" on and on—you see, Shirley has a very convenient memory. And then she's going to tell you about Harold. Like she knows. He and Sylvia are very happy.

Harold: No, they're not happy.

Melvin: You see, now she doesn't like Sylvia.

Harold: It has nothing to do with Sylvia—it's Harold. He's . . .

Maxine: And Harold runs the business?

Melvin: I run the business.

Daniel: Dad runs the business.

Melvin: I run the business.

Harold: Oh, really.

Melvin: Harold answers the phone—I run the business.

Harold: (*Extinguishing the second cigarette.*) I didn't know that.

Melvin: What are you—Harold—he's got ideas—he likes to talk, you know, he doesn't know what he's . . .

Maxine: Well, he's young. We're all young.

Harold: Like what?

Melvin: What?

Harold: "What?" Like what?! Like what doesn't he know?

Melvin: He doesn't know what he's talking about. He gets ideas from

Daniel:	Melvin:
Anyone want more cake?	some . . .
	You know what he does?

Harold: I've had enough cake.
Melvin: No—you know what he does?
Harold: No, tell us what he does, Melvin. In your own words—you tell us.
Melvin: I'm gonna tell you, yea, you know what he does? He labels things, you know. He thinks he knows—he sees . . . he says such and such is sick—you know he uses these words like they have a meaning—this is what the Nazis did—they started to label.
Harold: What are you talking about?
Melvin: No—Harold likes to label—he—
Harold: We heard that already.
Melvin: He's like you, Shirley.

[Harold lights the third cigarette.]

He gets an idea in his head—he says this one is sick, this one is such and such—this one is a fascist—you see, it's like McCarthy—someone starts calling someone else—and you have a witch hunt—you know—you have labels.

Harold: No, Melvin is angry because Harold called him a bigot. He said that—
Melvin: Yea—no—you see—you see—he's got a label. This is what happens—he gets—and it's very simplistic—and he gets this from Shirley.
Harold: But Melvin, I don't think you're a bigot. You're not a bigot. A bigot is someone who is prejudiced—who holds prejudice against a group of people. You're not like that, sweetheart. You're not a bigot.

You're a racist. You're a racist oppressor.

	Melvin:
Harold:	No,
Yes you are.	no—you—
Oh, yes you are.	wait—

Harold: In 1966 we almost lost the business because Melvin—because a federal investigator discovered Melvin had twenty-four illegal Mexican boys working at his—

Melvin: Oh, come—I don't need this. I was giving these kids a break.

Harold: You were giving them a break! Give me a break, you bullshit artist. You never hired a black until 1969—and only then because someone was going to drag you to court over it. The only reason he hired these Mexican fellas is he found he could pay them for—hey—hey—come on—come on—what—what were you paying them? What? Less—less than half the minimum wage! Less than half. We almost lost the business. Luckily, Melvin found this Hollywood lawyer—Alan—whatever his name was—who arranged some kind of pay-off.

Melvin: All right—so I'm not going to stick around—you wanna—

Harold: Oh, I could tell you a lot of interesting stories about my fath—abababababababout Melvin.

Melvin: You see, this is what happens. Shirley likes to get excited—

Harold:	Melvin:
No, it's true.	She doesn't like—

Harold: He gets it from his mother, Elsie—and his father—except his father lost his mind in 1958 and spent the last ten years of his life sitting around their apartment in his underpants with his testicles hanging out reading thirty-year-old newspapers. "The Stock Market Crashed." "We know, Moishe, it happened in 1929—why don't you put some clothing on?"

Melvin: You know—so Shirley didn't like my father—you know why? You know why?! Because he wasn't fancy like her family—you know. And my mother was very socially minded.

Harold: Oh, yea, Elsie, the good-will ambassador. She once sent five dollars to the March of Dimes and bragged about it for the rest of her life.

Melvin: All right—so I'm gonna go.

Harold: She was horrible—horribly prejudiced.

Melvin: This is—excuse me—this is why we had to put Shirley away—you see—because she has fantasies. My mother was frightened—she was traumatized because she was once beat up—she was mugged by a black man.

Harold: Oh, bullshit! Bullshit are you full of shit you're so full of shit! Your mother wasn't mugged. Some kid ran off with her purse at the airport—he never laid a hand on her.

Melvin: And you don't think—

Harold: Yea, and besides that was 1964. I first met the woman in 1952. From then until the day she died every other word out of her mouth was shvartzer. The shvartzers this, the shvartzers that, the shvartzers this, the shvartzers that.

Just before she died, Melvin bought her an oil well in Pacific Palisades—one of those little oil wells that bobs up and down and up and down. She'd have herself wheeled out into the middle of the oilfield every afternoon. She's sit in front of the goddamn thing for hours watching it bow to her. "Yes, Elsie. Whatever you say, Elsie."

Melvin: All right—so Shirley doesn't tell you how the woman suffered—

Harold: No, I'll give her that much at least, hers was not an easy life, believe me—between her meschuggener husband who drove her—

Melvin: You know, you'll find this interesting, Maxine, my grandfather—my mother's father was exterminated in—

Harold: That's right. She lost her father, Tsimon, in the concentration camp.

Melvin: That's right. And you know you just sit here—

Harold: I know it was terrible.

Melvin: You don't get over that kind of thing.

Harold: He sent his wife—your great-grandmother, Miriam, to America with Elsie and her older brother, Jacob—who went on to a great career as a necrophiliac.

Melvin: For Christ sake.

Harold: Meanwhile, he stayed in Europe—

Melvin: He stayed in Europe and made the sacrifice.

Harold: Oh, sacrifice, my ass. This was 1913. He ran off with a dressmaker from Strie in Austria where they came from. Her name was Reckle.

Daniel: How do you know?

Harold: I know from your great-grandmother. I know from Miriam. She told me she heard that he and the dressmaker—Tsimon and the dressmaker—were at each other's throats from the day they met until—

Melvin: Miriam—yea—another one with a great imagination.

Harold: She told us. She once met a survivor from the concentration camp at some benefit in Philadelphia who had been in the same boxcar with them. He said, "What, Reckle and the boyfriend? Sure, I remember them." They bickered all the way to Dachau. (*After a pause.*) He would refer them as Heckle and Reckle.

(*Aside in his own voice.*) I gotta get out of this place.

(*In Shirley's voice.*) Okay, time's up, gotta go.

[Harold extinguishes the last cigarette.]

Maxine: Can I wrap something up for you?
Harold: No thank you, darling. I've had enough.

So, I leave you.

Maxine, honey, welcome to the family.
Maxine: (*As she embraces Harold.*) Oh, thank you.
Harold: Saul, it was a pleasure talking to you.
Uncle Saul: What?
Harold: Yea.
Uncle Saul: Good.
Harold: Maxine . . . Danny . . . you'll be good to each other?
Maxine: We will.
Daniel: We will.
Harold: (*Under his breath.*) Like hell you will.

Melvin, drop dead.
Melvin: Yea, you go straight to Hell.
Harold: If I do, I'll save you a seat. No, better—you can sit on the floor.
Melvin: You came back from the grave and tried to kill me.
Harold: Yea, well, good—we're even. Good-bye.

[Harold exits.]

SYLVIA'S EPILOGUE

[From offstage, Sylvia's voice.]

Sylvia: (*G to E.*) Haaaaaaaarold.
(*B flat to G.*) Haaaaaaaarold.
(*G sharp to D sharp.*) Haaaaaaaarold.

[Daniel, Maxine, Melvin, and Uncle Saul exit as Sylvia enters with a wooden park bench, places it down center. During the first two paragraphs of her monologue, she clears the stage of the other furniture.]

(*To the audience.*) Enter Sylvia. This is Sylvia's epilogue. Attempt is made in monologue below to convey all information within the context of dramatic action without trespassing into self-conscious or alienating, unnaturalistic techniques—i.e., absurdism, surrealism, what have you.

The scene is a park located in the Eagle Rock district of Los Angeles. By day, a children's playground, by night a scene of men engaged in sexual activity. Offstage right a troop of Boy Scouts are seated at picnic tables painting Easter eggs. No attempt, however, should be made in production to inform the audience of the significance of this setting. Clearly, the coincidence of Eagle Rock and Boy Scouts is telling—one immediately associates to Greek mythology—how Zeus, infatuated with the Trojan prince, Ganymede, swept down upon him from Olympus as an eagle and carried the handsome youth up into Heaven. Interesting as well the "rock" in Eagle Rock—no doubt a scrotal reference. The time, we note, is Easter: one, a resurrection symbol—as in the Dante *Comedy*—new life, new beginnings, etc. Second, the Easter Bunny—significant in its association to the hare—an animal symbol associated with gay men in Medieval Europe. And finally, recall the celebration of the Christian Easter falls near the Jewish Passover—another new life, new beginning symbol—but also, and more important, I think, an example of liberation from slavery, the severance of bondage, and of course the commencement of wandering around in the desert for years and years. (*As she sits on the bench.*) It is regretted that Yom Kippur could not be utilized—tying in atonement for sin, judgment of God, etc.; but, you know, you stick in as much as you can. Take it away, Sylvia.

Well, Harold, it's been weeks—a month now since you disappeared. Your car was found parked here, outside this park. I wonder what's become of you? It's good you're gone, you know. I couldn't bear you any longer. I packed and split the day you evaporated. No joke; not knowing you were gone, I left. That's some coincidence.

You took a copy of our wedding picture. Why was that? It would take one hell of a steady hand to snap our portrait, Harold—you and I. And I don't mean an "I" in your cold shadow. I mean an equal "I" a fleshed out "I" in equal light. Sharp the eye that would evoke with single-mindedness the constellation of attractions, yes, and disappointments that have made our little marriage, Harold; then plot them undistracted without tangent on a graph and show the evolution—the collapse. Thank God for that collapse.

Oh, look. The moon is up—full circle in the sky. (*To the audience.*) They say the moon was Nemesis—raped of course by Zeus—who else? She'd taken flight from him as a goose, but he became a swan and triumphed over her. Of course, in its original form, "the love chase myth," the Great Goddess would hound the Sacred King through his seasonal changes of rabbit, fish, bird, and grain of wheat—then finally devour him. With the advent of the patriarchal system the chase reversed; the nymph fled the god.

(*To herself.*) It's getting dark. That troop of kids is taking off. I gotta go.

[Sylvia rises from the bench and exits. Light is extinguished. End of play.]

She Stoops to Comedy

T. Ryder Smith (left) and David Greenspan (right) in *She Stoops to Comedy.* Playwrights Horizons, New York, 2003. Photograph by Sara Krulwich/ *The New York Times*/Redux.

She Stoops to Comedy

First produced by Playwrights Horizons, New York City, from April 3 through April 27, 2003.

Alexandra Page	David Greenspan
Kay Fein	E. Katherine Kerr
Hal Stewart	Philip Tabor
Eve Addaman	Mia Barron
Alison Rose	Marissa Copeland
Jayne Summerhouse	E. Katherine Kerr
Simon Lanquish	T. Ryder Smith

Set Design by Michael Brown
Lighting Design by Matt Frey
Costume Design by Miranda Hoffman
Directed by David Greenspan

Characters:

Alexandra Page—an actress, assumes the character of Harry Samson
Alison Rose, Alexandra's lover—also an actress
Kay Fein, close friend of Alexandra—an archeologist or a lighting designer
Hal Stewart—a filmmaker
Eve Addaman, Hal's girlfriend—also a filmmaker
Jayne Summerhouse, rival to Alexandra—also an actress, she's studying film
Simon Lanquish—an actor

Setting: The stage of course.

Time: As indicated.

Notes:

Alexandra Page is played by an actor, not an actress. At no time in the play is that actor in drag.

A cast of six. One actress plays Kay Fein and Jayne Summerhouse.

A bed. Four stools. Legs down left and right that serve as offstage. Cell phones are to be mimed. No sound effects!

Alexandra should be visible during her first "offstage" scene in the bathroom. During the final scene, she must be out of sight, truly offstage prior to her entrance.

The actors must never step out of character to comment on the play. They must remain in character and in the play when faced with incongruities or sudden "revisions."

Alex: The urge then to move across the words the page to paint a character on the stage.

The impulse then to translate onto the stage. The stage I say as fast as flexible as the page.

This then to make through revision the stage a play of words moving its characters its plot its action.

Okay fine you say so what a comedy perhaps not funny. Words then you see as you hear them not always connected but enough. This is the way I'll do it.

An actress, name: Alexandra Page. Her lover, Alison Rose. An actress also. Alexandra Page and Alison Rose. This is not funny. Okay, fine. Kay—Fein. Their friend, Kay Fein. Alex's friend, Kay Fein. An archeologist just back from a dig. A room with curtains and a bed and a door and an offstage. Okay. Fine. Talk, Kay. Talk, Kay Fein.

Kay: Alex, what're you doing?

Alex: What am *I* doing? What're *you* doing? I mean here. I thought you were on a dig.

Kay: I was. I'm back. What're you doing in there?

Alex: I'm changing. I'll be right out. I was shocked to get your call, Kay. Shocked. Where were you again?

Kay: In Egypt. I was in Egypt. You know, the usual stuff. My hands filthy with the past. Ancient history under my fingernails. And then that call from Charlotte—at my hotel—in Cairo—that you and Alison had split up.

Alex: And you dropped everything?

Kay: I rushed to London, I flew to New York.

Alex: You flew?

Kay: Well this is 1950.

Alex: How fast we move—the modern age. And yet at times, Kay, it all feels so post-modern. Whatever that means.

Kay: Well, if it doesn't mean anything now, it will probably mean something then.

Alex: I don't know how it happened. Oh, Kay. A fight, of course. One of the many. I too am an actress. That's her talking. I had just gotten back from the coast. A small part in a big picture. After all these years on the stage, but I am a stage creature—a creature of the stage—and film, you know, the motion picture—I mean what does it do for me? What does it—what has it done for me? Hope Court had a tiny role a cameo, precious little Hope—and Laurence Lawrence—after that scandal in the men's room—you naughty boy I told him he wasn't amused. And Hal, a man of the theater or so he says, now he's making pictures, trying to make it in pictures—I played his sister's best friend. I was horrid—to everyone. Abysmal. And the food! Well, I got home—

Kay: I got home after the dig in Egypt and Charlotte told me that you and Alison had split up.

Alex: She told you what?

Kay: She said she heard from Jayne Summerhouse—

Alex: Jayne Summerhouse? Foreshadowing.

Kay: That you and Alison had split up.

Alex: Who said that, Jayne said that? That's ridiculous. No. We had words, yes, but that has nothing to do with the fact that Alison is not in this scene. Alison was cast in *As You Like It.*

Kay: The one by Shakespeare?

Alex: I think so. We fought about what? I don't remember these things. Her not spending enough time with me. She's been taking this acting class. We were arguing about the kitty litter. It hadn't been changed. In days. It was her fault. Clearly. Or maybe it was my day to do it. It's of no importance. We were fighting and she said I didn't I wasn't interested enough in her career. I too am an actress, that's her talking. And anyway she left for Maine, someplace in Maine—don't come unless I call you it may be horrible and I don't want you to see it and tell me and then their Orlando was arrested. Some incident in a men's room—I don't ask for details—the naughty boy.

Kay: I hear that Hal is directing *As You Like It.*

Alex: Which is not how he likes it. The movie was a bomb. His three-picture deal is kaput.

Kay: Some place in Maine, I hear.

Alex: There's no place in Maine, believe me, I've been there. Some avant-garde take I guess on the play. A post-modern spin.

Kay: Well this is 1990.

Alex: And you know Hal. Don't you?

Kay: He's a film director, isn't he?

Alex: Small independent films. I had a role in one, one scene against Humé Hubert, this young French Canadian actor with a speech impediment. He's gonna be a major star.

Kay: I don't understand what's going on, Alex. Stay in the present. Leave the past to me.

Alex: Kay, it's simple. I did this film—it was how many years ago I don't remember—1995 or 4 or 3. So it was about two years ago. This is 1997. I guess I was awful because they cut me and replaced me with another actress. I had this one scene opposite the lead, Humé Hubert.

Kay: The young French Canadian actor with a speech impediment? I hear he's going to be a major star.

Alex: That's the one. Anyway the actress I guess they replaced me with was believe it or not worse than I was—or something—they said I wasn't speaking to the rest of the picture—whatever the fuck that means—but then this actress they got—I don't know what happened. Somehow or other I ended up back in the film.

Kay: I like Hal's movies, he's kind of avant-garde. Whatever that means these days.

Alex: It means nothing. The avant-garde is over. Or at least it is for me. But he's not avant-garde—he's just—he just has taste, he's intelligent. He's not spelling the whole thing out. You do that—and if you're somewhat intellectual, not just intelligent but intellectual—you're considered avant-garde. Don't ask me. And you're not, you never were. And he's never directed a play before and he has some ideas, I guess about a play doing a play a Shakespeare play like a film because Shakespeare I think he feels practically invented the cinema. Whatever that means. I don't care it sounds interesting and Alison—who has spent years too many years in one revival of *Oklahoma!* or *Carousel*—I mean for God's sake, how many times can you be a cock-eyed optimist in Pittsburgh—don't get me wrong I like those things—or at least I liked the albums—one revival after the other and for Alison to have a chance to play Rosalind I mean she met Hal at a dinner party for the film I was in and cut from and then put back into and he liked her and he read her and he cast her and he didn't cast me didn't even audition me but that's all right, I understand.

Kay: Alex. Pause. So she's cast as Rosalind, that's exciting.

Alex: It's thrilling. And she's a nervous wreck. I was coaching her, we were fighting, I was jealous, she was nervous, we were fighting and now she's fine. She left for Maine, they lost an actor—Hubert. He was playing Orlando.

Kay: The young French Canadian actor with a speech impediment.

Alex: Naturally. Well we all knew he'd be a major star. He's in L.A. Doing something.

Kay: But Alex let's go back.

Alex: How far?

Kay: 1970?

Alex: Oh, Kay!

Kay: For atmosphere, not continuity.

Alex: Well just for a moment.

Kay: I mean your career.

Alex: My career?

Kay: The roles you've played, Alex. Hedda, Phaedra.

Alex: (*Fehdra*) Phaedra. 1998. We're back.

Kay: Just recently, three Phaedras.

Alex: (*Fehdras*) Phaedras. Four of them—those two modern adaptations—one of them set on the moon for Christ sake all of us wearing those stupid space suits—ahahaah—then the Euripides finally the Racine. I'm fed up with Phaedra—why doesn't she just get over it.

Kay: Cleopatra, Clytemnestra.

Alex: All out of town—of course. Except for the one on the moon. How embarrassing. And for no money. She left on Saturday. They begin rehearsal on Tuesday.

Kay: In Maine?

Alex: Some shed near a pond. Heavens, the mosquitoes. Poor Hal, losing Humé on such short notice. Hell, I'd play the part. I'm so tired of the roles I get cast in. These angry, depressed women. Why do people think I'm so angry? I'm not angry. For God fucking sake. I'm not depressed. Today. I'd love to play Orlando.

Kay: Audition.

Alex: What?

Kay: I'm kidding.

Alex: (*With a bray of laughter.*) I should audition, shouldn't I?

Kay: Cut your hair, put on a suit or something, and show up.

Alex: Right. Like I could pull that off. With my figure. I've gotta lose some weight.

Kay: Well, finish getting dressed, I'll take you out for breakfast.

Alex: Thanks. Phone rings.

Kay: Hello. Oh hi, Seymour, it's Kay. Alex, it's your agent.

Alex: I'll be right out.

Kay: No, she's changing. Metamorphosing. Well, you know her, the bathroom is her temple. She makes obeisance to the gods. No, I just got back into town. No, that was an earlier draft, I'm no longer an archeologist, I'm a lighting designer. I was in Cleveland. *The Matchmaker, Salesman.* Minneapolis. The Molnár play—the funny one—and then something else—I can't remember the names anymore—it all seems like one endless play. No, I loved it—sort of. *Oedipus.* Yes, but that's months away. In two weeks. Kind of vacation. In Maine. But then I'm lighting—you know Hal Stewart? The film director, right. He's doing

As You Like It. Yes, Alison. She's fine, she's nervous. Hysterical that's she's going to be alone.

Alex: I'm not hysterical.

Kay: Sure. Oh, she'll love that. 'Bye love. He said call him tomorrow. They're doing *Hamlet* in Buffalo. They wanna see you for the Ghost.

Alex: You're kidding!

Kay: Alex, I'm bewildered. What is it with the contemporary theater? This penchant for cross-dressing. Men around the cauldron. Noras with five-o'clock shadow. It's the year 2000, but I mean really.

[Enter Alexandra disguised as a man.]

Alex: It's funny, isn't it.

Kay: Yes and—

[Kay turns, sees. Screams.]

Oh, my God, who are you? Alex. Alex, there's a man.

Alex: Kay, it's me.

Kay: Don't you come near me or I'll . . . Alex?

Alex: What do you think?

Kay: You're not serious.

Alex: Of course I am.

Kay: I see it all.

Alex: I thought you would.

Kay: You're . . . "changing." Orlando.

Alex: First I have to audition. Think I'll get it?

Kay: (*Stunned.*) You look like a man.

Alex: I told Hal, after I read the script I told him I said, I'd love to audition. He said, no, I know your work from Jeff's play. I said, Okay, but I've never done a film before. Expanded the role when he thought of me. Cut me all the same. Now I audition.

Kay: Your hair!

Alex: Does it look too butch. I hate those dykey cuts.

Kay: You cut your hair and dyed it.

Alex: Dyed it? I had the dye taken out. Did you really think I was a redhead?

Kay: After all these years. Have I been so deceived?

Alex: Kay, I am an actress. Please keep that in mind.

Kay: I feel like I hardly know you.

Alex: It's just a costume. A few odds and ends.

Kay: Where are your breasts? What's that between your legs?
Alex: Surely you've seen one of these before.
Kay: Not on you.
Alex: There's an open call at 1:00. It's amazing what you can do with a little spirit gum and an Ace bandage.
Kay: You have a cock.
Alex: (*Holding groin.*) Wanna touch it?
Kay: (*Recoiling.*) Ahahaah!
Alex: It's just chicken wire and polyester stuffing.
Kay: Where'd you get all that hair?
Alex: (*Arms, legs, and chest.*) It's Laurence Olivier's.
Kay: (*Disbelieving.*) Alexandra Page!
Alex: He always shaved his legs for roles in tights. I got it from this guy in my building.
Kay: Would you be real.
Alex: I am. The hair on my ass once belonged to Vivian Leigh.
Kay: You're going to audition for the role of Orlando. But why the anatomy?
Alex: I'm not taking any chances. Remember the wrestling scene? Who knows what I'll be asked to do.
Kay: But Alex, do you really think you can pull this off? And what's your motivation for all this?
Alex: How the hell should I know? Oh please don't examine the script too closely, Kay, we'll all be in trouble. Jealousy. Rivalry. I don't know. Look at a re-run of *Lucy.* I'm grabbing at straws. Why did she do half those things? Jayne Summerhouse. There you go. She's a treat—I mean a threat. It was a typo.
Kay: Jayne of course, she had a thing with Alison years ago.
Alex: A thing *for* Alison.
Kay: Or so you tell yourself.
Alex: Well, there you have it, motivation. I don't want Alison to sleep with Jayne Summerhouse. Or the fact that all I do is play tragic women in creepy modern adaptations. Blanche in a bathtub, Beckett in a tube stop, Congreve at the corner saloon.
Kay: Oh, stop acting.
Alex: I will not. I love it. I love to act. And when I do get a chance to play one of those roles straight, it's in some boring production with some dweepy director who doesn't know the difference between convention and the conventional. No life! And I'm tired of it. I just wanna have some fun for God's sake. I'm tired of sitting on my ass.
Kay: Well there's your motivation.

Alex: Huh? Right! Fine, whatever. And don't get me started on new plays. What I think of some of those. We'll get to that later. What was the question?

Kay: I don't remember.

Alex: Do you think you can pull this off?

Kay: Right.

Alex: I don't give a damn. The worst that can happen is I'm discovered. Uncovered. Another masquerade. Well, so what, it's my nature. I'm not afraid.

Kay: But sweetie can you act—really act—like a man?

Alex: Oh man, man. Woman, woman. What's the difference?

Kay: There is a difference. I mean you look like a man. But can you play the part? And I'm not talking from a distance, when you're on the stage painted with light. I mean in the flesh. Can you convince those in life, convince yourself?

Alex: I don't have to convince anybody, darling. That shit is for amateurs. The whole world's a fucking drag show. Look at them, they're all in costume. I'm not playing anything. I'm not acting. I'm not pretending. I don't have to act like a man. I don't know what a man is, or a woman. What is man? What is woman? Who in their right mind knows? Go back to Egypt. Dig! I guess you're an archeologist again. See what you find. I'm off to Arden. And why the hell not?

[Enter Hal, Eve, and Alison. Exit Kay.]

Hal: Sorry to keep you waiting. I'm Hal.

Alex: (*Her hairy arms.*) I'm hairy. Samson. Harry Samson.

Hal: Harry?

Alex: Samson. Harry Samson.

Hal: Well thanks for coming in. This is my assistant, Eve.

Alex: Eve?

Eve: Addaman.

Alex: Addaman?

Eve: Eve. Eve Addaman.

Alex: Eve Addaman.

Hal: And this is our Rosalind, Alison Rose.

Alex: Alison?

Alison: Alison. Alison Rose.

Hal: Alison 's Rosalind.

Alison: Alison Rose.

Alex: Rosalind.

Alison: Alison.
Alex: Alison.
Eve: Rosalind. Rosalind's Alison.
Hal: Alison Rose.
Alex: Eve. Hal. Harry. Samson. Alison Rose. Alison's Rosalind. Alison Rose.
Hal: I think you've got it.
Alex: It's nice to meet you.
Hal: Just give us a minute to get organized.
Alex: Sure.

[Exit Alison.]

Hal: We'll start with the opening speech to Adam.
Alex: Okay.
Hal: Then look at the scene between you and Rosalind.
Alex: Right.
Hal: (*To Eve.*) Can we get rid of this bed?
Eve: Sure.
Hal: (*To Alex.*) Looks like someone just finished a production of *Cat on a Hot Tin Roof.*
Alex: (*With reference to the bed, chortling.*) Oh right.
Hal: You know the play?
Alex: Done it—twice.
Hal: Play Brick?
Alex: Not really.
Hal: (*To Eve.*) Actually, you know, why don't you why don't we leave it, that way there's something to sit on.
Eve: Okay.
Hal: (*To Alex.*) You have a picture, resumé?
Alex: No, actually, I don't. I just got back into town, haven't unpacked my stuff. I just ran down here when I heard you were seeing people.
Hal: That's all right, we know what you look like. Where have you been . . .
Alex: Working?
Hal: Yea.
Alex: Are you familiar with theaters in Montana at all?
Hal: Nope.
Alex: Yea, I've spent a lot of time last few years working in Montana. At the uh Montana Rep.
Hal: Great.

Alex: Yea.

Hal: Who's directing up there?

Alex: Directing? Oh . . . you know, what's her name—my God I've worked with her for years I can't believe I—Levi. Simple. Levi Simple.

Hal: Name is familiar.

Alex: Yea, he's been—she's been—he's been up there . . . since the beginning.

Hal: What kind of stuff they do?

Alex: Did *The Guardsman*—old Lunt/Fontanne vehicle. That was fun—farce, kind of. Um . . . *Biff at Colonus.* Kind of an experimental piece—didn't really pan out—interesting idea, though. And then just your . . . standard stuff, usual stuff . . . that gets done . . . across the country . . . all the time . . . Everywhere.

Hal: Well great. And here's Alison.

[Enter Alison.]

Alison: Sorry. Sorry. I got stuck in traffic. The trains.

Hal: No problem. We've got one more audition. If you don't mind waiting.

Alison: No.

Hal: (*To Alex.*) This is Alison Rose. She's playing Rosalind.

Alex: Hi, nice to meet you. I'm Harry. Samson. Harry Samson.

Alison: Hi.

[Long handshake, they look at each other.]

Hal: So give us a minute. (*To Eve, surreptitiously.*) Interesting chemistry between them.

[Alex and Alison finally let go hands.]

Alex: (*Off long handshake.*) Oh, sorry. Must be a little nervous.

Alison: That's all right, don't be. Is this your first time doing Shakespeare?

Alex: Oh, no, un, no, I've uh, done a little. Not too much. Quite a lot.

Alison: Then I'm the one that should be nervous.

Alex: Why do you say that?

Alison: My first role, really. In Shakespeare. In a Shakespeare.

Alex: Huh. You've been doing . . .

Alison: Musicals mostly. Mostly musicals. Musical comedy.

Alex: Musical comedy?

Alison: Musical comedy. Musical theater, musical comedy. Musical comedy.

Alex: Musical comedy.

Alison: Did *Pygmalion*—not too long ago. A few years ago. In high school.

Alex: Oh, right, sure.

Alison: Shaw.

Alex: Right.

Alison: *My Fair Lady.* That was interesting. But mostly . . . musical . . . comedy.

Alex: Musical comedy.

Alison: Musical theater, musical comedy. Musical comedy.

Alex: I'm sure you'll do fine.

Alison: Hope so. You've been . . .

Alex: Out of town lately a lot. Just got back in really—going back out again—I hope—if I get . . .

Alison: What brought you back?

Alex: What?

Alison: What brought you back?

Alex: Well, I uh split up with someone, recently. Woman I was living with.

Alison: Oh really? Me too.

Alex: Yea. What?

Alison: I haven't told—well, yet. It's terrible I know, I just figure this summer, get some space—I can . . . you know.

Alex: God. I'm shocked. About how hard it is when you—

Alison: Breaking up?

Alex: Yea. Yes. I mean for me.

Alison: Really? Did she break up with you or did you break up with her? I guess it's always kind of a mutual thing whether you know it or not. I mean you saw it coming, yes?

Alex: No. Not really. No. I was—it was kind of a . . . I was kind of you know . . . shocked I guess.

Alison: You were—were you married?

Alex: Yes. No. I mean for all intents and purposes.

Alison: Same with us. We lived together for years. Did she work in the theater?

Alex: In a way. Kind of . . . depends on what you think theater is.

Alison: What do you mean?

Alex: What do I mean? It's difficult to say—at this moment—but uh. What about the uh . . . Boy this is an old draft, isn't it?

Alison: It sure is.

Alex: This breaking up stuff, I completely forgot about the man you were with? Was he—

Alison: A woman.

Alex: I'm sorry?

Alison: A woman. He was a woman. Is a woman.

Alex: Oh, I'm sorry. I mean about—

Alison: And she does—it's all right—works in the theater.

Alex: Wasn't working . . .

Alison: Out between us? No. But she doesn't know I mean I haven't told her yet but I told you that I didn't, didn't I?

Alex: I think so.

Alison: And you've been working—

Alex: Out of town mostly. Going back out again—I hope—if I get—

Alison: What . . . what brought you back?

Alex: I've been just tired of what I'd been doing. Kind of getting into a rut and I thought I'd just kind of mix things up a bit trying something new I hadn't done before. Plus my girlfriend is uh I don't know you know what I mean she's doing something for the summer in a show and so my agent got a call about a . . . well, you know what I mean.

Alison: Sort of.

Alex: It's tough—relationships.

Alison: In a way. In a way. She's very self-involved.

Alex: Your girlfriend.

Alison: Lover.

Alex: Ex-lover.

Alison: Right. She's always reminding me—everyone in fact—that we're not girlfriends we're lovers, that we're not girls anymore.

Alex: I see her point.

Alison: But it's very annoying. Kind of pretentious the way she says it. Correcting people all the time about it. Somewhat arrogant.

Alex: Did you ever tell her that?

Alison: I can't remember. What about the woman you were with?

Alex: Was she self-involved?

Alison: No, I mean—

Alex: Yes, in her own way. In her own quiet way. Has a way though of making it appear as though I'm the one that's self-involved. When in truth we both are.

Alison: Interesting.

Alex: Yes. But you were going to say?

Alison: Nothing. Nothing.

Alex: Your ex-lover anyone I might know?

Alison: You might. Actually, though, I'd rather not . . .

Alex: Oh, sure, sorry.

Alison: It's fine. I was kind of blabbing.

Alex: Should be—shouldn't be getting involved with—in other people's situations.

Alison: Don't worry about it.

Alex: Problem I have.

Alison: It's all right. We'd probably have a lot to talk about.

Alex: I'm sure we would. Who knows? Maybe we'll . . .

Hal: Hey, guys—I'm wondering—Alison would you mind if it's okay with Harry, how would you guys feel about reading a scene together?

Alex: Love it.

Alison: Okay.

Hal: Great, well welcome to Maine.

Alex: Thank you.

Hal: You guys come up together?

Alison: We were on the same train but didn't know it.

Hal: You're kidding.

Alex: Yea.

Hal: That's wild.

Alison: We shared a taxi from the station.

Hal: You guys come up together?

Alex: We were on the same train but didn't know it.

Alison: I didn't even know he was cast.

Hal: We didn't call you?

Alison: No.

Alex: We shared a taxi from the station, got acquainted a bit more. Dropped off our stuff at the hotel.

Hal: Great. Okay. It's gonna be great. I'm so excited. I'm really excited, think you guys are going to be great together. Going to be explosive.

Alex: Oh yea.

Alison: This is the theater.

Hal: It is. Now.

Alison: It's beautiful. What was it before?

Hal: It keeps changing. It's been a million things. It used to be a rehearsal hall. Before that someone lived here. Right now it's a theater.

Alison: Incredible.

Alex: Theater.

Hal: Yea.

Eve: Gotta get rid of this bed.

Hal: Oh no, leave it. I have this idea about using it. In the production.

Alex: Really?
Hal: Oh yea. Something really kind of interesting. But . . . well, you'll see.

[Jayne Summerhouse and Simon Lanquish enter with luggage.]

Jayne: (*With energized, dramatic fatigue.*) Hi.
Hal: You're here!
Jayne: We got lost.
Simon: Of course.
Jayne: Took the wrong road. Went down the wrong path. Made the wrong turn.
Simon: What else is new?
Jayne: But we're here. And don't you love us for it.
Alison: Hi Jayne.
Jayne: Alison! I can't believe it I'm so excited. So excited. I was so excited about doing it with you. This.
Alison: Me too.
Jayne: Just like old times. I won't elaborate.
Alison: Oh yea.
Jayne: (*To the others.*) We were undergrad together. In the dorms. Those awful curtains. So tacky. Then me going on to grad school. In Seattle. Really getting the training I needed. It was great. I work. I've worked. And you—musical theater. So talented. Raking in the bucks. Those national tours. I was envious. Then I got the soap. How's Alex?
Alison: She's good. She's okay.
Jayne: I miss her. I love her. Give her my best. Give her my love.
Alison: I will.
Jayne: I haven't seen you for ages.
Alison: I know.
Jayne: (*To Alison.*) Well you know I've been insane. I went back to school. Did you know that?
Alison: No, I didn't.
Jayne: Oh yes.
Alex: For acting?
Jayne: (*Looking over Alexandra.*) Film school. Columbia. (*Back to Alison.*) The program's incredible. The money I put away from the soap. Thank heaven that's over. It was fun. My character had a web site. But here I am. In the flesh. It's great the way this worked out. For the summer. Making a film while I'm up here. A pseudo-documentary about reality in the theater. Hal's my mentor. I had to beg him. (*To Alexandra, imperiously, offering her hand.*) Who are you? I'm Jayne.

Alex: (*Accepting her hand, shaking.*) I'm Harry.

Jayne: Airy?

Alex: Harry. Samson. Payne?

Jayne: Jayne. Summerhouse. Are you part of the cast? Or are you one of the technical people?

Hal: Harry is our Orlando.

Jayne: Oh, no! What happened to Hubert?

Hal: He had to drop out. (*To Alexandra.*) Humé Hubert was going to originally be playing Orlando.

Alex: Oh gee.

Hal: He's in L.A. Doing something.

Jayne: I'm devastated. What's he doing? I don't want to know. He was so right. So perfect. Everything about him. Brilliant. And that unique speech pattern.

Hal: (*To Alexandra.*) Do you know him?

Alex: I may have worked with him—once—a while ago. I think.

Hal: Hey Simon. Let me introduce you.

Jayne: Silent Simon. Thinking. Evaluating. Playing it cool. Keeping to himself. Maintaining a distance. Let others come to him. At first, then boom, he won't stop talking. I'm teasing, I love you. We work together always. On almost every project. It's not intentional. I don't know how it happens. Neither does he. A surprise every time. Unless we've chatted the night before. Oh my God. So am I. That's amazing. It'll be great. It'll be fun. What a blast. We'll have dinner every night. Someone to talk to. Someone to listen. The audience thinks the others can hear this and maybe they can or maybe they can't, it being kept purposely ambiguous. If they can hear it—what I'm saying—the other characters—me rattling on in this fashion, it can be interpreted either as a depiction of psychotic behavior—clearly she's insane—or given the permissiveness of theatrical artifice, an exercise in brutal satire. If, on the other hand, the speech can be heard by the audience only, what is it then but a manifestation of my inner turmoil. Satire achieved, surely, and the vague emptiness that inhibits inhabits inhibits my soul. Laugh if you must and I hope you do. I am a character in fiction. I'm meant to be funny. And I intend to be.

Hal: (*Introducing Simon to Alison.*) Do you know Alison Rose? Alison is our Rosalind. Our Ganymede.

Simon: I think we've met. Through Alexandra Page. I was Gooper in *Cat* in Phoenix.

Alison: Oh, I think so, yes.

Jayne: That was one of Alex's campier performances if I remember correctly. I came out to see it. I was dating what's his name—Joe—who played Brick. That doesn't make any sense, I'm a lesbian. Maybe I was dating the lighting designer.

Alison: Kay Fein.

Jayne: I was dating Kay Fein. No, that's no good, she was probably an archeologist at the time. I was there in Phoenix—doing something else. Or I was playing Mae. That's perfect. Simon and I were working together. And I was dating Kay. She *was* a lighting designer then. Or are Kay and I ever in the same city together?

Simon: It doesn't matter.

Jayne: I'm sorry. I interrupted. But she *can* be over the top sometimes. Alex. So cartoony. And talk about chewing the scenery. I've seen her use a curtain rod for a toothpick. I love her give her my love.

Simon: Anyway we have met, it's nice to meet you again.

Alison: Likewise.

Simon: Looking forward to working with you.

Hal: Simon's playing Touchstone.

Simon: "And as cast." Whatever that means.

Hal: I'll tell you in a minute. (*Introducing Simon to Alexandra.*) And this is Harry Samson.

Simon: (*Offering his hand.*) Simon Lanquish.

Hal: And everybody knows Eve.

Simon: Eve.

Eve: Addaman.

Alex, Alison, Jayne, and Simon: Addaman?

Eve: Eve. Eve Addaman.

Alex, Alison, Hal, Jayne, and Simon: Eve Addaman.

Alex: More of the cast is coming up later?

Hal: Oh, that's what I was going to tell you. I have this idea, I'm going to do—being doing the play—with only four actors.

Jayne: What?

Alison: Only four?

Simon: Is that what you meant by "and as cast"?

Hal: I have this idea. I'm going to be doing some doubling. And then I'll fill in the rest of the cast with some local actors. Local people.

[The actors stare blankly.]

I think I can keep the cast down to ten. It'll be more than just the four of you. You'll all be playing most of the major roles—some of you will.

And then we'll have some local folks playing roles—make it kind of a community event. And Eve's gonna play a role also.

[Eve holds up her hand.]

Eve: I'm playing Adam, the old man.
Jayne: That's interesting.
Hal: Now you guys need to deal with your luggage and where you're staying, right?
Jayne: (*As Celia.*) I cannot go no further.
Hal: Wait, back up further.
Jayne: I'm confused. Have we just arrived, or have we been here for a while?
Hal: (*After a brief hold.*) What do you mean?
Jayne: (*To Alison.*) Because you say, This . . . Well, this is the Forest of Arden.
Simon: Where are we?
Hal: Right.
Jayne: (*Pointing in the script for Simon.*) Here, honey. Rosalind, Alison, disguised as Ganymede.
Hal: That's right.
Simon: I see.
Jayne: So we've just arrived.
Hal: That's right.
Jayne: In Arden.
Hal: Yea, I think so.

[Hal looks to Eve, who nods.]

Jayne: (*As Celia.*) I pray you bear with me, I cannot go no further.
Simon: (*As Touchstone.*) For my part, I had rather bear with you, than bear you.
Hal: Good, okay. Make sense.
Jayne: Yea. (???) But it's a double negative, isn't it—cannot go no further. Why don't I just say, I cannot go further, or I can go no further? Am I really saying, I can go further?
Hal: (*Consulting the text.*) I pray you, bear with me, I cannot go no further—I don't think so. I think you're just saying you can—you can't go any further—but you say, I cannot go no further—I think that's just how she says it. I think that's the way you talk.

Eve: It's archaic.

Hal: Right. Just as the way we speak may seem—will seem archaic—confusing—you know in a hundred years—or three hundred years. Or even now. The way we talk.

Jayne: That's what I love about Shakespeare. It's like a foreign language. Not like Chekhov, where everything is spelled out.

Hal: Un huh. (*After a brief pause.*) Okay, great. Why don't we take a break.

Eve: Ten minutes.

Jayne: (*To Alison—with girlish excitement.*) It's going so well. Don't you think?

Hal: (*To Eve.*) This day's a disaster.

Alison: (*To Jayne.*) I think so.

Jayne: (*Spotting Simon exiting, lighting up a cigarette.*) Simon, I'll go with you. (*As they exit.*) Honey, you shouldn't be smoking.

[Alison sits near Alexandra. Eve and Hal confer.]

Alex: Hi there.

Alison: Hi.

Alex: How's it going?

Alison: Okay. I think. How does it look?

Alex: Okay. It's very early. You're doing well though.

Alison: You think?

Alex: Oh, yea.

Alison: Do I seem like a musical-comedy actress up there?

Alex: What's a musical-comedy actress?

Alison: I don't know, superficial, artificial.

Alex: No.

Alison: I'm trying not to act.

Alex: What do you mean?

Alison: Like a boy.

Alex: Like a boy?

Alison: I mean . . . I am.

Alex: Right.

Alison: Trying to pretend—I am this woman and how she would . . .

Alex: Yes.

Alison: Disguise herself.

Alex: Un huh.

Alison: I don't know what I'm saying. Not . . . act it, but . . . just . . . kind of . . . act. Pretend. Behave.

Alex: That sounds good.

Alison: All the musicals I've been in over the years I've watched others—they won't relax—it's not that they're—that the *material* is artificial—it is of course—but that *they* are. These performers. And I've worked so hard at it. And thought so what it's only in a musical—what does it mean what would it mean in a play—not that I'm ready for Ibsen—but this—

Alex: A comedy.

Alison: Yes. Light.

Alex: But serious.

Alison: Yes. There's more—he's a genius—to it. But the principle applies. And that's the thing. One of the things. About my relationship. With Alex.

Alex: Your ex-lover.

Alison: (*Startled by the "ex."*) What? (*Recovering.*) Oh right—ex-lover. That she would never appreciate, or understand—what I was trying to accomplish. In the form. I mean she would compliment me—try to be helpful. But she judged the form, not the content. Or at least not the content of me.

Alex: I see.

Alison: (*After a pause.*) I'm gonna get my hair cut for this. A buzz cut.

Alex: A buzz cut?

Alison: Think I could look like a boy?

Alex: I don't know, what does a boy look like?

Alison: Not like a girl.

Alex: Oh right. But you don't want to look too much like a boy.

Alison: Why not?

Alex: Well, half the fun is knowing, you know, you're a girl—a woman.

Alison: Really? For who?

Alex: That you're a woman? Unh, I don't know, the audience, I suppose. Orlando.

Alison: You think Orlando knows Rosalind is really a woman?

Alex: I don't know—yet. I'd like to think he doesn't, but I'm not sure. Or maybe he's not sure.

Alison: That's one of the things I like about what you're doing.

Alex: What's that?

Alison: It was odd when Hal cast you. I thought . . . I mean I enjoyed your audition. It was fun.

Alex: Un huh.

Alison: I guess I thought though you weren't my vision of what an Orlando should be.

Alex: What did you have in mind?

Alison: I don't know. I guess someone a bit . . . straighter.

Alex: You don't think I'm straight?

Alison: (*Laughing.*) No, I mean . . . Well, you know Hubert—who was going to be playing the part . . . he's very . . . masculine—and—

Alex: I'm not masculine.

Alison: No, I mean—this is not coming out right—but—like—when you called the other day about having dinner after rehearsal.

Alex: Un huh.

Alison: Which I really enjoyed by the way. I mean for a minute I thought—when I picked up the phone—and this is not a criticism—I thought it was a woman on the other end.

Alex: Huh.

Alison: I mean, has anyone ever—

Alex: Because I have a high voice?

Alison: Yea, I mean, you know, I think you're—I could see like . . . I'm losing language. I once saw a production of this play?

Alex: *This* play.

Alison: The one we're doing, right. And there were two guys—one was playing Rosalind—but he didn't do it in drag—just a suggestion of something. It was wonderful—a wonderful production. Most of the audience walked out. And both the guys were good-looking guys, but the Orlando was particularly . . . he wasn't beefy, but he seemed like a straight guy who maybe wasn't or maybe he was. With you . . . it's like—like when they did it, I knew who the man was and who the man wasn't, who the woman was—even though they were both men.

Alex: Right.

Alison: With you . . . I just don't think of you as . . . that kind of man.

Alex: Sure.

Alison: So it's different. I like it.

Alex: Do you?

Alison: Yea. It's not what I imagined. (*Pause.*) Can I ask you a personal question?

Eve: We're back.

Alex: (*Still looking at Alison.*) Okay.

Hal: I want to try this idea I talked to you about the other day, Harry.

Alex: (*To Hal.*) Un huh.

Hal: In the wrestling scene. And Simon.

Simon: Right.

Hal: I'd like you to just throw the lines for Charles the wrestler to Harry. I know you're Touchstone. But just say the lines for Charles. And Harry. I want to see what it's like if you're kind of wrestling with yourself. You know what I mean? Grappling with yourself. So in other words there would be—there wouldn't be another actor you'd be struggling with—it would be yourself.

Alex: Okay.

Hal: Can we try that?

Alex: Sure.

Hal: Are you cool about doing this without your shirt?

Alex: Oh sure. You want me to do that now?

Hal: If you don't mind. I want to see what it's like seeing you taking off your shirt.

Alex: Okay.

Hal: You ready Simon?

Simon: Yep.

Hal: Here we go. Down and dirty.

[Alexandra unbuttons her shirt, takes it off, begins wrestling, grappling, struggling with self. Simon knocks on door.]

Alex: (*Facing upstage, as if having released her breasts.*) Who is it? (*That was a little high in the voice. Lower.*) Who is it?

Simon: It's me, Simon.

Hal: You can even try bending over.

Alex: (*To Simon.*) Okay.

[Alexandra bends over, grabs shirt from floor, holds it up as if covering breasts.]

Hal: (*To Alexandra.*) Or get on your knees.

Simon: Am I coming too early?

Hal: Do you want to use knee pads?

Alex: (*To Simon.*) No, it's fine.

[Alexandra feels under the pillow of bed, searching for Ace bandage.]

Hal and Simon: (*To Alexandra.*) Are you sure?

Alex: (*To Simon.*) Yea.

Hal: (*To Eve.*) Why don't you get the knee pads for Harry. Look in the closet.

Alex: (*Momentarily abandoning search under pillow.*) The closet.

Eve: (*To Hal.*) Where's the key?

Alex: (*To Simon.*) The what?

Hal: (*To Eve.*) Is it in your pants?

Alex: (*To Simon—feeling crotch.*) What?
Simon: (*To Alexandra.*) I didn't say anything.

[Eve finds key in pants.]

Eve: (*Holding up key.*) Here it is, be right with you.
Simon: (*To Alexandra.*) Take your time.
Hal: (*To Alexandra.*) Just take your time.

[Eve exits. Alexandra finds Ace bandage under other pillow.]

Alex: (*To Simon.*) Be right with you.
Hal: (*To Eve.*) Eve, do you need some help with the door? (*To Alexandra.*) Hold on one sec.

[Hal exits to Eve, Alexandra exits to offstage bathroom with shirt and Ace bandage.]

Simon: Do you need some help with the door?
Alex: (*From off.*) Hold on one sec.

[Alexandra returns tucking shirt into pants. She adjusts her polyester penis.]

(*Adjusting polyester penis.*) Come on, get over there, would ya. (*Zipping pants, buckling belt.*) Stupid thing, it's been in my way since the beginning.

[As if before a mirror, Alexandra touches chest, making sure bandage is secure. Flexes muscles. Final pouf of hair. Alexandra opens door to Simon.]

Hey, buddy, come on in. Sorry.
Simon: No problem. (*Scanning Alexandra.*) What's up? Alex takes a furtive glance at groin. Checking to see theatrical member not rigidly misplaced into unwanted boner. This then macho slash gay-farcical opening of scene. Re-enter for different tack.

[Simon retreats, knocks. Alexandra opens door to Simon.]

Alex: Hi.
Simon: Hi. Here then both characters evince shyness, Simon for reasons of attraction to Harry, Alex for fear of intimate discovery. This pseudo-

ambiguous gay date-like opening of scene gives preferred flavor of possible male interaction.

Alex: Sorry, just getting myself together.

Simon: No problem. Here might say "adjusting your make-up, checking your eye-liner?" Or he perhaps, "just putting on my girdle," or better I to initiate effeminized remarks, "putting on your girdle, rip in your pantyhose?" He then to respond in kind, suggesting either conduct straight men might engage in with each other or with gay men or with women—gay or straight for reasons various; *or* it might suggest two gay men long accustomed to the habit of mocking women, women viewed inevitably inferior; this behavior real or imagined on the part of women a means for gay men to negotiate feelings of inferiority and insecurity. This tactic taken though the scene proceeds in unwanted direction. Simon no queen. Not given to queer innuendo.

Little behind?

Alex: (*With hand on bottom.*) I beg your pardon?

Simon: Unnecessary to shun all forms of ribaldry. Some jokes consistent with light-hearted nature of entertainment. The "beg your pardon" line a clear reference to Ludlam's *Irma Vep,* certain to be appreciated by all those familiar with the piece.

You did say 7:30?

Alex: Oh yea, no, you're right on time.

Simon: Advance the plot with a scene of unwanted advance.

Alex: Is Jayne meeting us?

Simon: No, she's getting together with Alison?

Alex: Jayne and Alison? Getting together?

Simon: They may meet us later.

Alex: What about Hal and Eve?

Simon: I'm not sure what they're up to tonight. Day off tomorrow.

Alex: Boy, I could use it.

Simon: So could I. How will it play out? Does this scene foreshadow any unanticipated coupling? Couplings?

Alex: Just us two then.

Simon: Yea. Maybe.

Alex: Let's go. Here we are. Little noisy—pooh, and smoky. Shall we get a booth? I'm starving. Yikes, that country music. I guess they don't have a no-smoking section. Oh, I forgot, you smoke. Anything without meat?

Simon: If it bothers you I'll . . .

Alex: Oh, don't worry about it.

Simon: I should stop. You're a vegetarian?

Alex: I try to be.

Simon: I should have thought of another place, I'm sorry.

Alex: It's all right, I'll find something, I didn't mention.

Simon: They're sitting on the bed, as if at a table, holding empty glasses for props—or maybe just miming it. Local beer for Alex/Harry, gin and tonic for Simon.

Alex: So Jayne and Alison went out together. That's interesting.

Simon: What do you find interesting about that?

Alex: About them going out together? Nothing. Nothing really. (*Pause.*) Where did they go?

Simon: Dinner, I think. They were gonna take a walk together around the pond.

Alex: At night? Together? Alison and Jayne?

Simon: You seem very interested in Alison.

Alex: Who me? In Alison? Why do you say that?

Simon: You just do. I know you've been spending a lot of time together out of rehearsal.

Alex: Just getting to know each other. Running lines. Getting acquainted.

Simon: You know she doesn't like men.

Alex: I do know that, yes. Absolutely.

Simon: She split up with her lover recently.

Alex: She mentioned something about that.

Simon: Alexandra Page. I've worked with her.

Alex: Oh right. I've heard she's an interesting actress.

Simon: In the right thing. She's limited.

Alex: Un huh. Well, we're all limited, I think—in our own way. I think.

Simon: I didn't know them well—as a couple—but from what I heard—from Jayne—what Jayne heard—from somebody—I think it's very good for Alison. To be on her own. I don't think she's really had the chance to explore herself with Alexandra around.

Alex: Yes, Alison intimated that.

Simon: What about you?

Alex: Have I explored myself?

Simon: Are you involved with anyone? I heard you split up with someone recently.

Alex: Yes, that was rough. But I think perhaps it's for the best.

Simon: They nurse their drinks. You've been involved with mostly women?

Alex: Almost exclusively.
Simon: But not exclusively.
Alex: When I was young—younger—not too young, I got a late start—so to speak—I did have a couple of experiences with men.
Simon: Mm mm.
Alex: I was attracted to women, but still afraid to . . .
Simon: Did you like it?
Alex: With men? Not enough to continue. Why do you ask?
Simon: I was just . . . curious. You seem like . . . maybe you never met the right man.
Alex: I don't think there is the right man. For me. (*Pause.*) What about you, Simon? Have you met the right man?
Simon: Simon stares blankly.
Alex: Are you okay? You've hardly touched your hamburger.
Simon: I'm on a new medication. It's upsetting my stomach.

I broke up with the man I was seeing, I met him on Fire Island, we were together for nine months, it was a nightmare.

I met him at Splash, I met him at the Monster, he lives in my building, he goes to my gym. I met him online, I met him at church, we met at a party, he temps for my agent, we use the same laundry, I know him from group therapy, we're in the same running group, we met on the street. We get together we can't stop fighting, he says something I react, I think he's attacking me which he is in a way he thinks I'm being too judgmental or controlling, I get insulted, I get paranoid, we end up fighting, he went on tour so I proposed we stop seeing each other. What could he do but accept my proposal?

Plus I have AIDS. Which doesn't mean anything. It means something—which is why I shouldn't be smoking. My T-cells are good, my viral load is stable—for the most part. I also get testosterone injections to boost my immune system.

That's one way it could go. Or just oblique flirtation, confusion of sexes—given Alex's disguise. Nothing boiling over—like Jayne's always saying—mostly to myself. Let's forget this entire scene, shall we. I met Harry at his hotel room, we've had dinner, I'm drinking a little too much, I'm attracted to him, I'm a little desperate, I'm feeling that way, I'm out of town—it's easy to have a crush on another actor in that circumstance. Or at least it is for me.

Then Alison enters.
Alison: Hi.
Alex: Hi. Where's Jayne?
Alison: I'm sorry?
Alex: About what? I mean Jayne, Simon says—
Simon: Simon says Jayne and Alison were having dinner.
Alison: Oh right, and then we took a walk over to the lake.
Alex: You mean the pond?
Alison: The pond, yes.
Simon: How was it?
Alex: Where's Jayne?
Alison: She got muddy.
Alex: Jayne did?
Alison: She was on the ground for a while. At the lake.
Alex: You mean the pond.

[Alison pulls out a cell phone.]

Alison: (*Pulling out her cell phone.*) Do you mind if I call Alex? We haven't spoken today. I want to catch her in case she goes to bed early.
Alex: You think she's home?
Alison: Why wouldn't she be?
Simon: I thought you and Alex split up.
Alison: We still talk.
Simon: Alex's cell phone rings.
Alex: Oh, that's me. How funny.
Alison: I'm trying her cell phone.
Alex: Excuse me one second.
Alison: You can stay here.
Alex: It's all right. It might be my girlfriend.
Simon: Your ex-girlfriend?
Alex: We might need to talk about something.
Alison: I wonder why she's not picking up?
Simon: Alex crosses stage, goes into the men's room.
Alex: Hello. (*That was a little low in the voice. Higher.*) Hello.
Alison: Hi honey, it's me.
Alex: Hi honey.
Alison: Is this a good time?
Alex: Oh sure.
Alison: I thought I'd try you on your cell in case you were out.
Alex: Oh no, I'm here.

Alison: At home?
Simon: Alex signals a guy he's not using the urinal.
Alex: (*To guy.*) Go 'head, no, I'm fine.
Alison: What was that?
Alex: Nothing, go ahead. How's it going up there?
Simon: And then some stupid, comic, farcical dialogue.
Alison: I've been spending a lot of time with him, he's a really nice guy.
Alex: That's nice. Is he a good actor?
Simon: Will she ever stop fishing? Let's fast forward.
Alison: He's very attractive. I find myself strangely attracted to him.
Alex: You mean like sexually?
Alison: Well, I don't know, not really, kind of.
Alex: Kind of? Sounds like you have a crush on him.
Alison: Oh Alex, for goodness sake. I can understand you being jealous if I was spending time with another woman, but this guy is a guy.
Simon: Toilet flushes.
Alison: What was that?
Alex: I'm in the subway.
Alison: I thought you were at home.
Alex: I'm coming home, going home, I'm on my way.
Simon: Oh where were you? Seeing a show, a film, a movie, blah blah blah. Alex steps out of men's room, remains out of sight. Alison hears same country western song through phone she hears in restaurant.
Alex: What a coincidence. I just walked past a bar, they must have the same station on.
Simon: In New York, that they have in Maine?
Alex: I'm so glad to know it's going well.
Alison: It is, I'm feeling very good. I can't wait for you to see it.
Alex: Oh, right. I have to make plans how to get up there.
Simon: You'll hear about that in the final scene. Alex is slowly making her way back to the booth.
Alex: Love you.
Alison: Love you too.
Simon: "Love you?" I'd never know the two of you split up.
Alison: Yea, well we're—(*To Alexandra.*) Finish your phone call?
Alex: Yea, my girlfriend.
Simon: Alex sees somebody enter the restaurant.
Alex: (*Pointing.*) Oh look.
Simon: Alison's cell phone rings.
Alison: (*Into phone.*) Hello.
Alex: It's Jayne.

Alison: (*Into phone.*) Hi Jayne.

Simon: (*Referring to the character that enters.*) That's not Jayne.

Alex: Who else could it be?

Alison: (*Into phone.*) Oh Jayne, you won't believe it. Guess who just walked into the restaurant?

Kay: Hi troops.

Alison: (*Into phone.*) Kay Fein.

Alex: Oh. Kay. What are you doing here?

Kay: (*With meaning.*) Do I know you?

Alison: (*Into phone.*) I will. Did you get cleaned up?

Alex: (*Secretly to Kay.*) I thought you were in Egypt, your hands filthy with the past.

Alison: (*Into phone.*) You tripped, I know, I felt so bad. Well as long as you're okay.

Kay: (*With meaning.*) Egypt?

Alex: (*Secretly to Kay.*) Aren't you an archeologist?

Kay: (*To Simon.*) I think I'm a lighting designer.

Simon: I think so too.

Alex: Oh, right. I'm thinking of a different Kay. I must be thinking of a different Kay.

Alison: Hi Kay.

Kay: Hi doll. (*Kissing.*)

Alison: Great to see you.

Kay: (*To Alex.*) And you're . . .

Alex: Harry.

Kay: (*Seeing Alexandra's hairy arms.*) I know.

Alex: Samson.

Kay: (*Wryly.*) Harry Samson?

Alison: (*Into phone, but with glance toward Kay and Alexandra.*) Uh huh.

Kay: (*Secretly to Alexandra.*) How's it going?

Alison: (*Into phone, but with glance toward Kay and Alexandra.*) Okay.

Alex: (*Secretly to Kay.*) Fine.

Simon: Harry's playing Orlando. He replaced Humé Hubert.

Alison: (*Handing phone to Kay.*) Here. Say hello.

Kay: (*Into phone.*) Hello? Hi Jayne. Long time no see. I just got here.

Alison: (*To Alexandra.*) They used to see each other.

Alex: I see.

Kay: (*Into phone.*) Oh, I'd love to see you. Would that be possible? Why not?

Simon: Tell her to come over.

Kay: (*To Simon.*) She says she can't. (*Into phone.*) I see. Right now? Well where are you? Offstage?

Alex: (*To Kay.*) That's the name of the hotel.

Kay: (*To Alexandra.*) Oh how clever. (*Into phone.*) The Off Stage Hotel, I think I can find it. Do you want to talk to Alison again? See you soon. (*Closing phone, to group.*) She's lonely, she wants some company. I just hope we don't have a scene. That would be impossible. I'll take my chances. I'll pick up some pizza. I'll see you guys later.

[Kay exits.]

Simon: A few more drinks—for Simon. His sad life. The girls listen. Alison and Alexandra.

Alex and Alison: We're women, not girls.

Simon: He starts lines from the play. Lines of Touchstone.

Alex: We gotta get him back to his room.

Alison: Here, give me the check, can you get him outside?

Alex: I think so. Do you need any money?

Alison: Oh no, it's all right. Alex never has any money. I'm used to paying the check.

[Alison exits.]

Simon: Alexandra shoulders Simon to the exit. That cool night air in Maine.

Alex: Slowly, Simon, one step at a time.

Simon: A full sky of stars, not like what you see in the city. They'll make their way beneath this heavenly blanket.

Alex: We gotta wait one second for Alison.

Simon: I want to sleep with you Harry. I want to have sex with you.

Alex: You may think you do sweetheart, but believe me, it's not gonna be worth your while.

Simon: I find it sexy when a straight guy calls me sweetheart.

Alex: Why the hell would you wanna have sex with a straight guy, Simon?

Simon: I know. I don't know. I just do. I always have. You wanna sleep with Alison, don't you, and she's not straight.

Alex: I find Alison attractive, but I'm not making any moves on her. Do you need to take any more medications tonight, Simon?

Simon: Don't remind me. Shit. No, I'm done for the night. Only with meals.

[Alison enters. Her hair is short. A boyish cut.]

Alison: Hi, sorry. They were running my card.
Alex: What happened to your hair?
Alison: It's cut for the show. You think it's too short?
Alex: No, it looks good. Let's go.
Simon: If I was lying on the couch in my sparsely furnished hotel room—as I will be tomorrow on my day off—staring out at a small patch of sky and a jutting of trees, morosely going mad in the middle of the afternoon, lonely out of town, refusing to call my therapist, this is what I would be thinking.

Who needs a play about a gay man who occasionally drinks too much—with AIDS no less? Who needs another play about him?
Alison: Are you sure this is the way, Harry?
Alex: Positive. Pretty sure.
Simon: Who needs a play about a gay man who's entered into a series of failed relationships and finds as he grows older he's drawn into relationships with younger and younger men? Who needs another play about him?
Alison: I think we've covered this ground already, Harry.
Alex: Trust me.
Simon: Who needs a play about a gay man who gets turned on by straight men and can't even go to a gym because he might try to pick somebody up and once got punched in the face for trying and could never go back to that gym again? Who needs another play about him?
Alison: This is getting scary, Harry. I think we're going into the woods.
Alex: Believe me, I've been here.
Simon: Who needs a play about a gay man who attends meetings for sexually compulsive behavior and goes right from those meetings to a bar or a bookstore or the pier or a men's room in the subway? Who needs another play about him?
Alex: Keep going.
Simon: Who needs a play about a gay man who dreamed of being a fine actor and of one day leading a troupe that would bring Shakespeare to minority children finding himself on his forty-sixth birthday trying to seduce a fifteen-year-old Hispanic kid outside of Splash, pleading with the kid to come home and have sex with him and even though he himself has had twenty years of therapy is shocked when the kid says, go home with you alone to your apartment you might try to kill me, what do you think, I'm crazy, man? Who needs a play about him?

Alison: Oh, I think I know where we are.

Simon: Who needs a play about a gay man so fearful of what life holds he can't get out of bed in the morning, the recess under his quilt the closest he can get to either the womb or the grave? Who needs a play about him?

Who needs a play about an aging homosexual who's had and has—thank you very much —issues with his mother and I'm sorry we've gone over the terrain before but let's face it when you grow up in the home of the oppressor in this society who the hell do you think you're going to identify with more, a man or a woman! and Jesus Christ, who doesn't have issues with their mother? Who needs another play about him?

Who needs a play about a gay man who fucked-up as he is goes to the theater and sees one quote end quote positive image of gay people after the other acting like the biggest fucking queers in the world—or worse a singing transvestite in a supposedly serious musical who dies from AIDS and comes back from the dead—and funny that never happened to any of my friends!—making the same damn hairdresser jokes they've been making since the day one—"those brave and idiosyncratic characters who were here before AIDS and will be here when it's over"—and women from Westchester with too much make-up who look like drag queens themselves laughing their asses off or crying at this shit beside men in Levis and pink and powder-blue sweatshirts with one earring laughing and crying just the same, but that's what masochism is I suppose, victory in defeat, and one of the reasons this fucked-up man is in the audience is because he has an audition for this stupid play on Monday—and wants the goddamn fucking job—and who imagining the accolades he'll receive for his performance fucks up his audition so badly he doesn't even get a call back? Who needs another play about him?

Alex: Come on Simon, we're almost there.

Simon: Who needs a play about a man who's thrown seventy-five percent of his life away, squandered opportunity after opportunity and finds himself in middle-age the stereotype of a self-loathing homosexual, the only difference being that he doesn't camp it up? Who needs a play about him?

Alex: Simon, we're in the hotel. But where is your key? I can't find your—

Simon: God have mercy, God have light,
Get me through this goddamn night.

Night follows night follows every tomorrow,
What man doesn't deal with, man has to swallow.
Who needs another play about him?
Who needs another play about him?
Who needs another play about him?
Who needs another play about him?
Who needs another play—

Alex: What did you say, Simon? Did you say something?

Simon: What? Nothing, oh sorry, I was thinking to myself. I don't know where it is—the key.

Alex: (*To Alison.*) Let's bring him to my room. (*To Simon.*) Simon, you're going have to sleep on my couch.

Alison: Why don't we just get the manager to open his room?

Alex: Well for one thing it's a plot device to get you and Simon into my room. But if you want to be a stickler about it, there's nobody at the desk after eleven.

Alison: Right, we'd have to wake somebody up. And they're so grumpy here.

Simon: I'll be fine on the couch. I hate to put you out, Harry. And I apologize for what I said before. And about you and . . . (*With a glance at Alison.*)

Alex: It's all right.

Alison: What's that mean?

Alex: Nothing, come on. I'm just down the hall.

[Enter Hal and Eve.]

Hal: It's a little rough—

Eve: Us being lovers—

Hal: Her working as my assistant.

Eve: They've returned to the hotel after dinner, entered their room. Tomorrow they plan to take a drive, have a picnic near a lake. Some time alone together.

Hal: She's worked—been working as my assistant—

Eve: One of his assistants on a number—

Hal: On a few of my films—as one of my assistants—which is kind of rough, you know, kind of male-female power thing in a way—according to her—which I can understand.

Eve: They've taken off their coats—it grew chilly on the walk home, he's gone into the bathroom to pee, the sound of his urine hitting the porcelain, she's taken from her coat pocket several stones and a pine cone she collected on the walk home, places them on the wood floor, examines them, arranges them. When he returns he'll ask her are those the rocks you got on the way home. Yes and the pine cone.

Hal: And—you know, that was one thing—and then I got this call from a friend of mine—

Eve: This friend of his—Charlotte—she'd taken over this theater space and she asked him—

Hal: She asked me about coming up directing a play—

Eve: Which he'd never done before.

Hal: And I'm working on the financing for a new film I want to do—

Eve: A play—funny, I've had more experience in the theater than he has—

Hal: She comes from a dance-choreography background—

Eve: And as an actress—

Hal: She goes into the bathroom. He never hears or rather rarely hears her on the toilet. For one thing she closes the door, which he rarely does. Never does. And besides, he's picked up his cell phone checking his messages. His DP—he thinks of him as his DP, Alan, has called, left a message he wants to talk. He calls him, leaves a message to call him tomorrow anytime, forgets they have plans to have a picnic. Toilet flushes, well at least he knows when she's through. He sometimes forgets to flush the toilet, never mind putting the seat down. She returns hears him on the phone.

Eve: Cell phone. Pine cone.

Hal: She says to herself.

Eve: And I needed the money—

Hal: Well she didn't really need the money—but we thought—

Eve: We thought about traveling in the southwest, this summer—planned, actually, to go before Charlotte called and asked him to come up—

Hal: Asked me if I was interested in coming up, directing *As You Like It.*

Eve: He wanted to do it—he didn't really want to go to the southwest, that would have been more for me.

Hal: Both of them are in the bathroom now, brushing their teeth, playfully—but what is playfully?—pushing each other away from the mirror.

Eve: And they're talking about nothing much by now, regressing as they often do before bed, taunting each other in childish ways, teasing one another, venting their hostilities obliquely, she laughing more than he, he having a talent to amuse, both of them hurt by the other's remarks, it all a game, empty.

Hal: So she figured—

Eve: I figured I didn't want to go to the southwest alone—
Hal: Which I proposed—
Eve: And I could—I suppose—use the money, so he—
Hal: I offered her like to work as my assistant, stage manager, prop mistress-kind-of-everything-person, you know, so she wouldn't—we wouldn't be separated all summer—or for most of the summer.
Eve: They're undressed by now. I'm in my late twenties, she's thinking, he's in his early thirties. Pine cone, cell phone.
Hal: What'd you say?
Eve: Pine cone, cell phone.
Hal: What's that about?
Eve: Nothing.
Hal: And when the show goes up, I'll go back to New York, see if I can close up some of the financing for the new film—and she'll—
Eve: I'll stay here, run the performances.
Hal: So I think she's a little frustrated—because she'd like—what she'd like to be doing—
Eve: Is making films of my own.
Hal: She's not really interested in the theater.
Eve: Though I come from this dance-choreography background. My mother was a choreographer.
Hal: She's got a lot of issues with her mother.
Eve: I've made two films.
Hal: Interesting experimental short kind of films about light, very different . . . difficult . . . different from mine.
Eve: Very different from Hal's.
Hal: They've made love. Now they're cuddled up together in spoons. The stars outside the window.
Eve: So you see how it all—
Hal: It's kind—
Eve: It's been difficult. And I haven't said much—to anyone, about it. But. Well.
Hal: They have a fight the next morning.
Eve: It's very complicated.
Hal: Women and men and women.
Eve: Very complicated.
Hal: Very complicated.
Eve: Good night, sweetheart.
Hal: Good night, sweetheart.

[They're in bed by now.]

Alex: Okay, here we are. Moving on. Easy Simon.
Simon: I'm okay.
Alison: Harry, there's no couch.
Alex: What?
Alison: There's no couch. Where is Simon going to sleep?
Simon: Yea, where am I going to sleep?
Alex: Oh right, there's no couch. I forgot.
Alison: He can sleep in the bed with you.
Alex: (*Indicating Hal and Eve in bed.*) There won't be room.
Alison: Oh right.
Alex: (*To Simon.*) I guess you'll have to sleep on the floor.
Simon: Well, how about if I sit in a chair and pretend I'm sleeping on the floor?
Alex: (*After thinking about it.*) That's fine.

[He does so—sits off to the side.]

Alison: You have a nice room, Harry. My God, you have a kitchenette.
Alex: It's an efficiency.
Alison: None of the other rooms in the hotel have one.
Alex: I know—there's a big joke near the end of the scene—I needed a garbage disposal.
Alison: That's so nice. (*She's close to him.*) Harry. Your arms are so hairy.
Alex: I know.
Alison: I'm attracted to you, Harry. Did you know that?
Alex: Uh huh.
Alison: Are you attracted to me? I think you are.
Alex: Of course, I am. You're a beautiful woman. And I'm a man. I've dreamt of having you in my arms.
Alison: Oh.
Alex: But Alison. You're on the rebound. I don't want you using me like some kind of sex toy.
Alison: It's funny. I'm not usually attracted to men.
Alex: Usually? What does that mean?
Alison: It's funny. I've never been attracted to a man before.
Alex: And my girlfriend and I, we're . . . kind of in a strange place with each other . . . right now. I've got to be careful.
Alison: There's something soft and gentle about you Harry. You're not just some stupid stud.
Alex: Well, I hope not.

[They kiss.]

Oh, Alison.

[They kiss again.]

I'm in love with you. I've been in love with you since we first met.

Alison: Then why don't you ever show it?

Alex: I have difficulty with my feelings.

[Alison touches Alexandra's chest.]

Oh, don't touch me there. I'm very sensitive there. Are you wearing a bandage? I had a slight injury. Your arms are a little sticky. I don't know how to explain that. The fact of the matter—and then of course there's Simon laying on the floor here. (*Indicating where Simon is not, Simon waves a hand from his seat.*) What if he should wake up? With all that's going on, I'm concerned I might not be able to perform properly. I mean I'm sure I would. I'm an attractive man.

Alison: You are. You're cute. You're sweet. I bet women go crazy over you.

Alex: Some do.

Alison: Let's turn off the lights.

[The lights dim.]

(*As if to the lighting booth.*) Thank you.

[You know who enters in pajamas. Hal and Eve sit up in bed to watch. Alexandra and Alison stand to the side.]

Jayne: Oh Kay, that was wonderful.

Alex: A scene, of course, between Kay Fein and Jayne Summerhouse.

Kay: Jayne, I can't believe I let you talk me into that.

Jayne: Kay, I didn't talk you into anything? Did you or did you not tell Charlotte you were hoping we'd have some kind of reunion when you got up here?

Kay: And she told you?

Jayne: Since when has Charlotte ever kept a confidence? You knew the minute you told her the first thing she was going to do was tell me. That's probably why you told her in the first place.

Kay: Well I'll say one thing about you Jayne . . . You know, I think we should start the scene over. It means a whole different thing if we've had sex.

Jayne: (*Disappointed.*) All right, fine.

Kay: And another thing completely if we haven't. Sex is so easy.

Jayne: Speak for yourself. That was good pizza. Thank you for bringing that over, Kay.

Kay: My pleasure.

Jayne: I can't believe I let you talk me into it, though. You know I have to watch my weight.

Kay: Jayne, you're always talking about your weight. You look fine. You look terrific. Stop fishing for compliments.

Jayne: It's so good to see you Kay. I've missed you. When Charlotte told me you were coming up I was so excited.

Kay: You're studying film.

Jayne: Yea. And.

Kay: Well, isn't that something.

Jayne: Do you want to have a conversation about it?

Kay: Well, wouldn't it be a good way to get reacquainted, talk about our lives?

Jayne: And you'll talk to me about your work as an archeologist or a lighting designer?

Kay: Something like that.

Jayne: We'll review the specifics of our history together or not together. Reminisce how we met, where we met. Spend these precious moments we have together in idle chit chat.

Kay: I don't consider these things necessarily idle.

Jayne: Let's cut to the chase, Kay. If this were a play, do you think an audience would want to sit through the back story, the exposition.

Kay: Fine.

Jayne: Why didn't things work out between us, Kay?

Kay: Damn it. I knew the minute I walked in here we'd have a scene.

Jayne: Well that's what life is, Kay. Scenes. One after the other. Episodes, chapters, events. You never know how it's going to play out. Two women who haven't seen each other for years, both single—still—approaching middle age—fine, arrived at.

Kay: One of them, or so I heard from Charlotte—who's taken steps to change her life, going back to school—

Jayne: Yes, the money I stowed away from the soap to study film. And dumped that god awful therapist—

Kay: The one that kept telling you to seek your goodness, discover your flower, open yourself to munificence? That was money well spent.

Jayne: Now I'm seeing Simon's therapist—he tells me how narcissistic I am, how self-involved—what about discovering my flower, opening myself to goodness—he practically guffaws in my face.

Kay: Uh huh.

Jayne: Uh huh? What about you Kay, are you a cipher? Say something about yourself.

Kay: Cipher? You know next to Alexandra Page you are the most abrasive woman I have ever known.

Jayne: Known? You mean like in the biblical sense? I always knew there was something between you and Alexandra.

Kay: And here we have a demonstration of your paranoia—if you're even being serious—or of your inclination to melodrama. That's a trait you and Alex have in common. I never slept with Alex—I never had any interest in sleeping with Alex—nor to the best of my knowledge has she did she ever have any interest in me—in that way—

Jayne: Yea—well—

Kay: You've always had this some kind of odd rivalry with Alex—this competition. Which was ridiculous. For all your shenanigans, Alex was never half the actress you are—you know it and she knows it. You've worked much more than she has—and got paid for it more than she has.

Jayne: Not that that necessarily means—

Kay: It doesn't mean everything, it sometimes doesn't mean anything, but in this case at least it means something. And how dare you—dare you even Jayne—

Jayne: Little more pizza?

Kay: Shut up for a minute and don't change the subject.

Jayne: (*In coloratura.*) Wha—?

Kay: You have an awful habit of doing that, Jayne. Besides, you don't need any more pizza. You can ill afford the calories.

Jayne: (*As an intake of breath.*) Ahh!

Kay: For you to accuse me of infidelity. You—and talk about your—there's another example of your rivalry with Alexandra—flirting with Alison—

Jayne: I haven't seen Alison for years until—

Kay: You know what I mean. And the promiscuity—or the attempt at it—before I met you and after we split.

Jayne: Well, I'm sorry Kay. Unlike you I don't live in the past. I did feel—I still feel—shit—that women—I'm a woman—and we should have the right to explore ourselves sexually just as much as any man. I want—I wanted—I'm older now—I wanted—I still want—the prerogative ascribed to men, not to be tied down exclusively to one person for my entire life. People have affairs. You know it as well as I do. The heterosexual construct of marriage is a no-win situation.

Kay: What do you mean by marriage? Monogamy?

Jayne: Of course.

Kay: Well when it comes to heterosexuals, monogamy is a relatively recent innovation.

Jayne: Isn't that just like you, Kay, to throw around your weight as an archeologist.

Kay: (*Devilishly.*) Let's not start talking about weight.

Jayne: (*Fuming.*) You can't live up to it and nobody or at least nobody I know—that we know—does—ever does.

Kay: Alex and Alison do.

Jayne: Yes! and they split up.

Kay: I don't know anything about that. I've not been in any of those scenes. The point is—despite their problems—which are many—they have stayed together—now I realize that's complicated because the reasons some people do stay together—well, it's complicated.

Jayne: Dependency. Alison is—

Kay: Granted, unhealthy forms of dependency—but it's not been all bad—and they do struggle—hell, they've stayed together longer than most of the straight couples we know.

Jayne: What's your point, Jayne?

Kay: Kay. I'm Kay—you're Jayne.

Jayne: What? Oh, shit. This is so confusing.

Kay: What *was* my point? This perpetual tangentia. Oh, yes—not living up to the heterosexual construct of marriage. See—you're laughing—the minute I repeat it you know how ridiculous that is. I mean the sight of you that evening, Jayne, with a cigarette in one hand and a light beer in the other standing in the crowd outside The Cubby Hole. If you knew how ludicrous—

Jayne: They happen to have a very nice vegetarian menu.

Kay: You were eating a burger.

Jayne: I needed the protein.

Kay: You sure as hell didn't need those french fries.

Jayne: It came with the order.

Kay: Jayne, the only people who advocate fluid relationships are the ones that can't tolerate solid ones. Look at Charlotte—she spouts the same baloney. Well Charlotte hasn't had a long-term relationship since Winnie-the-Pooh. Now she's into "Asian" men—and excuses it with multiculturalism.

Jayne: You moved away from me.

Kay: From you? How do you move away from somebody who's always on the prowl. "I want to be a wolf. I have desires—"

Jayne: I said that when I was younger.

Kay: Why would any person in their right mind, Jayne—man or woman—want to claim the male prerogative? It's one of the most unfortunate developments since the Stone Age—or before—even if it did have its evolutionary moment or two. It makes you think that God really is a man. Who but a man would be stupid enough to create male behavior? And believe me, I have no investment in the matriarchy. That's as much of a dead end as the other. The priestess of the moon humping the phallus of the adolescent sacrifice.

Jayne: (*On the verge of tears.*) I was just having a beer.

Kay: Honey, it's as old as Abraham throwing Sarah to the pharaoh.

Jayne: Now you stop right there, Kay. I may not be observant, but I am of the Jewish persuasion. Please do not besmirch the reputation of the patriarch.

Kay: Just because you initiate a religion doesn't mean you can't be a schmuck every once in a while.

Jayne: Oh cut him some slack, Kay. He came from Sumeria. He never had the benefits of a religious education.

Kay: Well now we're just being silly.

Jayne: Now? (*After a pause.*) I've missed our fights, Kay. There's nothing like a good fight.

Kay: (*Gently—but seriously.*) Mrs. Molloy. *The Matchmaker.* You can't fool me, I lit you when you did it.

Jayne: Oh right. I guess you did.

Kay: Come on, Jayne. Let's not get sentimental here.

Jayne: (*After a pause.*) Okay. Fine.

[Eve and Alison move from their respective positions, take stools, sit beside each other down right.]

Alison: What now ensues at this the peripeteic stage of the drama?

Eve: In answer: the requisite scene of sexual farce between Alexandra and Alison.

Alison: What sight first greets the audience as this the penultimate scene unfolds?

Eve: Alison pulling Harry towards the bed.

Alison: Describe the threat of intense physical compromise to which Alexandra now anticipates being made subject.

Eve: The descent of Alison's hand in the direction of the artificial groin.

Alison: What tack does Alexandra employ to prevent contact with that aforementioned hand?

Eve: Interception. Meeting that hand with her own in the region of her navel, she deftly removes it to her lips.

Alison: What tender words does she enunciate upon the kissing of that sweet hand?

Eve: Uh, Alison?

Alison: And Alison's response?

Eve: Harry.

Alison: What next occurs?

Eve: Placing her left hand on the back of Alison's head, bringing their mouths together, Alexandra engages Alison in a manner worthy of Belmondo.

Alison: What phrase might best describe the purpose of Alexandra's maneuver?

Eve: An effort to buy some time.

Alison: Given the moment of opportunity, what action does Alexandra perform?

Eve: Maintaining a steady and enjoyable swishing of tongues, holding still the back of Alison's head in her left hand, she dips her right hand into the cavity of her back pocket.

Alison: What thought occurs to Alexandra as she proceeds in this fashion?

Eve: She wonders if Alison thinks he's taking out protection.

Alison: And is she?

Eve: In a sense. Extracting her cell phone from the recess of her pocket, locating the appropriate button, she applies the appropriate pressure.

Alison: And what happens?

Eve: Alison's cell phone rings.

Alison: State concisely the successive events.

Eve: In brief: Alison detaches herself from Harry, removes her cell phone, flips it open, sees it is Alex who is calling and, with Harry's encouragement, repairs to the bathroom where she might converse with Alexandra in privacy.

Alison: Given that this leads by means of shame and embarrassment to Alison's subsequent departure and jettison of the anticipated scene of sexual deception, outline the scene as initially imagined and reasons for its revision.

Eve: Again in brief: inspired by Singer's *Yentl,* the final subterfuge was to be accomplished by means of a candle, extinguished for maximum darkness, inserted in place of the prop penis, which given its flaccidity, was made pulver in the garbage disposal. Hence the need for the kitchenette. But this evoked an inevitable dilemma. It is one thing to deceive a woman with whom you desire no further contact, another a partner to whom you hope ultimately to return, and with whom you have enjoyed conjugal intimacy. Further, if the trickster evaporates at the end of the drama, good enough, but Alexandra is no disappearing act. She must live in the world, and as such must conduct herself accordingly. Thus Alison's removal became an absolute necessity, and is if I may say accomplished with commendable brevity.

Simon: Staring at the door after Alison's departure, Alexandra hears the sigh of a recumbent Simon.

Kay: Grateful for four weeks out of town in which her off time was used at a local gymnasium, she lifts the sleeping figure from the floor and onto the bed.

Alex: Turning back the sheets, she removes his shoes and socks, strips off his pants and shirt, folds them neatly, places them on a chair. She knows how horrible it is to wake in yesterday's clothes. His white briefs, the hair on his legs and back. So this is Simon. A real man.

Eve: What picture composes itself in Alexandra's mind—Simon's elevated rump before her?

Alex: I like it when straight men call me sweetheart. His briefs pulled down, the candle in his ass.

Simon: But what does Alexandra do?

Alex: Pull up the sheet, brush the hair from his eyes, consider her own sins.

Kay: What sins are those?

Alex: Too many to enumerate. It comes down, I suppose, to a lack of love.

Hal: What sight greets Alexandra as she moves from the bed to the window?

Alex: The sky of stars. The peeping universe. At every moment we're watched. A million eyes. It sees what we do.

Eve: Does she sit now by the window?

Alex: Yes and weeps. Her own life, the sleeping figure. Those of the comedy. And all the sleepers.

Alison: Do some sleep in hunger?

Alex: Yes.

Alison: Do some sleep in fear?

Alex: Yes.

Alison: Do some sleep well?

Alex: I suppose. A few.

Alison: Do you? Do I? And how does the night proceed?

Alex: Like an old woman in a dark dress, slowly trudging along. At first she was a young woman draped in indigo, now her steps falter as she approaches the dawn.

Alison: Do you mean we're growing older?

Alex: Oh, sweetheart.

Kay: Speak of the forms of comedy as you understand them.

Alex: There is comedy, there is tragic comedy, comic farce and comic tragedy—and other permutations. Beckett I think was wrong, the master I think was wrong. His plays are comic tragedy not tragic comedy. For they end in despair.

Simon: Do you propose the happy escape from misery?

Alex: If only I could. Not how we behave but how we should behave.

Hal: What happens when the old woman stumbles?

Alex: She falls into her grave. It's dawn.

Kay: And after that?

Alex: Another day, another dollar. Another evening.

Kay: And how will that evening begin?

Alex: With a new scene. You see, I'm always one step ahead of you.

Alison: Alex, do you know what time it is? We're going to be late.

Kay: One question last?

Alex: Yes.

Kay: Does Alison know of Alexandra's masquerade? Has she known from the very beginning?

Alex: I can do no more than refer you to the reviews Lynn Fontanne received when she played Ilona in *The Guardsman,* the play on which this play is modeled. Ilona claims to have known all along it was her husband, Nandor, in disguise. There is this twinkle in her eye. But you're never quite sure what's behind that twinkle. (*To Alison.*) I'll be right out.

[Alexandra exits.]

Alison: You've been in that bathroom all night. What are you doing?

Alex: Changing.

Alison: Again?

Alex: We've got plenty of time, keep your shirt on.

Alison: It's so good to be home.

Alex: I missed you this summer. It was hard your being away.

Alison: I really appreciate your coming up to see the show.

Alex: Oh, it was my pleasure. I wish I could have stayed longer—you know—more than one night. You were so good, I was so proud of you. I thought everybody was quite good. Jayne and Simon—and that young woman . . .

Alison: Eve.

Alex: Eve.

Alison: Addaman.

Alex: Addaman?

Alison: Eve. Eve Addaman.

Alex: Eve Addaman. She was very good.

Alison: She ended up directing the play.

Alex: You were telling me. Now tell the audience. But tell them as though you're telling me. That's how plays work every once in a while.

Alison: Well, either Hal had to get back to New York all of a sudden because of financing for his film, or there was some big artistic emotional brouhaha and he left under less than agreeable circumstances.

Alex: That's amazing.

Alison: Or perhaps he left for a more plausible reason.

Alex: Or maybe he didn't leave at all. Maybe it was amicable. Perhaps they ended up co-directing.

Alison: She was amazing. I mean she stuck to Hal's original conception—basically—but she had—she just has a much better way with actors and she really understands the stage. And the changes she did make made everything make so much more sense. I guess the idea originally was Eve's anyway.

Alex: Really? Well I thought it was terrific. And it was nice seeing Jayne. She was actually civil to me.

Alison: I think Kay's being up there had a very nice influence on her.

Alex: I'll say. It was great seeing them together. I never thought that would happen.

Alison: Well, that's the magic of the theater for you.

Alex: And Simon. Poor Simon. I don't know what to say about him. (*Pause.*) Do we have any more exposition?

Alison: That depends on how much longer you stay in the bathroom.

Alex: Well, I want to look nice for Jayne's screening.

Alison: It's just for her class up at Columbia.

Alex: *A Pseudo-Documentary About Reality in the Theater.* What an interesting title. I wonder what it's about? Ask me something about Kay.

Alison: Will Kay be there this evening, or did she return to Egypt?

Alex: I think from this point on, wherever you see Jayne you'll see Kay. She's finally decided that she is a lighting designer.

Alison: Really?

Alex: Yes. She says that archeology is a thing of the past.

Alison: (*After a pause.*) Uh huh. You know I wish you could have met Harry when you were up there.

Alex: Oh yea, I would have loved to have met him. I really enjoyed his performance. Did you like working with him?

Alison: He said he would meet us after the show. In fact, right after I left you at the box office, I went backstage to look for him. He was just getting to the theater. I told him we'd all be getting together that evening and he said he'd join us. But then he never showed up at the restaurant. I guess his girlfriend—ex-girlfriend—girlfriend—came up that night. At least that's what he told me.

Alex: Uh huh.

Alison: I looked for you in the audience during the curtain call, I couldn't see you.

Alex: Oh, I was there all right. And like I say, I really admired your work. You didn't push, acting like something that you weren't. It was clear and direct. I was inspired by what you did.

Alison: Thank you, honey.

Alex: And I liked what's his name too. The guy that played Orlando.

Alison: Harry.

Alex: Harry, right. I thought he was very good. (*Pause.*) What did you think of his performance?

Alison: I thought he was all right.

Alex: Um mm.

Alison: But you know who I think would be really good in that role?

Alex: Who?

Alison: You.

Alex: Me?

Alison: Uh huh.

Alex: Why do you say that?

Alison: I don't know, I just have this feeling. And guess what?

Alex: What?

Alison: Hal has decided to revive the production this fall in New York.

Alex: You're kidding.

Alison: Eve is directing, Hal is producing. Jayne and Simon are doing it, they've asked me and I think they're going to ask . . . you.

Alex: Me? I didn't think Hal liked my work as an actor.

Alison: Oh, I think he sees things in you that perhaps he didn't see in the past.

Alex: Uh huh. What about Eve? Does she—I don't even think she knows my work?

Alison: I think she has some acquaintance with it.

Alex: Uh huh.

Alison: Simon and Jayne loved the idea.

Alex: They did, huh?

Alison: Kay had a few reservations initially, but I think—

Alex: She now . . . too—

Alison: Sees—

Alex: Yes. Uh huh.

Alison: Think about it honey. It would be a lot of fun to work on something together. Especially now that I'm more my own person. I think I could be helpful to you.

Alex: I'll think about it.

Alison: All right. But in the meantime stage time is very different from real time and we don't have any more time. It's either now or never. Enter in all your glory.

[Enter Alexandra. She is exactly as she was when we last saw her: i.e. the actor is ***not*** *in drag.]*

Alex: Here I am. How do I look?

Alison: Just like yourself. Beautiful.

Alex: Oh, please. (*Giving Alison her back.*) Here, zip me up. (*Bending slightly and as though pulling her hair over her head to expose the zipper.*)

Alison: You look good in this dress.

Alex: I gotta lose some weight.

Alison: I thought you said you cut your hair.

Alex: Oh I did say that didn't I. (*Turning to Alison.*) I look okay?

Alison: Ravishing.

Alex: Come on, you're the pretty one in this family.

Alison: Your arms are so smooth. Did you get a waxing?

Alex: Um hum.

Alison: So smooth.

Alex: (*Quietly, directly.*) I love you.

Alison: (*Quietly, directly.*) I love you too. You will think about doing the play, won't you?

Alex: Think about it? It's not like I have any other offer. And it would be nice to work together. Maybe we could help each other.

Alison: Um hum.

Alex: And a comedy. Life is so hard. It's so good to laugh. To make other people laugh.

[Pause. Then Alison exits. Alexandra follows, stops, holds near the exit, speaks to the audience.]

(*To the audience.*) We're just pretending there's a door here. And I'm going to leave it open. I could close the door, but I think it's more interesting to leave it open. And besides, I trust you all completely.

[Alexandra exits. End of play.]

The Argument

Based on *Aristotle's Poetics: The Argument* and *Plato and Aristotle on Poetry* by Gerald F. Else and on the *Poetics* by Aristotle, translated by Gerald F. Else.

David Greenspan in *The Argument.* Target Margin Theater/The Kitchen, New York, 2007. Photograph by Hilary McHone.

The Argument

First produced by Target Margin Theater and premiered at The Kitchen, New York City, from June 14 through June 30, 2007.

Aristotle David Greenspan

Lighting Design by Natalie Robin
Costume Design by Asta Bennie Hostetter
Directed by David Herskovits

Character:

Aristotle, a philosopher trained by Plato

Setting:

Athens.

Note:

Modern dress, no toga.

Aristotle: The art of poetic composition in general
and its various species,
the function and effect of each of them;
how the plots should be constructed
if the composition is to be an artistic success;
how many other component elements
are involved in the process and of what kind;
and likewise all the other questions
that fall under this same branch of inquiry—
these are the problems we shall discuss.
Let us begin then in the right and natural way
with basic principles.

Epic composition and the writing
of tragedy—and also comedy,
composing dithyrambs and
some of the making of music
with the flute or the lyre: these are all,
in point of fact, *imitative processes*—
though they differ from each other in three ways: (1)
by having different *means* (or *media*),
(2) by having different *objects,*
and (3) by having different *modes* of imitation.

In terms of means: the aforementioned arts
all carry on their imitation
by means of *rhythm, speech,* and *melody*—
but with the latter two (speech and melody)
used either separately or together: thus,
the arts of flute or lyre—or any similar
instrument—such as the panpipes—
produce their imitation using only melody
and rhythm, while such arts as the
Socratic dialogues or other works in prose
or verse use only speech and rhythm. Parenthetically,
some people lump together poetry
with anything composed in verse. In fact,
the title poet is at times applied
to anyone who versifies a subject; yet Empedocles—
whose treatise *On Nature* has
pronounced artistic qualities—

has nothing in common with Homer
except for the fact that he writes in verse.
Poets imitate, they don't hold forth;
hence Homer is a "poet," Empedocles
a "scholar." And a scholar—
no matter what he thinks—
or thinks of himself—is not a poet.

Now certain arts use all the media
we specified (rhythm, speech, and melody):
the dithyramb does so,
and so does tragedy and comedy. But there is a difference:
tragedy and comedy are sung at points,
at some points only spoken; in the choral dithyramb—
the singers sing from first to last—which
makes for a great deal of singing.

Objects of imitation:
since those that imitate, imitate those
in action—it follows those they imitate
must by necessity be either
worthwhile or worthless people
(for clear characteristics
do tend to develop in men of action—
we are what we do):
thus Homer imitated serious men
and Hegemon of Thasos (the inventor
of parody) imitated rascals. And thus,
the difference between tragedy and comedy
coincides exactly with this master-difference: namely,
the one (tragedy) imitates noble types,
while the other (comedy) imitates
what we sometimes refer to
as low-down no-'count types.

Modes of imitation;
and this is the third and final way we have
of differentiating these arts; for it is possible (possible)
to imitate the same objects
in the same media by: (1) narrating and dramatizing

(as Homer does), (2) only narrating,
and (3) only dramatizing. So in a way
Sophocles would be the same as Homer
since both have imitated noble specimens,
and in another way is Sophocles
the same as Aristophanes, for both
have imitated characters by dramatizing them.

Why do humans imitate?
It stands to reason there are two operative causes: (1)
imitation is congenital to human beings
(we learn our first lessons
through imitation), (2) there is the pleasure all men take
in works of imitation. A proof of this
is there are things we view with horror
in life, but whose images—
even when executed in detail—
we view with pleasure. Think
of animals that frighten us or of cadavers.
The cause of this? Learning is a pleasure—
not only to philosophers, but to man in general—
though admittedly the grade of pleasure lessens
the less men care to know.

Now since imitation does come naturally
to us, it was in the beginning those
most gifted in respect
to rhythm, speech, and melody, who
developing their gifts little by little,
brought forth poetry
out of improvisation;
and the poetic enterprise split
in accordance with the two kinds of characters
who were prone to imitate: namely,
the soberer spirits who imitated noble types,
and the vulgar ones
who were imitating the other type—
producing lampoons and invectives at first
while the serious ones were producing hymns. Hymns.
And things of that sort.

In the invectives,
in accordance with what is suitable,
iambic verse first made its appearance;
and that is why we call it iambic, because
it is the verse in which they used to iambize—
that is lampoon—each other—because iambic meter
is closest in rhythm to back-and-forth speech unlike
the weightier hexameters
used in the hymns. The hymns.

Now once tragedy (and comedy)
had been partially brought to light by Homer
(for just as on the serious side
he constructed dramatic imitations, so too
he was the first to adumbrate the forms
of comedy by composing
iambic verse that was not invective
but an imitation of the *ludicrous*), and thus
those who were in pursuit of these two kinds
of poetic imitation (tragedy and comedy), became in one case comic
poets instead of iambic (lampooning) poets
and in the other case producers of tragedies
instead of hymns. Hymns.

Now Aeschylus was the first
to expand the troupe of supporting actors
from one to two,
shorten those damn choral sections and see to it
that the dialogue was given precedence—and
at the same time
the verse became iambic—
because in the beginning
(when they used the tetrameter)
the composition was more given over to dancing
and spectacle—but when speech came along
the very nature of the enterprise turned up
the appropriate verse
and the verse
was
iambic—
because iambic is the most speech-like

of verses—and an indication of this
is that we speak more in iambics
than in any other kind of verse
in conversation with each other—
whereas we utter hexameters but rarely—
if ever—and when we do
we abandon the characteristic tone-pattern
of ordinary speech—and any of us—
any of us—
could count on one hand
the number of times we've spoken to another person
in tetrameter. And this is what we are getting at,
which is the victory of speech
over music and over dance. And later on
we will discuss why and why it remains
crucial if we are to have dramatic imitations.

On to comedy momentarily. Comedy as we said
is an imitation of persons who are inferior—
not however going all the way to full
villainy, but imitating the ugly of which
the *ludicrous* is one part—the ludicrous
being a failing or a piece of ugliness
which causes no pain—
or at least no lasting pain; thus,
to go no further, the comic mask
is something ugly and distorted
but painless. Back to tragedy.

Epic
poetry follows then in the wake
of tragedy and what do we mean
by wake? We mean
as a speedy vessel cuts through the sea
and a slower vessel travels behind it,
so epic poetry follows tragedy up the point of being (1)
full-length, (2) an imitation, (3)
in verse, and (4) of people
who are to be taken seriously; but
being primarily narrative in character
here the epic differs from tragedy. Further,

so far as length is concerned
tragedy tries as hard as it can
(or at least it should)
to exist during a single daylight period. But let us be clear
lest future generations think we mean by this
that tragedy (or comedy)
must represent the events of a single day—
one can imagine the confusion
that would lead to: no, what we say
is that dramatic presentations begin
in the morning and conclude
before nightfall—for as we know,
stage lights will not be invented
for over two thousand years, so for now
(so for now) only love, war, wine, or thievery—
or some combination thereof—
occupy our species after sundown. I clarify
lest we be misinterpreted.

Tragedy, then, is a process
of imitating
an action
which has serious implications,
and by means of language
made sensuously attractive
is enacted by the characters
themselves
and not presented by means of narrative
through a course
of pity and fear
completing the purification
of tragic acts
which have pitiful
and fearful
emotional characteristics.

Now first of all,
since actors perform the tragic imitation
by acting it, the adornment of their visual appearance
(the masks and costumes)
will inevitably constitute some part

of the making of tragedy; as will song
composition and verbal expression.
Next, since it is an imitation of an action
and is enacted by the characters, and since
those characters must necessarily have
certain traits both of character
and thought; and since the imitation of the action is
the *plot*—by which I mean
the structuring of the events—
it follows then
that tragedy—as a species—
has only six constituent elements; and they are
(1) plot, (2) characters, (3) thought,
(4) verbal expression, (5) song composition, and (6)
visual adornment, and there is nothing
(nothing) beyond these six.

The greatest of these elements
is the structuring of the incidents—
the plot: a tragedy cannot exist without a plot;
but it can without characters; because
if one strings end to end speeches
that are expressive of character and thought
one still will not achieve the aim of tragedy;
the job is much better done
by a tragedy deficient
in respect to character
but one that has a plot. Besides,
the most powerful means tragedy has
of swaying our feelings,
namely peripeties and recognitions,
are elements of plot.

So plot is the basic principle—the heart and soul
of tragedy—the characters come second.
Third in rank is thought—the passages
in which characters try to prove
that something is so or not so. But character—
which we rank second—before thought—
includes the kind of thought
which reveals the bent

of a man's *moral* choice. Fourth,
verbal expression, and I mean by this
conveyance of thought
through language. The point here:
thought does not exist in drama
unless the characters express the thought
in speech.

Song composition
is the greatest of the sensuous
attractions, and the visual adornment
of the characters can have strong
emotional effect but is the least connected
with poetic art; in fact—
and this is fundamental: the force
of tragedy can be felt
without the benefit
of public performance or of actors.

But a plot (no matter its length)
is not unified, as some people think,
because it has to do
with a single person. A large—
indeed an indefinite number of things
can happen to a given individual—
some of which go to constitute
no unified event. And in the same way
there can be many acts
of a given individual from which
no single action emerges. Hence it seems clear
that one might depict the life
of anyone—of a particular philosopher,
for instance—thinking this particular philosopher—
whom for the sake of the argument
we'll call Plato—
because this "Plato"—
because he was an individual—
a single person
it would be wrong to think
(because he is an individual
a single person)

that the plot of our imagined play
of this particular philosopher—
given the large—indeed
indefinite number of things
that could conceivably have happened
or happen to this character—this Plato—
would necessarily be
a single unified plot. No. But Homer,
superior as he is in all other respects
appears to have mastered this point.
For in composing an Odyssey
he did not incorporate every thing
that happened to Odysseus. He composed
the *Odyssey* around a unified action of the kind
we have been talking about. And
so should it be—when we—if we
compose our play of our imagined Plato.

From what has been said
it is also clear the poet's job
is not to report what has happened
but what is *likely* to happen:
what is *capable* of happening. Thus,
the difference—as we said earlier—
between the historian and the poet
lies not in their utterances being in verse
or prose (it would be possible
to translate into verse Herodotus' work;
but it would not be any less a history
with verse than it would be without it—or
if someone were to take my lecture here
for instance,
versify it and set out to make some drama
from it, hoping to capture what
implicit drama there might be in my
delivering this particular lecture at this particular time
and in this particular place—given the circumstances
that have instigated its composition—well,
or say for instance—the particular philosopher
that we imagined—our Plato—
say he were some other teacher's teacher

and had come
for reasons various to compose
a dialogue—a Socratic
dialogue—which we established
as one of the poetic imitative arts—
and in this dialogue—this
Socratic dialogue—he throws the poets out
of his ideal State with barely
a garland or two
to hide their nakedness, issuing a challenge—
not to poets themselves
but to some unnamed lover of poetry—one
whom he considers having no poetic talent
whatsoever—issuing this challenge
to one he trained himself philosophically—
to step up to the bar and offer a defense
of poetry, and this particular philosopher—
our Plato, ironically—for the sake of the argument—
and the potential imitation—
is himself [or was] a gifted imitative poet. And in the course
of what we may soon come to call
a dramatization
the circumstances that have led
to the or a poetically gifted philosopher
taking the stance he has or does
against the art of poetry—despite the reasons he himself
offers—might be revealed but we get
ahead of ourselves, don't we. For the proposition
entails not only parceling out
other bits of information—
it must come—
as you might well imagine—
at the opportune moment); no, the difference
between the historian and the poet
lies in the fact that the historian speaks
of what has happened, the poet of
the *kind* of thing that can happen. Hence, poetry
is a more philosophical and serious business
than history; for poetry speaks more
of universals, history of particulars. Universals
in this case being what kind of person

is likely to do or say certain kinds
of things, at a given time—
and in a particular way. That
is what poetry aims at—even if it gives
its persons particular names afterward—
a Pentheus, a Patroclus, a Peleus, a Plato.

So, some plots are simple, others
complex. By simple plot
I mean the development of one which
being continuous and unified,
the reversal
comes without peripety or recognition;
and by complex plot
one in which the reversal is continuous
but with recognition or peripety
or both.

Peripety
is a *sudden* and *unexpected* shift
of what is being undertaken
to the opposite. For example in the *Oedipus*
the man who has come,
thinking that he will reassure Oedipus, that is,
relieve him of his fear with respect to his mother,
by revealing who he (Oedipus) really is,
brings about the opposite. And recognition,
as indeed the word indicates, is a shift
from ignorance to awareness.

The finer recognition is one that happens
at the same time as a peripety, as is
the case of the *Oedipus.* Naturally,
there are other kinds of recognition: it is for example possible
for one to take place
in relation to chance occurrences,
and it is possible to achieve recognition
even if a person has not acted
(and by acted
I mean performed the tragic act
and by tragic act I mean

the violent act—
the act of violence—a *pathos*).

Peripety, recognition, *pathos—pathos*
is a destructive or painful act
such as deaths on stage, paroxysms of pain,
woundings—all that sort of thing. The *pathos*
is the foundation stone
of tragedy. Peripety and recognition
are limited to complex plots, indeed
they constitute the definition of
a complex plot. The *pathos*
on the other hand
can be equally well-embodied
in a simple plot. In fact
it happens that the happening
or (listen closely) the *threatened happening* of a *pathos*
is the *sine qua non* of all tragedy.

All right, on to the good stuff:
complex plots. If the job of tragedy
is to arouse pity and fear,
and if peripety and recognition arouse
them, the complex plot is the kind
one wants. And since
the construction of the finest tragedy
should be not simple but complex,
and at the same time imitative
of fearful and pitiable happenings
it is clear that (1)
neither should virtuous men
appear undergoing a change
from good to bad fortune—
that is not fearful, nor pitiable,
it is morally repugnant—which is fine,
but that's what it is; (2)
the wicked from bad fortune
to good—that is the most untragic of all—
it has none of the qualities
one wants from tragedy—it is productive
neither of ordinary sympathy, pity,

or fear; (3)
the really wicked man
changing from good fortune to bad:
all right: that kind of structure
will excite sympathy
(if you're lucky) but neither pity
nor fear, since the one (pity)
is directed towards the man
who does not deserve his misfortune
and the other (fear) towards the man
who is like the rest of us—and I won't even bother
with the fourth pattern
which is a shift of the good man
from bad to good fortune—
that is so obviously untragic as to not need mentioning—
I hope. So, what is left? What is left is
the man who falls between these extremes.
Such is a man who is neither a paragon of virtue
nor undergoes the change to misfortune
through any real badness
or wickedness but instead
because of some *mistake.*
A mistake. By someone who's not
perfect and who the hell is?

Now it is possible for the fearful
and pathetic effect to come from
the actors' appearance—
and by that I mean their costumes.
Oh come on, how many times
has Aristophanes jeered
at Euripides' *Telephus*—the king
arousing the commiseration of the audience
by his appearance in rags. (I mean I loved it,
but it's so cheap.) It is also possible for
the fearful and pathetic effect to arise
from the very structure of the events—
the plot. The plot
must be structured
in such a way
that even without benefit of visual effect

the one who is hearing the events unroll
shudders with fear and feels
pity
at what happens: as one would
experience on hearing the plot
of the *Oedipus.* I mean here
the bare plot, unclothed in speeches,
verses, images, music, etc.

Now it is possible, (1)
for the act (the tragic act—
the act of *pathos*) to be performed
knowingly and wittingly—Euripides
did it that way
in the murdering of the children in *Medea*—
(2) it is possible
to refrain from performing the deed,
with knowledge (and I'll tell you what that means in a sec), (3)
it is possible to perform the fearful act,
but unwittingly, then recognize
later, as Sophocles' Oedipus
does and in that case
the act (the tragic act—the violent act—
the act of violence) is outside the play,
(4) while intending
because of ignorance
to perform some fearful crime, it is possible
to recognize
before one does it. And there is no other way;
for one must either do the deed
or not,
and with or without knowledge
of what one is doing.

Of these modes,
to know what one is doing but hold off
and not perform the act (number two—
the one I was going to tell you about): the worst (the worst!):
it has the morally repulsive character
(and by morally repulsive I mean filthy,
I mean polluted)

and at the same time it
it is not tragic; for there is no tragic act
and by tragic act I mean
the violent act—
the act of violence—the *pathos.* Performing the act
with knowledge (*Medea*—number one)
second poorest. Better it is
to perform the act in ignorance
and recognize what one has done
afterward (number three); for the repulsive quality
(the pollution) does not attach to the act, and the recognition
has a shattering emotional effect. The catharsis
is a purification—of whatever is filthy
whatever is polluted
in
the
pathos—the foundation stone
of tragedy. The filthiness inheres
in a *conscious* intention to kill a person—
particularly one who is near and dear. And it adheres.
An *unconscious* intention to do so,
i.e., without awareness—
as Oedipus did not know that the old man that he killed
at the crossroads was his father—
would therefore be pure, *katharos.* But the purity
must be established to our satisfaction.
Catharsis would be then the process
of proving that the act was pure
in the sense that the person who committed the crime
committed the crime by *mistake.* How is this proved?
It is proved by the remorse of the doer, which shows
that if he knew the facts
he would not have done the deed. In the *Oedipus,*
the self-blinding satisfies; it then effects
purification of the tragic deed
and so makes Oedipus eligible for our pity. We do not
the spectator experience purification ourselves—
we are not purged. The question before us here
is whether we will think of literature
as a therapeutic device and we the spectators
as patients and of course the answer

is no. Why when we come for pleasure
should we expect to be cured?

And now we're going to go back up—which I didn't expect to do—but something has occurred to me; and so we are going to back up and I'm going to try bring it all together here. You see how I have been emphasizing the close affinity between *fear* and *pity*. We *pity* in the case of others that which we *fear* in our own. In both cases the emotions are aroused by things close at hand. But *fear*—*fear* is distinct from *pity*—they differ in the psychic distance they imply. We *fear* that which is about to happen or seems likely to happen to ourselves, we *pity*—feel *pity* for that which happens or is about to happen to another because it *might* happen to us.

He was wrong about the stage—Plato—he was wrong—not just the stage, the *drama*. The *drama* by its very nature separates its characters from us and necessarily thus alters the relation between the two—*pity* and *fear*—for *tragic fear* cannot be felt directly or overtly for ourselves, it necessarily applies only to the protagonist—the character. We fear for him, we fear for her, we fear for Plato has indicted the poets—he throws the poets out of his ideal State alleging they misrepresent the truth. Poets feed and nourish the irrational in man he says by making him indulge emotions especially the emotions of *pity* and *fear*—I rule out these objections immediately—simply because they are not tragic, they don't arouse tragic emotions. I appeal to the psychological facts; we feel not *fear* or *pity* but *repugnance* when a good man falls in suffering or when a villain prospers—the unaided moral sense of ordinary people will perform the duties of the censor. Plato lays the duty of the censor on philosophers, but we do not need to be saved from immoral stories by decree or revelation or by philosophers thank you very much—our own unconscious screens the reversals of fortune presented by the drama according *pity* and *fear* to some but not to others. The emotions—our emotions are not merely irrational as Plato has made them out to be, they have also that rational side—or are at least amenable to reason. In the first place, emotional effects are brought before the bar of reason by the spectator himself. He judges (1) whether the hero is like us ourselves and (2) that he does not deserve misfortune. If the judgment runs to the contrary on either account, the effect is not *tragic*. The mode that Plato would approve—good things for good people, bad things for bad people—is ruled out—it does not produce *pity* and as *pity* will affiliate itself with reason, I for one accept it as legitimate and he and I part company. He was my teacher, I loved him, but we part company. The special pleasure—and it is a pleasure—of tragedy is neither simply intellectual or simply emotional but has its roots in both these realms. It is a pleasure springing from emotion, but emotion authorized and released by an intellectually constituted structure of an action. The emotion flows unimpeded because when we feel it, we feel it is inevitable and justified.

Best of the modes is the last
(number four): I mean
a case like the *Iphigenia in Tauris* of Euripides.
Iphigenia is about to kill her brother, Orestes,
but does not do so
because she recognizes him first. It is enough
to call forth the tragic emotions
of pity and fear without
completion of the *pathos.* As was said,
the happening or
the *threatened happening*
of a *pathos*
is the *sine qua non* of all tragedy. And as in the *Iphigenia*
the *pathos* in the *Oedipus*
is kept offstage and out of the story—
it has already happened: the genius
of Sophocles is that he manages to sublimate
his plot structure into a pure nexus
of recognition: he achieves in number three
the effect of number four; thus
accomplishing a *tour de force:*
the full impact of the pathos
without giving us one.

There are other things I say in my *Poetics*—
I take you (with some cuts) only half way through
the argument—or what is left of it—
who knows how much of it is lost. I want to tell you
something else. It's true what people say of me—
that I have little feeling for the magic of words—
I'm a botanist for Christ sake;
and though I very much enjoy the theater—
and welcome the newer dramatists—

it's to the older plays—the plays of Sophocles
and Euripides to which I am drawn—and to this day
I thrill to the dramatic genius of Homer—
these are the things I grew up on. What I'm saying is
I'm not a literary type—
I couldn't for the life of me
compose a real play. But if I could,
the plot I would lay down
unclothed in speeches, verses,
masks, or music—it would be
of a particular philosopher—
who in his youth wrote tragedies
and dithyrambs—but tore them up for
Socrates—that is for philosophy. Yet he remained, despite
the stance he took against his old
idolatry, one of the great dramatic geniuses
of all time—though comic
by nature—much more akin to Aristophanes
than say Aeschylus. And he perfected
a poetic form known as the
Socratic dialogue. And though there was
a Socrates, the Socrates of our
philosopher is not the Socrates
there was; the Socrates that he
created is a poetic
imitation. And the particular philosopher
that I would imitate wrote once a dialogue
about a dinner party for a tragedian who had
just won first place at the festival—a comedy
that will not stay in the comedic mode.
Everything rolls on in a golden flow
of humorous invention—as each participant
discourses on the nature of love. But Socrates
begins and ends the evening alone—
in solitary meditation. And notes are struck
of spiritual anguish, unassuageable longing,
and shame—which is
the antithesis of comedy: the self-reproach
of the soul that sees the truth
but has not followed. Then Socrates
discourses on the worthiness

of poetry as an enduring spiritual
legacy—and further,
insists on the essential unity
of tragedy and comedy, and this takes on
symbolic character: the particular philosopher
who for the sake of the argument
we have called Plato—is now the true
dramatic poet—a comedian
by virtue of the same knowledge that makes him
a tragedian: he can produce a drama—
heretofore unknown—that seems now comic—
now tragic—because he alone—our imagined
philosopher—has knowledge enough
to distinguish the *appearances* of tragedy and comedy
from the *reality* and *truth* behind them.

Of course he wrote this dialogue
in the first enthusiasm of his love affair
with Dion, a political adviser to the throne of Sicily,
as the two of them attempted to transform
an intemperate tyrant
into a philosophical monarch.
But the true sterility of their relationship
and the failure of that enterprise
cast later a blight on our philosopher's view
both of poetic and political creation—
long before the tragic *denouement*
of his lover's assassination.

When we read in the *Republic*
that poets leave no spiritual legacy
and truth behind them, we must remember
that our philosopher had once been
magnanimous enough to acknowledge that the truth
was quite different.

So I accepted the challenge
and offered a defense of poetry
which is itself
tragically flawed. Based too narrowly
on the overwhelming importance

of plot against all other elements,
I found no room for *Oedipus at Colonus,*
The Trojan Women,
The Orestia—and (I suppose) countless
other works. There are some things
I fear, not dreamt of in my philosophy.

But that is the wonderful thing about making mistakes,
isn't it? Someone always comes along
to correct you.

When next we meet,
we shall take up the subject of comedy.

End.

The Myopia, an epic burlesque of tragic proportion

David Greenspan in *The Myopia.* The Foundry Theatre/Atlantic Stage 2, New York, 2010. Photographs by Jon Wasserman.

The Myopia, an epic burlesque of tragic proportion

First produced by The Foundry Theatre, Melanie Joseph, Artistic Director, at Atlantic Stage 2, New York City, from January 6 through February 7, 2010.

Performed by David Greenspan

Set and Lighting Design by Peter Ksander
Directed by Brian Mertes

Note:

The Myopia is performed as a solo—in the "story-telling" tradition. One actor plays all the roles, speaking the stage directions in brackets as narration. The actor is confined to a chair for the entire performance. He does not move from that chair.

Act 1, Flare-Up

Characters:

The Raconteur
Narratage in the form of Stage Directions
Yetti, an old hag
Koreen, Yetti's daughter
Febus, Koreen's suitor, later her husband
Barclay, product of Febus and Koreen
Second Self, Barclay
Warren G. Harding, a character from history
Florence Harding, Harding's wife
Old Timer, a country fellow
Henry Cabot Lodge, Senator from Massachusetts
Will Hays, Republican Party Chairman
George Harvey, Editor, *North American Review*
Charles Curtis, Senator from Kansas
Frank Brandegee, Senator from Connecticut
Selden Spencer, Senator from Missouri
Reed Smoot, Senator from Utah
William Borah, Senator from Idaho
Joseph Frelinghuysen, Senator from New Jersey
Medill McCormick, Senator from Illinois
James Watson, Senator from Indiana
Henry Haskell, Reporter, *Kansas City Star*
Irvin Kirkwood, Reporter, *Kansas City Star*

Setting: Various.

Note: Yetti speaks with an East European accent.

Prologue

Raconteur: I've been thinking about pictures. I've been thinking about pictures and how one might make pictures on the stage, which is not to say that I've been thinking about stage pictures. On the contrary.

I've been reflecting on the difference between the image and the imagined, and the relationship of imagining to thinking—and I've been thinking about thinking, but for the moment that's tangential.

I've been thinking how a picture is a picture of something, but not the something it is a picture of. And the same for film—which is after all pictures, and for anything that is a picture even if it is not a picture but a recording of something, but not the something it is a recording of. And others have addressed this issue more astutely than I. If you wish, see me after, I refer you.

But that this is not true of live signals, broadcast or monitored, might lead one to consider the televising of something, which is not by necessity a recording though it is by necessity a transmission. Here again others—I must refer you to others—though I will say that television, no matter how it is maligned, shares with the *theater* the capacity of presenting things actually happening. Of course this is true with radio, but I'm not thinking about radio because with radio there is no picture—other than the ones one must imagine—which is to say I am thinking about radio.

But—well—others—others will address these issues. I cannot—other than to say there might be a lot of confusion about the theater—with some expecting of the theater what is inherently untheatrical, and some in the theater providing this—some of these some being sometimes successful—abandoning action for image in ways that are thrillingly theatrical—forcing one in one's confusion to wonder whether what one has been thinking all along has not more to do with the stage than the theater, the stage being a platform for drama, the theater not that same thing entirely.

But—well—so—anyway, thinking about pictures—a picture being a picture of something but not the something it is a picture of, I've thought about the theater, which is not a picture of something, though one might make pictures in it. And not only have I thought about the theater which is not a picture, I've thought about the theater because it is not a picture, thinking instead it is what is happening in it. And that no matter what is happening in it—even if what is pictured happening has already happened, or didn't happen, or never happened, or never will happen, you know on some level—and I think you know that you know—something is actually happening. And of course this is the difference. Nothing happens in a picture—it's already happened—whereas in the theater what is happening is actually happening—it is happening as it happens—it is an act. A picture is never an act!

So thinking how it might be useful to distinguish if one could the difference between the stage and the theater—a distinction I think marvelous to navigate—the stage from the theater—I've made what I'm doing and what I'm about to do. And if you were to ask me is what I do on the stage a play, I could not be certain, I could not say. If you were to ask me is what I do on the stage theater, again, I could not be certain, I could not say. Of only one thing can I say and of it be certain, and that is that what I do on the stage is an act! And it is full of imitations. And if not imitations, impersonations. And it is actually happening, happening as it happens, happening as I speak. And this has been a Prologue and is a moment more until it ends, and then the next thing begins, and this next thing—this thing to begin—why, it is called *The Myopia.* And it is an epic burlesque of tragic proportion. Ding, ding, ding, ding. And the curtain is rising on its first act, entitled *Flare-Up,* and this is scene one:

SCENE 1

[Light illuminates Warren G. Harding, immobile, seated in an easy chair in his room in the La Salle Hotel—Chicago, June 12, 1920. The chair is directed upstage right at an angle of (say) 45 degrees, facing an open window, blind down. Now and again, a faint breeze rocks the blind. Light cuts in at the edges of the blind—more so as the blind is rocked. Try as one might to keep it out, the world gets in. Beside the chair, left, a tall standing lamp. Beside the chair, right, a doilied table with a phone. The lamp is dark, the phone is silent. Down left, an elegant writing table and a matching straight-back chair. Further down left, a door—ajar. Light from the corridor slices through the crack, slashing the back of Harding's head, making distinct cerebral division between the right and left. Sound, now, of foot traffic in the corridor, buzz of voices. Night fades as the sun rises. This can be determined by witnessing the change in light evidenced at the edges of the blind, particularly as the blind is rocked. As light pervades, Chicago awakens. Through the window come the sounds of the street, sparse at first, denser with time. Sound and light coincidental. Harding sits out of it. Time passes. Light is extinguished.]

[Light illuminates Harding as before—except the window blind is up, thus making visible a rectangle of starry sky—paled to some extent by the city's light. As night fades, the sun rises. Light burns in at Harding, his hands clutch the arms of the chair, his head, turning left, pushes deeper into the cushion. As light pervades, Chicago awakens. Through the window come the sounds of the street, sparse at first, denser with time. Sound and light coincidental. Harding stays—unmoved. Time passes. Light is extinguished.]

[Light illuminates Warren G. Harding, immobile, seated in the straight-back chair, pushed slightly back from the elegant writing table. The blind is up. Earliest dawn. Harding is directed, though, down left, toward the door—ajar—and the muffled tread and buzz beyond. Thus, he faces darkness, having turned from the outer light in favor of that dim interior illumination, which falling in harsh precision on the longitude of his left eye foments a dropping of his blind—leaving him monoptic, stymied in a painful wink. Time passes, light pervades, Chicago awakens. From shadow, now, behind Harding, a woman appears, her features indiscernible. It is Harding's wife, Florence, commonly referred to as "the Duchess." She speaks.]

Florence: (*Tired exasperation.*) Wurr-n. (*Hold.*) Wurr-n.

[Curtain as light is extinguished. Noise of the change behind the curtain.]

SCENE 2

[Noise subsides. Curtain. Light illuminates a seascape—the ocean downstage, beach upstage. A gray brick tower stands right of center, its single window—like a single eye—open to the ocean; and situated in such a way that only a sliver of the orifice is visible to the audience. Left of the tower, a small square of cultivation—a vegetable garden. Various green leaf vegetables sprout from the earth. The rest of the terrain is sand and sparse beach grass. Yetti is working in her garden. Elderly, short, plump, bit bosomy, slightly hunchbacked, shock of dry, white hair. She wears a simple dress and tennis shoes. She calls out to Koreen, directing her speech to the ocean side of the tower. Koreen responds from within the tower—unseen.]

Yetti: Yoo hoo. Yoo hoo. Nice weather, ain't it?

Koreen: It's all right.

Yetti: (*To herself.*) The sun is shining on the ocean. There's a nice breeze. It's not too hot. I'm never so happy since I built this tower.

(*To Koreen.*) You got a good view from up there, ain't you?

Koreen: It's all right. Are we out of coffee?

Yetti: (*To herself.*) I spend my days working in my garden by the sea—tending my lettuces. (*To Koreen.*) We'll have a fresh salad today for lunch. (*To herself.*) Tender green leaves.

Koreen: We're out of coffee, and I'm down to my last couple of cigarettes. You gotta do something.

Yetti: You smoke too much.

Koreen: What do you mean I smoke too much? Don't tell me I smoke too much. You're always telling me.

Yetti: Koreen, for Christ sake, can't we have a nice day today? I'm trying to show you a nice time! There's a good view from where you are, ain't it? (*To herself.*) I love to sit by the window and watch the sea on a sunny day. (*To Koreen.*) Can you see some wildlife—some porpoises or turtles? (*To herself.*) The wonderful panorama of life!

Koreen: I need coffee, Mother.

Yetti: Koreen, why don't you go wash your hair?

Koreen: Don't tell me what to do. I hate being cooped up like this.

Yetti: Come on, sweetheart, you're not cooped up.

Koreen: I can't even stand.

Yetti: Try to relax.

Koreen: (*To herself.*) I gotta get out of this place.

Yetti: You know what Doctor Edelman said.

Koreen: Oh, look at this, my last cigarette. I can't believe we're out of coffee.

Yetti: There's a can behind the farina in the green cabinet.

Koreen: What?

Yetti: I say, there's an unopened can of coffee behind the farina in the green cabinet.

Koreen: Oh, holding out on me, ay? Why didn't you say so before, before I got worked up? Now where is it?

Yetti: The green cabinet—top shelf.

Koreen: Jesus Christ! Why'd you stick it in there? My hand barely fits. I'm so swollen.

Yetti: Take it easy.

Koreen: (*To herself.*) Why am I being tortured like this?

Yetti: You see it? It's right behind the farina.

Koreen: I see it. Oh boy, coffee!

Yetti: You got it?

Koreen: (*To herself.*) I'm in such pain.

Yetti: You see it?

Koreen: There we go, I got it. Hey, this stuff is regular. I need instant coffee. I don't have time to stand over a goddamn percolator all goddamn day.

Yetti: What's 'a matter?

Koreen: This is regular. I need instant! Instant coffee! I am suffering! What am I suppose to do with this shit?

Yetti: Koreen, for god's sake, it takes ten minutes! Put it up, go wash your hair, and when you've done, there'll be fresh coffee for you!

Koreen: Oh, shut your goddamn cunt. You think I can wash my hair before I've had a cup of coffee? Are you insane? And now I'm out of cigarettes!

Yetti: You smoke too much!

Koreen: Fuck you!

Yetti: Koreen, please, I'm begging you not to start with me. I don't know how much I can take today. I'm—

Koreen: Too bad about you and how much you can take. You know what I need.

Yetti: (*To herself.*) Impossible!

Koreen: Let me out and I'll go into town for them myself.

Yetti: You can't go anywhere. Go wash your hair.

Koreen: I'm gonna burn my goddamn hair. I'm sticking my head over the burners—right now.

Yetti: Koreen, stop it. Stop it!

Koreen: I'm turning on the flames.

Yetti: Koreen! What are you doing?

Koreen: I'm gonna burn my hair off. You'll never get up here again.

Yetti: Koreen, don't be stupid!

Koreen: Here we go. Flame on!

Yetti: Koreen, I'm warning you!

Koreen! Koreen!! All right, all right, I'm going into town. I'll get you your cigarettes. Just turn off the gas. Come on. Okay?

Koreen: (*After a pause.*) Make sure they're Salem.
Yetti: Fine, just turn off the gas!
Koreen: The gas is off. Don't forget the coffee. Instant!
Yetti: All right, in the meantime you'll go wash your hair.
Koreen: Yes, Mother.
Yetti: And rinse it good.
Koreen: Fine. Cigarettes and coffee. Hurry back. I'm desperate.

[Yetti grabs her purse and rushes off.]

(*To herself.*) Wash your hair. Oh boy, all this hair. When will I be free?

[From within the tower, the sound of water running from a faucet.]

Water is so goddamn hot. Why doesn't the water work? You either freeze or burn in this place. All right, where's the shampoo? Where'd she put the shampoo? Och, here it is—cheap stuff she buys. Why is she so cheap? Your mother is so cheap. Oh, God how I suffer. People in Africa don't suffer the way I suffer. I've never been happy. Never will be happy. Everybody suffers. Why do we suffer?

[Sound of running water stops. Koreen sings "Funny Girl." Shampoo bubbles float out the window.]

Funny, did you hear that? Funny.
Yea, the guy said, honey, you're a funny girl.
That's me, I just keep them in stitches, doubled in half.
And though I may be all wrong for the guy,
I'm good for a laugh. Da da da da—

[Koreen hums the tune, rinsing the shampoo from her hair. Enter from left, Febus, driving a '53 Oldsmobile. He's just back from THE WAR! Balding, nearsighted—he wears thick bottle glasses. Febus stops his car, sticks his head out of the window, listens to Koreen singing. Koreen's hair piles out the window, reaching the ground. She shakes it gently, to dry it in the sun. Febus gets out of his car, approaches the tower. He climbs Koreen's hair.]

I guess it's not funny.
Life is far from sunny.
When the laugh is over and the joke's on you,

A girl ought to have a sense of humor.
That's one thing you really need for sure
When you're a funny girl.
The fella said a funny girl.
Funny how it's not so funny, funny girl.

[Febus climbs Koreen's hair, arrives at the tower window, looks in.]

Febus: (*To himself.*) What a beauty!

[Febus climbs through the window. Curtain as light is extinguished. Noise of the change behind the curtain.]

SCENE 3

[Noise subsides. Curtain. Light illuminates a square of beige carpet, bordered on its upstage perimeter by a thin veil of beige drape. Vague light—as if the outside—beyond the drape. Barclay is situated on the carpet. Barclay is an illuminated globe of singularly ocular appearance. His inner light pulses erratically as he speaks. He is raised several feet off the carpet, cradled in a four-pronged metal stand. Barclay speaks to his Second Self.]

Barclay: Now do I remember me. I fancied me a drama of me parent's nightmare marriage—a mythologic burlecue of endless discord. Savages were they! This play to be my revenger's comedy. Thus did I return, finger the wreckage. But what manic distraction. I could not spin their conflict into play. They "played" the same scene time and time again. Obsession with the "drama" altered me. Fixed in purpose I hardened. I find myself self-rendered thus. A fragile globe. Unlife-like shell. Encased. Immobile!
Second Self: And stuck in your head.

["Erh, erh."]

Barclay: What was that?

[From behind the drape, the sound of a passing seagull.]

Second Self: A passing seagull, Barclay.
Barclay: I see. The sea.
The childhood sea.
It batters me still with memory.

Second Self: Yes, Barclay. Avoid it as you would, you find yourself in your father's room—engirdled in the dark. Until you go dark. All gone dark.

[Light is extinguished. From the dark, Barclay's voice.]

Barclay: All gone dark!

[Light illuminates the space as before. The Second Self has vanished.]

In dearth of light, I whisper me, create something! From this, say I? What else? my teasing reply. What a task? What a task? And I, having rifled through my father's books and papers, finding nothing, it would seem, feeling nothing, it would seem. What a task? What—

[Curtain as light is extinguished. Noise of the change behind the curtain.]

SCENE 4

[Noise subsides. Curtain. Light illuminates the seascape. If you look closely, you might see a thin strand of silken ladder dangling from the sea side of the tower. If you look closely. Now look again. The vegetable garden has been trampled by something. Or someone. Enter from right, Yetti, carrying a brown paper bag loaded with cigarette cartons and jars of instant coffee.]

Yetti: (*Calling out.*) Koreen. Koreen, I'm back. I got you everything you want, sweetheart. Today is our lucky day. They were running a special on . . . I . . .

[Yetti notices the ladder—gasps, drops the bag—cigarettes and coffee all over the sand.]

(*Under her breath.*) Koreen.

[Yetti rushes to the tower, grabs hold of the ladder, climbs.]

(*Calling.*) Koreen? Koreen?!

[The ladder falls from the window.]

Koreeeeeeeeeeeeeeeeeeeeeeeen!!!

[Curtain as light is extinguished (thud! Yetti: Ehh!)—and cornet music from off left. Music to continue—as will the noise of the change behind the curtain.]

SCENE 5

[Noise subsides. Cornet continues off left. Curtain. Light illuminates Ohio. Three miles to Marion on the road from Caledonia. July 1, 1882. Dusk. Rose-streaked sky. As the scene progresses, the sky darkens. Enter from left, Warren Harding, riding an old sagging mule, tooting away on his cornet. The mule is burdened with a few satchels and household items—beat-up pots and pans. The mule comes to a halt. Harding finishes his tune, "Camp Town Ladies," then looks up at the sky.]

Harding: Well, how do you like that? The evening shades are falling. You like that? You like that, Dearie, "The evening shades are falling?" Sure you like that, sure you do. I wonder how far? I wonder. What do you think? What do you think, Dearie, you think it's far? You think it's far? Could be far, huh? Could be close. Could be close, could be far, we don't know. You think we'll make it? Think we'll make it before dark? We're not sure. What happens if we don't make it? What happens! We'll make it. We'll make it. All we have to do is get a move on.

[Enter from right an Old Timer, smoking a straw pipe. He moves left, stands unnoticed by Harding.]

What do you say, Dearie? Shall we get a move on? Shall we go? Come on Dearie, what do you say?

[Dearie doesn't budge. Harding performs a speech.]

Mr. President. Honorable judges. Respected audience. The question of morality and immorality on the stage today is one of the most important that can engage us. When we reflect upon the universal passion that has been exhibited to us through this species of amusement, when we further remember that some of the noblest productions of human intellect have been offered to the world through the medium of the stage, and lastly, when we bear in mind that the theater is one of the chief pleasures of the youthful members of society in all times and countries, we should realize at once that we have a topic worthy of debate.

Old Timer: She don't wanna move, huh?
Harding: Huh? Oh. Afternoon. Evening. Yea. He.
Old Timer: He?
Harding: He. He. He's a he.
Old Timer: Oh.
Harding: Yea. Dearie. He's a he. Mother named 'em.
Old Timer: That right?
Harding: Yea. I'm going to Marion.
Old Timer: That right?
Harding: Sure am. Far into Marion?
Old Timer: Will be on that mule.
Harding: Well, I'm hopin'.
Old Timer: 'bout three mile.
Harding: What do you say, Dearie? Three mile, huh, what do you say?

[Dearie doesn't budge.]

Meeting up with my folks. We're in from Caledonia. They are. Before that Blooming Grove. We're settling now in Marion.
Old Timer: That right?
Harding: Yep.
Old Timer: You makin' up a story before?
Harding: Oh no—no—no, that was—that was just un—that was un—that was just a speech. I was uh—done uh—I uh—did that speech. For a debate. College. Just graduated. Yea. Ohio Central!
Old Timer: That right?
Harding: (*Pointing.*) In Iberia.
Old Timer: Oh. You graduated, huh?
Harding: Oh yea. One of three. Just did. Class of '82. And that was uh—a speech I un . . . did—debated.
Old Timer: That right?
Harding: "Has the Stage a Moral Tendency?"
Old Timer: Huh?
Harding: That was the debate.
Old Timer: Oh.
Harding: I took the affirmative. I was assigned the affirmative. But I don't know, Hell—heck—you ask me, I wouldn't at all know. Not too moral to me. Not at all.
Old Timer: You been to the stage?
Harding: Who me? Oh me, no—never—couldn't—couldn't do. I mean, I'd like to go, but never have. But things I uh . . . hear, things they do,

don't—doesn't at all sound moral. I mean, could be moral, but doesn't sound. Things I hear they say.

Old Timer: That right?

Harding: Oh yea. And do. On the stage. All kinds of things. You know—(*Speechifying.*) tragedies of milk and water. Dramas of blood, uh . . . blue fire and slang. And uh . . . operas of the most irredeemable silliness.

Old Timer: That right?

Harding: Part of my speech. Yea. But uh . . . I'd like to go. See for myself. See what it's like. The Theater! 'specially some of them girlie shows. Wouldn't mind takin' in one of them girlie shows. At least one before I kick. What do you say?

[Dearie neighs.]

Hey, not you Dearie. You don't need to see any of them girlie shows. Don't want you getting all worked up in no girlie show. Imagine that. Big thing like that. (*Harding laughs.*)

Old Timer: What you plannin' to do in Marion?

Harding: Well, meet up with my folks first thing. They're in from Caledonia. Before that Blooming Grove. After that, haven't figured. Make some friends—that's what I like to do. Just fit myself in. That's always the first step. I find once you're well liked, all kinds of things happen.

Old Timer: What'd you say your name was?

Harding: Didn't say. (*Harding laughs.*) Harding. Warren Gamaliel. My father's Tryon. Tryon Harding. I'm Warren. Warren Harding.

Old Timer: Looks like he's ready.

Harding: Sure does. What do you say, Dearie—to Marion? Here we go. Well, thanks a lot. Thanks for your help.

Old Timer: Didn't do nothin'.

Harding: Well, thanks anyway. I appreciate it.

[Harding exits right on mule. Church bells ring. The evening shades are falling. Curtain as light is extinguished. Noise of the change behind the curtain.]

SCENE 6

[Noise subsides. Curtain. Light illuminates the darkened bathroom of a middle-class household. The door is closed. The single source of illumination is the outside. It enters through a small window placed high on the left wall. The window's glass is thickly frosted, thus permitting only the most meager light of an already gray dawn. Shabby throw rugs scattered on the tile floor. A beige rug—unprofessionally cut—limply hugs the base of the toilet. Febus is sitting on the toilet, his boxers at his ankles, his shirt covering his groin. He wears socks and sandals. Febus has aged since last seen. What little hair he had has gone gray, and his eyesight—never the best—has deteriorated to near blindness. At his feet, a princess telephone, the cord of which extends underneath the bathroom door. Before him, a small typewriter table on which is stationed a large reel-to-reel tape recorder. The reels are moving—the machine is recording. It will record the entire scene. The only other artifact of note is an old typewriter that has been dumped into the bathroom sink. Febus speaks into his mics.]

Febus: Okay, so then what? Then what? Then what do we got? We got . . . We got . . . We got . . . Okay, so then what do we got? We got—

[Telephone rings. Febus picks up.]

Hello? Hey baby. No, it's fine, it's fine. It's fine, she's sleeping. She's sleeping. Yea. Yea. Yea. Yea. Okay.

[Febus hangs up, returns to the problem.]

Now what?

[Telephone rings. Febus picks up.]

Hello? Hey baby. That's all right. No, she's sleeping—didn't I just say that? Well, why do I have to repeat myself? Why do I have to repeat myself? Yea, but I'm stuck, I'm stuck. I'm not getting anywhere, I can't get anywhere. I'm right where I was, that's where I am, I'm still there. "The evening shades were falling." You like that, "The evening shades were falling?" Or do you like, "The evening shades are falling?" Which do you like, "were" or "are," "are" or "were," which do you like? I don't like either of them. Maybe I should cut it. Should I cut it? You think I should cut it? What do you think? Maybe I'll leave it for now—I can always cut it later. You think I should cut it later? Or should I cut it now? Later or now? Now or later? What do you think? Maybe I'll leave it for now. I'm gonna leave it for now. "The evening shades—" Maybe I'll just say, "The evening shades." What do you think? You like it, "The evening shades?" You don't like it. Do you like it? Maybe I'll just cut it. I'm gonna cut it. Cut the whole thing, it's crap, right? It's crap! You think it's crap? Cut the crap or keep the crap? Keep it or cut it? Cut it or keep it? What do you think? Come on, I'm under pressure. Maybe I'll just keep it for now. You think I should keep it for now? I'll keep it for now. What do you think? That's what I'll do. You think that's what I should do? That's what I'm gonna do. That's what I'm gonna do. Or maybe I'll just put it in the stage directions. They can make it with the lights. What do you think, make it with the lights? Maybe it needs to be said. (*Intoning.*) "The evening shades." "The evening shades." Would you miss it if I cut it? You wouldn't miss it? You *wouldn't* miss it. You wouldn't *miss* it?! All right, I'll think about it. You think I should think about it? That's what I'm gonna do. That's what I'm gonna do. Yea, so how are you? (*Yawning.*) Un huh. Un huh. What time? That's good. Yea, near where they train the dogs. Sounds good. All right. Okay. Yea, big kiss.

[He makes a kiss into the phone, hangs up, returns to the problem.]

No more. No more what? What the Hell is happening? Nothing. Nothing is happening. So what?

[Telephone rings, Febus picks up.]

Hello? Hey baby.

[From off right, a groaning as if coming out of sleep. It is Koreen, waking.]

Koreen: No. No more. Oh. Please. Stop.
Febus: (*Into phone.*) Wait a sec.
Koreen: Stop, get off me. Get off me. Help.
Febus: (*Into phone.*) No, it's Koreen.
Koreen: Help. Help.
Febus: (*Into phone.*) Her medication is wearing off.
Koreen: Somebody help me. Help. Please.
Febus: (*Into phone.*) Her medication.
Koreen: (*Louder.*) Oh. No. Help. Help. (*Crying out.*) Aaaaah!! (*Shrieking.*) Aaaaaaaaaaaaaaaaaaaah!!!
Febus: (*After a pause. Into phone.*) Okay.
Koreen: (*Calling weakly.*) Febus?
Febus: (*Into phone.*) Hold on.
Koreen: (*Weakly.*) Febus?

Febus: (*Into phone.*) Wait a minute. (*To Koreen.*) What do you want?
Koreen: Where are you?
Febus: I'm on the phone, go back to sleep.
Koreen: Did somebody call?
Febus: What's 'a matter?
Koreen: Is it my mother?
Febus: No, baby, go back to sleep.
Koreen: My mother was supposed to call. What time is it?
Febus: It's just past six.
Koreen: What are you doing up so early?
Febus: (*Into phone.*) Okay—
Koreen: Where are you?
Febus: I'm on the toilet.
Koreen I thought you were on the phone.
Febus: (*Into phone.*) Okay, listen—
Koreen: Febus.
Febus: (*Into phone.*) I gotta get off. I'll see you later.

[Febus hangs up. Four knocks at the bathroom door.]

Koreen: Febus, what are you doing in there?
Febus: I'll be out soon.
Koreen: What'd you, got the phone in the john?
Febus: In case somebody called. I didn't want them to wake you.
Koreen: What are you doing in there?
Febus: I'm working on the play.
Koreen: Oh, for Christ sake.
Febus: I need privacy.
Koreen: That goddamn play.
Febus: What are you talking about?
Koreen: I can't believe you. What're you, sitting on the toilet writing your play? Someone should put that into a play.
Febus: Korky, go back to bed.
Koreen: I can't believe you.
Febus: You know, Longfellow used to work on the toilet, baby. All the greats.
Koreen: Henry Wadsworth Longfellow did not sit on the toilet writing a musical about Warren G. Harding.
Febus: Oh, what do you know.
Koreen: Besides, we're supposed to look at apartments today. You're not going to spend the whole day sitting on the toilet.

Febus: What are you talking about?

Koreen: Febus, we are suppose to look at apartments.

Febus: Come on, Korky, let me alone.

Koreen: Please Febus, don't do this to me. I can't live here anymore.

Febus: What do you want?

Koreen: I want to move! I want you to help me. Come on.

Febus: What are you talking about?

Koreen: Febus, please, don't aggravate me. You know I don't like it here. The rooms are too small.

Febus: What are you talking about?

Koreen: The rooms, Febus, the rooms.

Febus: Let me finish this and I'm gonna come out to you. Give me a minute.

Koreen: And I didn't sleep last night.

Febus: What?

Koreen: I couldn't sleep. I have nightmares. Always the same. Always the same. Oh, look at me. I'm so swollen. My whole body. How much longer can I live like this, Febus? How much longer can I live?

Febus: What's a matter? What do you want?

Koreen: We have to move, Febus! I can't bear it anymore.

Febus: We're gonna move—some day.

Koreen: Not some day, Febus. Now.

Febus: What're you, wanna move today? You think we're gonna move today?

Koreen: Oh Febus, don't do this to me!

Febus: These things take time, baby. They take time—and planning. You gotta have a plan.

Koreen: Febus, I made appointments.

Febus: What?

Koreen: What do you mean, what? I told you.

Febus: What appointments?

Koreen: I made appointments! To look at apartments. I made them earlier in the week. I told you this. I told you this!

Febus: I don't know what you're talking about.

Koreen: Oh Febus, don't do this to me!

Febus: What am I doing to you?

Koreen: You know goddamn well what you're—

Febus: Come on Korky. I don't wanna—

Koreen: Wait a minute! Wait a minute!

Febus: Listen, Korky, you got big ideas, you know—

Koreen: (*Getting more agitated.*) No. No.

Febus: All right, here she goes.
Koreen: (*Crying out.*) Aaaaaaaaaaaaaaaaaaaah!!!
Febus: See, now you're gonna get upset, baby. This is what you're gonna do.
Koreen: (*Pounding on the door.*) You bastard! You goddamn bastard!
Febus: (*Getting into the argument—on the offensive.*) That's right, Korky, let the whole neighborhood know what you're like.

[The bathroom door bursts open. Koreen's hand comes sailing through the doorway. Her hand is bigger than Febus.]

Koreen: You son of a bitch. Why do you do this to me?
Febus: A little louder, baby, come on. Let them know what you're like in Philadelphia.
Koreen: (*Pounding the floor with her fist.*) Damn it. Damn it.
Febus: (*With sadistic disgust.*) Look at that! Look at that! Like a goddamn animal.
Koreen: (*Sobbing, furious.*) Don't you dare call me an animal!
Febus: See that? See that? That's what you're like. Like an animal. For Christ sake.
Koreen: (*Reaching for the phone.*) Give me that phone!
Febus: (*Pushing her off.*) What're you, gonna try to hit me with the phone?
Koreen: Don't touch me.
Febus: Get outta here.
Koreen: (*Sobbing.*) I'm gonna call my mother. I can't take this anymore with you, Febus.
Febus: What'd you think your mother is gonna take you back, baby? Are you crazy?
Koreen: Give me that phone!
Febus: (*Pushing her hand off.*) She knows what you're like.
Koreen: Stop it, Febus! Stop it!
Febus: Everybody knows what you're like!
Koreen: Please, please, Febus. I beg you. Don't do this to me!
Febus: Look at you! Look at you!
Koreen: (*Wailing.*) Help! Help!
Febus: What're you, crazy? Are you crazy?!
Koreen: Help me. Somebody help me!

[Telephone rings.]

Febus: For Christ sake!

Koreen: (*Sobbing, furious.*) Oooooooooh. Oooooooooh, I could kill you!

Febus: I hope somebody's taking that down, baby—so you can hear yourself some day.

[Koreen growls, claws at Febus.]

You better watch it, baby. You're gonna swell up. You're gonna swell up!

Koreen: (*Wailing horribly.*) Noooooooooo! Nooooooooooooo!!

Febus: Get outta here! Get outta here!

[Koreen withdraws her hand, wailing, sobbing, growling as she goes. She scratches a gash in the floor as she retreats. The door closes. Muffled sobs now as she crawls away. Febus pounds his head.]

(*To himself, pounding his head with his fist.*) You see what I gotta live with now? You see what I gotta live with?

[Koreen continues to cry. Phone continues to ring. Reels continue to move. It's all recorded. Curtain as light is extinguished. Noise of the change behind the curtain.]

SCENE 7

[Noise subsides. Curtain. Light illuminates Barclay on his carpet, the square of which is littered with reams of paper. Barclay speaks to himself.]

Barclay: "The evening shades." "The evening shades." Oh how my dramaturgy is like my life. Both inscrutable.

[Barclay's Second Self appears.]

Second Self: Your papers, Barclay, in disorder, such disorder.

[Barclay screams at his Second Self.]

Barclay: Relentless entity, begone. I am the subject now of unsparing torment. Confusion! Fury! I have lost the thread of my narrative!

Second Self: Is't possible?

Barclay: No longer simple family play. I am engulfed now in extended scrutinization of that Warren G. Harding.

Second Self: Warren Harding? You were revenging yourself solely on your parents.

Barclay: Such was the plan. But flipping through my files, I lit on the prolonged episode: my father's great ambition to musicalize the former President. Forever did he promise composition, threatening my mother with the role of Harding's nagging wife, Florence. Oh, many were the dinner fork flung over that injury.

What, methoughts, were I to loop the whole farcical-tragic family spectacular—entwine it I say—with some stately pageant of American politicos? But the plot is hopeless. The language hopelessly baroque. And worse I can't determine which of all this shit has issued from me and which from him.

Second Self: Your father?

Barclay: Yes! My father, yes. That most original genius!

Second Self: Curious you can't determine where your father leaves off and you begin. I wonder that the two of you become like one man?

Barclay: Who? My father and I? No! Horrible. I will not complete the text. He begun it, I should leave it. Shouldn't I? Should I?

I find myself in my father's room. Bad enough! I wake here, discover me transformed into an ill-lit globe. Fine, I accept it. Now I glean my miserable excuse for a father and I become like one man, and that soon, if this Hell continues, there will be no distinction between us. One more monster. Let us pray for oblivion.

Second Self: Oh Barclay, your continual "drama"! Put your papers into order. Discover if you can where your father leaves off and you begin.

Barclay: Fine. I'll do it. I will create something splendid beyond belief. Then burn it before a live audience. Now that's theater!

[Barclay's Second Self evaporates. The lights come up to full. Barclay chews the scenery.]

These walls, these floors. It's all on my mind. Noise behind the curtain.

["Erh, erh."]

Oh, I am slain!

[Barclay continues his drama, he pulses idiosyncratically. He gets the hook.]

(*As he's pulled off.*) Hey, I'm not finished!

[Curtain, as light is extinguished. Noise of the change behind the curtain.]

SCENE 8

[Noise subsides—giving way to the sound of men coughing. Curtain. Light illuminates the Smoke-filled Room. Suite 404, 405, 406—the Blackstone Hotel, Chicago, June 12, 1920. Coughing continues throughout the entire scene—at points singular, at points choral, at points between. The dialogue always rising above. Smoke is everywhere, and virtually impenetrable. Figures appear—phantasmagorically—detected a moment, then—moving or stationary, quickly re-enveloped and invisible. The only entity visually persistent is Henry Cabot Lodge. Somehow his mouth and right leg are constantly visible. He alone does not smoke. He sits in a chair down right, right leg crossed over left, right leg eternally swinging. The smoke screen is forever replenished. There is the occasional striking of the match, the sudden flame, the lighting of the cigar, the match extinguished. Cards are shuffled and dealt—this can be heard. Drinks are poured—the sound of bottles clinking—dumped when empty into trash cans, liquid splashing into glasses, the rattle of ice. It's sweltering. The men wipe themselves with handkerchiefs, fan themselves with newspapers and straw hats. Lodge speaks.]

Lodge: Have another drink, Selden! We need to start talking about Senator Harding.
Borah: (*To Frelinghuysen.*) Hey Joe, what're you and Smoot talking about?
Frelinghuysen: Warren Harding.
Smoot: We gotta break the deadlock. (*Hiccup.*)
Curtis: Oh, but Henry, Senator Penrose has very little confidence in Harding.
Borah: (*To Smoot.*) Because of Cox?
Smoot: (*To Borah.*) That's right. We have to carry Ohio! (*Hiccup.*)
Lodge: (*To Smoot, Borah, and Frelinghuysen.*) What are you gentleman discussing?
Smoot: Harding. (*Hiccup.*)
Lodge: Ah!
Hays: Oh good night, Phipps.

Lodge: (*To Smoot.*) Wait. (*To Hays.*) Hays! Did you get someone, Hays?

Hays: Crane talked to Johnson. They want Johnson and Knox, not Knox and Johnson.

Lodge: I could have told you that! Too bad. Just as well. Deal again.

Hays: There's Coolidge.

Borah: Cautious Cal! (*Inquisitively to Lodge.*) Henry?

Spencer: (*Inquisitively to Lodge.*) Henry?

Curtis: (*Inquisitively to Lodge.*) Oh, Henry?

Lodge: (*To all his inquisitors.*) What?

Borah: He's the Governor of your state, Senator. You'd have to push him.

Lodge: No!

Borah: Why not?

Lodge: Nominate a man who lives in a two-family house? Never! Massachusetts is not for him! Besides, he's too old.

Curtis: (*To Lodge.*) Henry? Hoover!

Lodge: (*To Curtis.*) Oh, Charles. Herbert Hoover has about as much chance of being elected President as . . . Calvin Coolidge!

Smoot: That's right. (*Hiccup.*)

Lodge: Besides, it doesn't solve the Ohio problem at all. Let's review again. Wood and Lowden are unthinkable. Knox is nix. Johnson a disaster.

McCormick: My God, is Congress in session?

Lodge: Ah, the home state Senator finally arrives!

McCormick: Either that or the jails are empty. (*Laughs.*)

Curtis: Ah, Medill. Did you forget where Illinois was?

McCormick: Hey, what's drinking? You know I voted for Prohibition.

Lodge: We all voted for Prohibition. Have a drink.

Curtis: (*To Frelinghuysen.*) Oh, good night, Joe.

Lodge: (*To Curtis.*) Where is he going? (*To McCormick.*) Medill, you're fresh blood here. What are your thoughts this evening about Warren Harding?

Smoot: Hey, now we're getting somewhere. Getting back to Harding. (*Hiccup.*)

McCormick: Warren Harding? I love Warren Harding.

Lodge: Borah!

McCormick: But what are we talking about?

Smoot: His name's been bubbling up all evening. (*Hiccup.*)

Borah: What are you talking about? Are you talking about Warren Harding?

Lodge: There's a very strong possibility the Democrats will nominate Cox!

Smoot: We have to carry Ohio. (*Hiccup.*)

Lodge: Cox has carried Ohio twice now as Governor.

Smoot: That's right. (*Hiccup.*)

Lodge: No candidate of the Republican Party has ever been elected President without carrying Ohio.

Smoot: None. I feel very strongly about Harding. (*Hiccup.*)

Lodge: I remind you, in all this, we can never seem to eliminate his name. Who said—it bubbles up.

Spencer: Yea, like tar!

Lodge: Everything goes, Selden, Harding remains.

Spencer: But Henry, I can't think of a single man less qualified to be President of these United States than Warren Harding.

Lodge: It doesn't matter! He is the logical solution to the current psychological development. Hays! Harvey!

Hays: He's well liked. He looks like a President.

Curtis: Oh, Penrose said that. Penrose is keen on Harding.

Brandegee: He can take instruction. I don't think he has an original idea in his head.

Lodge: All the better!

Borah: Well, I like Warren. I always have.

Curtis: Oh, everyone likes Warren. George made that point. Beautiful speaking voice.

Brandegee: Yes, and he looks good. Like a leader.

Lodge: His availability is outstanding!

Borah: Well, this might mollify Johnson.

Lodge: Good. But let's not be definite. We must never be definite.

Watson: Evening!

Curtis: (*To Watson.*) Oh Jim! You're missing all the fun!

Spencer: (*To Watson.*) You coming? I'm going.

Borah: I'm out of here too.

Smoot: Good night. (*Hiccup.*)

Watson: Where in Hell are we?

Smoot: Harding. (*Hiccup.*)

Watson: Harding? Harding what?

Smoot: Gonna give 'em a run tomorrow. (*Hiccup.*)

Harvey: (*To Lodge.*) Haskell and Kirkwood are on their way up.

Lodge: Who?

Harvey: Guys from *The Star.*

Lodge: Oh yes, fine, reporters, you'll talk to them.

Watson: Why Harding?

Lodge: Only sensible decision, Jim.

Watson: Well, I like Warren. He looks like a President.

Hays: Right this way, gentlemen. Harvey, can you—
Lodge: (*To the intruders.*) Who's there? Stand and unfold yourself.
McCormick: Guys from *The Star*.
Lodge: Ah, Kirkwood, you're a newspaper man, tell us whom to nominate!
Kirkwood: I will not, Senator. That's your job, thank God!
Harvey: (*To Haskell and Kirkwood.*) Right this way, boys. (*To Lodge.*) Henry, you think you could help me? I might not remember everything.
Lodge: I'm not moving. Frank, get in there with them. Charles.
Watson: Boy, the air stinks in here.
Lodge: I need a drink. But I can't move. Who can get me a drink? Reed? Thank you. How are you, Jim?
Watson: What?
Lodge: How are you?
Watson: Fine. Tired. We all are.
Lodge: Not too much ice.
Smoot: There's none left. (*Hiccup.*)
Watson: Dirty business. Takes all day. All damned day. And now the night's no relief. Is it?
Lodge: No relief.
Curtis: (*Returning with the reporters.*) We'd like to give him a try. See how he runs.
Lodge: (*Aggravated.*) What's the problem?
Kirkwood: No problem, Senator. Just curious.
Brandegee: (*To Harvey.*) Pssst. He's the logical selection.
Lodge: (*Irritated.*) Yes. Didn't you explain it?
Curtis: Everything is fine, Henry, relax.
Lodge: (*To Curtis.*) Don't tell me to relax, I'm exhausted! (*To Reporters, spelling it out.*) He is the superior candidate. He is from a strategic state. He is experienced—politically. Very popular in the Senate.
Smoot: Very well liked. (*Hiccup.*)
Lodge: He's very well liked, do you hear that? His appearance is super presidential! And he listens to reason. We're tired of these Woodrow Wilsons—men who can't take advice.
Curtis: "Advise and consent." Remember that? (*Laughs.*)
Haskell: But the man is scarcely known out of Ohio.
Lodge: He'll be known tomorrow!

[Chorus of coughing grows.]

Curtis: Listen fellas, this ain't any 1880 or 1904. We haven't got ourselves any John Sherman or Theodore Roosevelt. What we got are a lot of second-raters. And Warren Harding is the best of the second-raters.

[Lodge is handed his drink. He takes it, sniffs it.]

Lodge: Perfecto!

[Coughing overwhelms the scene. Everyone but Lodge. He savors a moment his theatrical skills. Then, satisfied with his craft, brings his drink to his thirsty lips. His lips purse, he drinks—as curtain. And that's the end of the first act. There'll be a fifteen-minute intermission!]

Act 4, A Fall to Earth

Characters:

The Raconteur
The Orator and his Doppelganger

Setting: Irrelevant.

Note: The Doppelganger is Carol Channing.

Entr'acte

The Raconteur: The stage is shifting, but how at this stage shall we shift? How change? Must we depend on mortal mechanics? Better had we moral mechanics, and by changing ourselves change this illusory world we temporarily inhabit. Turntables, air casters, lifts, tracks, and drops—honey, who can afford these things? Of course we could hit up on the lighting designer—many were the times he changed the scene by changing the light. But what if we're short on circuits? I was once in a production of *Romeo and Juliet,* and one night a whole bunch of dimmers blew. What light through yonder window did not that evening break? It's true, all things grow dim—there is death—Everyman knows that. Let us be rid of these transient riches and face facts; we're broke! All we can afford is a noisy old traveler—and then we'd have to find someone to pull it. Better were we a Traveler.

But I have one other concern and that I think somewhat vain. I once attended a revival of a much-loved musical put on at one of our better furnished theaters. And it was wonderful. And there was a marvelous set. But the piece—having been staged so beautifully in that very beautiful way that some people stage things these days—the set-changes were made in front of the audience. And the actors helped make the change. But because the set was cumbersome the stage crew was required to assist, and since the crew was to be in plain view of the audience—the piece again being staged in that very beautiful way, the crew had to be costumed. And since the actors were dressed as turn-of-the-century roustabouts, so was the costumed crew.

But you know, you can always tell the difference between the actors and the stage-hands. I don't know why this is—but I think it is because there is a difference. The actors are always smiling or staying in character while they change the set. But of course you know and I know—and one hopes they know—all they're actually doing is just changing the set. And then the crew lumbers on in that grumpy but purposeful way, and they are not smiling and they are not even remotely in character. They simply are characters. In fact, what they are, are "characters in action"—that action being changing the set. And changing the set is the essence of what they are doing. And it really is, and it really is real, and it really is interesting; because not only are they actually doing something, they are really actually doing something. And you know it, and I know it, and they capture your attention. Or at least they capture mine.

And one particular member of this particular crew did capture my attention in particular; because not only was he actually doing something—really actually doing something—the other thing I found interesting about him was that though he was costumed—perfunctorily at least—as a turn-of-the-century roustabout—he was wearing a digital watch. And that was very interesting, because it made him—if somewhat surreal—nonetheless more real—more than the actors who were more than perfunctorily costumed. And he captured my attention. I didn't watch the actors—not that they were actually doing anything that actually needed to be watched—I watched him.

Now, am I to allow some surly technician to upstage me? Never! If anyone is going to upstage me, I'll be the one to do it. Which of course I already have. Because you see, while I was talking, and you weren't looking—you were listening—hopefully—I've changed the set.

[Two figures appear on the bare, impoverished stage. They are the Orator and his Doppelganger. The Doppelganger bears a striking resemblance to the actress Carol Channing.]

Doppelganger: (*As Carol Channing.*) The Orator—who in his Prologue conceived himself a Raconteur, but was transformed in the first act from that into Stage Directions—this Orator Explains how the second act, *Republican Ascendancy,* and this fourth act, *A Fall to Earth,* are cut. He says:

Orator: Act Four. There isn't any Act Four.

Doppelganger: Well that's exactly what he says. He says no Act Four. The second act it seems was Written then discarded, the fourth act Conceived but never written. And he tells you why. He says:

Orator: The second and fourth acts would have made the Inner Play.

Doppelganger: Oh, did you hear that—the Inner Play? Oh, say that again—would you, the Inner Play.

Orator: —the Inner Play, at one time called *The Second Part of Warren Harding.* Act Two being *The First Part of the Second Part of Warren Harding* or *The Second Part of Warren Harding Part One,* Act Four being *The Second Part of the Second Part of Warren Harding* or *The Second Part of Warren Harding Part Two.*

Doppelganger: Because you see—excuse me—there are two parts to Warren Harding, just as there are two parts to each and every one of us—which generally speaking is our inner play. But—

Orator: There is no play to play.

Doppelganger: Or so he says.

Orator: No play.

Doppelganger: So instead of Showing he is Telling, telling how he hopes to tell—

Orator: (*To Doppelganger.*) What happened?

Doppelganger: Exactly.

Gertrude Stein once said—you know she was talking about her writing plays—many plays, she said—and she—well, actually she was writing about her writing plays, but the writing she wrote was a Lecture to be spoke—so it was writing to be heard—she said I remember very well, she said, the first one she wrote, and she called it *What Happened, A Play*—always thinking that if you write a play you ought to announce it as such. She said she'd come home from a very pleasant dinner party and realized that something is always happening. Something is always happening, and that anybody, and I quote, anybody knows a quantity of stories and what is the use of telling another story since there are so many and everybody knows so many and tells so many, and she, naturally she, what she wanted to do in her play was what everybody did not always know nor always tell, and by everybody she naturally included herself. She said that she wrote *What Happened, A Play,* because she wanted to tell what could be told if one did not tell anything. In short, to make a play the essence of what happened.

Orator: And so she chose not in her plays to tell stories.

Doppelganger: But sometimes—excuse me—telling is not just telling something, it is telling of something—which is to say that telling is the essence of what happens.

Orator: I'll tell you something: I once participated in a reading of *The Tempest.* A play. By William Shakespeare. And after the reading, a playwright said to me how she didn't care for the opening of the play because "there was too much exposition." The scene in which Prospero narrates to Miranda their history, hers and his. "I would have cut it," she said, "gone right to the action." Which is interesting, because one of the things I find interesting about that scene is not just the telling of how they came to be on the island—

Doppelganger: Though dramaturgically, if I may say, it's shrewd—one character telling the other and the audience if they're listening understanding what happened.

Orator: Ah, but the telling of it. A father telling his daughter who he really is and who she really is, and why they really are where they actually are. And of course how he tells it and how she hears it.

It's telling how telling a telling can be.

Doppelganger: Can you imagine your own father sitting you down and telling you all this? Shakespeare knew what he was about and made a dramatic scene.

Orator: And so now I'm going to tell you—

Doppelganger: Me?

Orator: Yes, you—what exactly does happen to Warren Harding, and what he does to become President in 1920.

Doppelganger: Oh, but now wait a minute, you mentioned the second and fourth acts, what happened to the third act? And what happened to Barclay—our scattered Author.

Orator: The third act! I can't even talk about the third act—which was called *The Crack-Up*—other than to say that by the end—after trials and tribulations of the most absurd variety—the globe, Barclay—confronted with the myopia of his entire endeavor—if not his entire life—is—as the curtain descends—completely and totally shattered.

Doppelganger: Shattered? You mean—

Orator: Cracked-up. Shattered.

Doppelganger: Oh, dear.

Orator: But that's what happens. Things happen. We see things—about ourselves—and we are shattered.

Doppelganger: I think of that incredible scene—and I know you know it—in the play *Everyman*—where Everyman is just walking along, thinking God knows what, doing God knows what and Death—oh, you know Death—comes along and says we have an appointment, did you forget?

Orator: And that's what happens, we're walking along, mindless, absorbed in the progress of our "dramas" and we forget. But you know something?

Doppelganger: What?

Orator: The forgetting is telling.

Doppelganger: (*Laughing.*) Exactly. So there's no more Barclay.

Orator: (*Guiltily.*) A shard here and there.

Doppelganger: Good. Why hold on to parts of ourselves that are not viable?

Orator: It isn't germinative.

Doppelganger: Well I should hope not. And besides, we want to encourage new things to grow.

Orator: So—

Doppelganger: And you'll notice—excuse me—you'll notice there are no Stage Directions in this act. Did you notice that? Even though there might be Descriptions of stage directions.

Orator: It's telling how telling descriptions can be.

Doppelganger: And shorter.

Orator: Yes, sometimes a telling description is more concise, more to the point than a telling in showing.

Doppelganger: If it's not too long. People—who of course apprehend words by either reading or listening—might be willing to sit a long time apprehending words by reading, but might not be willing to sit a long time apprehending words by listening. Even if they're simultaneously seeing.

Orator: In reading one is going one's own pace, stopping and starting as one is choosing.

Doppelganger: Whereas in the theater—

Orator: You can't do it.

Doppelganger: Exactly. Which is actually one of the reasons the second, third, and fourth acts were cut.

Orator: The whole thing was just too damn long.

Doppelganger: Yes. And if they weren't cut we'd be sitting here for another three hours listening without having anything to look at.

Orator: And someone—I won't say who—wanted someone to listen. Because words written to be spoken are words written to be heard. And they must be played, played for others.

Doppelganger: Because even if in a piece to be played one might play by oneself—and some do it—or play oneself—and some do that—or even play with oneself—

Orator: Some even playing themselves playing with themselves by themselves—

Doppelganger: You mean on stage?

Orator: It's been done.

Doppelganger: Oh, goodness me. Still, one cannot play for oneself.

Orator: Oh, one can do it but if one does, what one is doing is just engaging in the fantasy of performance.

Doppelganger: Exactly! (*To the Orator.*) And you don't want to do that.

Orator: If what one makes is made to be played—which is to say made so that others might listen, it should be made so that others can listen.

Doppelganger: And playing oneself—excuse me—though it's different is related to being oneself. And whole schools of Acting developed so that actors could be themselves.

Orator: And some of us took some of those acting classes because we wanted to be ourselves and find ourselves, and eventually find ourselves to be big Broadway musical-comedy stars. Only to find there were no big Broadway musical comedies for us to star in.

Doppelganger: Well honey, there are very few.

Orator: And there was nothing—nothing to be done.

Doppelganger: Well, unless you just revive your old vehicles—and some people actually . . . do this.

Orator: And in one of these acting classes—which was really a singing class—we stood up in front of our class and our teacher and our teacher asked us how were we and we said okay or some said great and most said terrible and we were encouraged to get in touch with our feelings—to make that long-distance inside phone call—and some started to cry immediately—especially those who had been in the class for a long time, and they were feeling their feelings of generally pain and anger—and it is yes very much an essential part of being an actor—having access to pain and anger—actors generally speaking having to play people who are angry or are in pain because people who are not angry or not in pain are not generally speaking very interesting—at least not on stage—or at least not until the end of the play. So characters can be a bit scary—and the theater at times provocative. And Plato felt this, and railed against the theater, claiming that it stimulates indulgence of Natural Passions—and it took Aristotle—thank God!—his former Pupil to rebuke him in the *Poetics,* and to remind us that in the midst of rage, in the midst of a Passion—given that the passion is Pretend—we might as we Listen, See something—seeing a way of Learning—learning a Pleasure—learning having sometimes to do with seeing what is pride—pride being evil—evil finding expression in pain and anger—and so they expressed their pain and anger my classmate actors and I did too or tried—and it always came back to mom or dad—and what is that wonderful line from *The Boys in the Band*—

Doppelganger: It always comes back to Evelyn and Walt—

Orator: And obviously it's true. And so we stood up in front of our class thrusting our arms out yelling get off my back get out of my life fuck you mommy fuck you daddy—oh God, I swear we did this—and when we were fully in touch with all this pain and anger we sang our songs—"Raindrops on roses, and whiskers on—"

Doppelganger: Honey, honey, excuse me. Honey.

Orator: What?

Doppelganger: We're out of time.

Orator: What? Out of time? What do you mean? I haven't yet told what happens to Warren Harding.

Doppelganger: Well, I know, but you have to get to the Fifth act, and kill off the characters.

Orator: Do you hear that? There's no time. What happened?!

Doppelganger: (*Indicating her watch and his babbling.*) Well, I just—

Orator: Oh, never mind, what does anybody need to know about what happens! to Warren Harding or how what happens! might have been a play and might still if someone ever figures out why he wants to write a play that his father started years before as a musical comedy.

Harding never had a son which means the son he never had never had a father. And some of us who are sons feel that same way exactly. Yes, the only thing you need to know about Warren Harding is that he didn't want to be President, he just wanted to stay in the Senate. But he knew—because of the in-fighting in the Ohio Republican Party in 1920, that if he didn't control the Ohio delegates at the Republican national convention, he would lose control of his state's patronage, and if he didn't control the patronage, he'd never get back in the Senate—and so the only way he could stay in the Senate was by running for President—then drop out once his Senate seat had been secured.

But that's not what happens. And so even though he didn't want to be President he became President, suggesting that he didn't not want to be President enough.

Doppelganger: And how many of us at one time or another do things we know we shouldn't and don't want to but don't not want to enough.

Orator: And that perhaps not wanting to enough has something to do with not knowing why one does or why one does not. Because if one did might one not?

Doppelganger: (*Indicating the Orator.*) And like a man full of pride, pain, and anger who inherits this not wanting to know from his father and continues in this vein, thinking he is going somewhere—

Orator: When in truth he is going nowhere. . . . Immobile, stymied in a painful wink.

Though of course there would have been wonderful marvelous speeches and scenes—all culminating in Chicago as the smoke-filled Republicans descend upon their dark convention. And perhaps there will be some day be the act of the inner play, ending after Harding hoping to the end he will not be nominated engineers it so he must.

Doppelganger: It sounds like you know an awful lot about it. Perhaps *you* should write this play.

Orator: (*With a wink—of course.*) Perhaps I should. And of course the fourth act would have ended with the exact words Harding spoke the moment after he was nominated.

Doppelganger: Oh, say those words, would you—I find them very telling.

Orator: You mean right here, right now, on this very stage? Do we have the time?

Doppelganger: Well, we just cut three hours off the show!

[The Orator assumes the role of Warren G. Harding.]

Orator: (*As Harding.*) We played to a pair of deuces, and filled.

Doppelganger: Exactly. And as surely as I'm sitting here, and sitting here surely I am, that would have been the end of Act Four.

Orator: Act Five. *The Pull of the Past.*

Act 5, The Pull of the Past

Characters:

Narratage in the form of Stage Directions
Al Jolson, an entertainer
Febus
Warren G. Harding
Nan Britton, a young woman
Tryon Harding, Harding's father
Phoebe Harding, Harding's mother
Florence Harding
Koreen
Shav, Koreen's father
A Raconteur who is a Real Character

Setting: A setting.

Note: Shav speaks with an East European accent.

[Out of a great darkness comes the voice of Al Jolson. He sings.]

Al Jolson's voice: We think the country's ready
For another man like Teddy.
We need another Lincoln
To do the country's thinkin'.
Mi-ster Hard-ing
You're the man for us!

[A toilet flushes. Light illuminates Febus—in the bathroom, bent over the basin, washing his hands in the sink. The sun has set, the evening shades have fallen. The reel-to-reel tape recorder continues to record, but the tape has long run out. A smacking sound as the tape spins in infernal revolution.]

Febus: All day. All damn day. Shit out my brains. Now what?

[Febus straightens, stands before the cloudy mirror.]

I can't see myself.

[Febus shuts his eyes. Within the mirror, light illuminates Warren G. Harding, immobile, propped up in bed in his room in the Palace Hotel, San Francisco, August 2, 1923. In his hands, *The Saturday Evening Post*—an article about Harding, entitled: "A Calm Review of a Calm Man." But the President is not reading. His blinds are down, he has drifted into dreamy slumber.]

Harding: Gldphhhhhhhhh . . . Gldphhhhhhhhh . . .

[Harding dreams the theater of his entire existence, from boyhood gambol to backwater matriculation; from newspaper ownership, to Lieutenant Governor to Senator, to nominee, to President. All his relations come back to him—they blanket the stage. He calls from sleep.]

Carrie. Carrie.

[Carrie Philips appears, an elegant figure. She holds forth the love letters Harding scribbled to her from his seat in the Senate, page upon page decorated with hearts and kisses.]

Oh, Carrie.

[Nan Britton appears, pubescent, sporting a medical encyclopedia, pointing to pictures of human anatomy.]

Nan Britton: Oh, Warren, what rapture!

[Florence Harding appears in the person of a monumental fury. She throws a chair at Carrie Philips, and hires a private detective to shadow Nan Britton.]

Harding: (*Reaching for Nan's breasts.*) Nan, dearie.

[Nan flips the pages of her encyclopedia, displays a picture of pregnancy.]

Nan Britton: Oh, Warren. Milk of a most luxurious richness is't already issuing from both my breasts.
Harding: Oh, fuck.

[Characters of Harding's life now populate the stage: senators, congressmen, cronies, and crooks. World War I enters, commences, and concludes. Soldiers return from Europe, litter the stage, impoverished and out of work. Post-war chaos ensues: all over the stage there are race riots, crime waves, and a rise of fundamentalism. Down left, the Democratic Party is paralyzed by the social upheaval. Up right, the Republican Party capitalizes on the nation's discontent, begins its ascendancy. Harding's father enters, dragging an old sagging mule, waving his diploma as a homeopathic veterinarian.]

Tryon Harding: You have to aim high, son.

[Harding corresponds. With one hand, he writes dozens of letters, refusing consideration for the office of President. With the other hand, he writes hundreds more, asking to be considered as a second-, third-, or fourth-choice candidate; the right hand not knowing what the left hand is doing. The Republican Convention convenes, the Smoke-filled Room assembles. At its pontific center sits Henry Cabot Lodge. But so thick is the haze of tobacco, Lodge does not discern how his playlet is in vain. His entire performance a shallow act of virtuosity. For Harding has already sewn up the nomination. His letters requesting second-, third-, and fourth-choice consideration congeal into an iceberg of support. The convention sails blindly on, deadlocks, slams into the iceberg. Harding is nominated, then elected President. He becomes a political giant.]

Harding: We played to a pair of deuces and filled. But God, what labor.

[Nan Britton gives birth to a baby in a cheap hotel on the Jersey Shore.]

Nan Britton: Oh, Warren, she looks just like you.

[Harding's mother rises from the traps on her deathbed. She recalls her conversion to Seventh-day Adventist.]

Phoebe Harding: The millennium approaches, Warren! Prepare ye the way.

[The President is transported! He crosses the stage on a miniature train, weakened by a life of material and gluttonous excess, corrupted by a career of political shenanigans, proselytizing the nation about good old family values. He then boards a miniature boat, sails up left to Alaska, shivers in a blizzard, begins to cough up blood. He hobbles to San Francisco, collapses in bed, wakes.]

Harding: My whole damned life. What happened?!

[Harding has a massive and convulsive heart attack. He spits up his guts, goes dark.]

Glllll . . . .

[A knock at the door.]

Florence: (*Knocking.*) Wurr'n? Wurr'n?

[The door opens. Florence Harding appears, her features indiscernible. She steps forward, into some beautiful side light—but just as she does . . .]

Koreen: (*Knocking.*) Febus? Febus? I heard the toilet flush. Did you finish your play?

[Febus opens his eyes.]

Febus: What happened? I'm all done.

Koreen: I'm feeling much better now, Febus. I washed my hair in the kitchen, I did my nails, I straightened up last night's dinner dishes. I'm much more relaxed. I'm sorry to have disturbed you this morning, Febus. I know how important it is for you to write your play. It was rude of me to disturb you. It's just that when I woke I was frightened. There was a bad dream and I couldn't find you. I get frightened in the morning, Febus. I don't know what horrors the new day will hold.

[Febus washes his hands.]

Febus?

[The door slowly opens. Koreen's hand appears, offering some of her hair.]

See how I shampooed my hair? Feel how silky it feels.

Febus: Leave me alone, baby.

Koreen: Oh. Well, maybe you'll feel it later. And look, Febus—

[Koreen produces a newspaper.]

I went through the paper, and look what I found. There's a duplex for sale on Hamilton Drive in Beverly Hills. Fifty-five thousand dollars. See what it says? Bright, spacious rooms, high ceilings, two bedroom, two bath. That's just the first floor. The upstairs is smaller, but I was thinking we could rent that out, make a little extra money—help pay off the mortgage. Fifty-five thousand dollars is a fabulous price for Beverly Hills. And it's right near the park—you know where they do the dog training. You like that.

Febus: Korky, you're living in a dreamland. Where're we gonna get the money for a duplex?

Koreen: Fifty-five thousand dollars is not a lot of money, Febus. I'll ask my mother to help us out.

Febus: I'm not borrowing any money from your mother, Korky. I don't want to get obligated.

Koreen: It doesn't have to be an obligation, sweetheart. We could let my mother live above us. It's like she's paying a rent. The downstairs has two bathrooms. You could write all weekend and I'd never once disturb you.

Come on, Febus, be a good guy.

Febus: Leave me alone.

Koreen: I don't want to leave you alone. Come here. Come to Mama.

[Koreen extends one finger, tickles Febus.]

Febus: (*Pushing off her enormous finger.*) Come on Korky, cut it out. I'm washing my hands.

Koreen: You can wash your hands later. (*Playfully shakes Febus in her hand.*) Come on, big boy, dance with me.

Febus: (*Being shaken.*) Hey, easy does it.

Koreen: Write me a song about our new apartment. Write me a song about two people who buy a duplex on Hamilton Drive in Beverly Hills and live happy ever after.

Febus: Hey, come on. I gotta write my play.

Koreen: You've been writing your play all day. Now it's time for me. Besides, you said you finished your play.

Febus: That was just the book. Now I gotta write the music and lyrics.

Koreen: Oh come on, Febus, stop pretending. Who the Hell is gonna be interested in a musical about Warren G. Harding?

Febus: What're you talking about? This thing is gonna put me over the top.

Koreen: The top of my head. Come on, get dressed. I wanna drive over, look at this apartment.

[Telephone rings. Febus picks up.]

Febus: (*Into phone.*) Hello? Yes. Yes. This is he. Un huh. Un huh.

Koreen: Who is it, Febus?

Febus: (*To Koreen.*) Shhhh. It's somebody from work.

Koreen: On Saturday?

Febus: Shhhh! I gotta take it. Give me five minutes, would ya?

[Koreen pauses, her hand stiffens, shakes. Koreen withdraws her hand, closing the door behind her.]

Febus: (*Into phone.*) Hello? Hey baby. I'm sorry, I'm sorry—I stood you up, I know. I couldn't pull myself away. You know how I get—all wound up in my work. I get carried away. I thought I was on a roll. I thought something was happening. Then nothing came out. Not even the usual crap. I can't live with this shit inside me. It's choking the life out of me. I gotta get outta here. I gotta get out! Well maybe I should. What do you think? What do you think? You and me, head up north—you and me, up north, out of this stink hole.

Right now! We could meet in the park. You know, where they train the dogs. A new beginning. Twenty minutes. (*Big kiss into the phone.*) Big kiss!

[Febus hangs up, turns to the soiled mirror.]

I'm outta here!

[The bathroom door is broken down, shattered into splinters by Koreen's fist. She pulls what's left of it off its hinges, tosses it into the room.]

What the Hell are you doing? Have you cracked up?

Koreen: You bastard! You goddamn bastard.

Febus: What are you talking about?

Koreen: (*Sobbing.*) You told me you weren't going to see her anymore!

Febus: Hey, watch it, you're gonna ruin my whole recorder.

Koreen: I don't care.

[Koreen grabs at Febus. He puts up his hands to protect himself, feels in Koreen's hand the receiver of a wall phone.]

Febus: Oh, fuck.
Koreen: That's right, handsome. I picked up the extension! (*She hurls the receiver.*)
Febus: (*Ducking.*) Hey!

[Febus turns blindly around, winding himself in the wires of his tape recorder.]

You better watch it, baby. You're gonna swell up. You're gonna swell up!
Koreen: I'm as swollen as I'll ever get. I can't get any bigger.

[Febus grabs a reel from his tape recorder, aims at Koreen.]

Febus: You fucking whale!

[Febus casts his reel, but the tape unwinds, he is handcuffed in a tangle of Mylar.]

We're gonna have to call up Dick Edelman about this, baby. Maybe Dick—

[Koreen grabs Febus, pulls him toward the doorway. The phone cord gets twisted around his neck.]

(*Clutching his throat.*) Ran foul!

[Koreen lifts Febus in her hand, pulls him out of the bathroom.]

(*As he's pulled away.*) Korky, Korky, put me down. You're gonna wake up the neighbors.

[And out he goes—all wound up, carried away by his "work."]

[It is quiet now on the wicked stage. Light changes, night passes for day. As the sun rises, light falls into the bathroom. Fragments of the shattered mirror—which had fallen onto the beige mat that hugs the base of the toilet—glimmer in the sunlight of a new dawn.]

[The beige mat enlarges into a square of beige carpet, and those shards of mirror into the splintered remnants of a shattered globe. The beige carpet expands further, becomes a beach, and the shards of glass shimmering speckles on a stretch of beige sand. From the sand are formed the scattered stones of a fallen tower. All is quiet.]

[A screeching gull passes, "Erh, erh," heralding the arrival of some galactic presence. And sure enough. Enter Koreen. We see her now. She rises fifty feet into the air—her hair cropped short, she wears a shapeless shift. She performs a brief Dionysian dance, hums a Bacchanalian tune. Thus is she envisioned: a maenad in a muumuu. In one hand she holds the lifeless Febus. He hangs limp, a shred of telephone cord dangling from his neck. She looks around, sees the crumbled tower.]

Koreen: (*Calling.*) Mother? Mother, it's me. Mother?

[She turns to the sea.]

(*Calling.*) Shav! Shav! Shav of the shav-green sea. It's Koreen, your daughter. Lift up your head to me.

[An offshore tempest. Shav's head emerges from the foam. A large green head, bearded, crowned.]

Shav: Koreenala, what are you doing here?
Koreen: I'm looking for my mother.
Shav: She's gone.
Koreen: What?
Shav: Gone.
Koreen: Gone? You mean . . . When?
Shav: Ages, ages ago.
Koreen: Why didn't someone tell me?
Shav: We tried to reach you. Your phone was always busy. What are you doing here?
Koreen: I came home. My marriage fell apart.
Shav: What happened with your hair?
Koreen: I cut it off.

Shav: Your long beautiful hair. You had from when you were a little girl. Why'd you cut it off?

Koreen: I guess I'm not a little girl anymore.

Shav: What's that you got in your hand?

Koreen: My husband. I killed him.

Shav: Why'd you do that?

Koreen: I got worked up. I couldn't contain myself.

Shav: You shouldn'ta killed your husband.

Koreen: I've had a hard life. Nothing really worked out for me.

Shav: You had every advantage, Koreen.

Koreen: Did I? What happened?

Shav: I couldn't say.

Koreen: Each day is misery. I can't go back to the apartment. The rooms get smaller and smaller. I'm so swollen.

Shav: Poor girl.

Koreen: I thought if I came back. I thought if I came home. But look, the tower has fallen. There's no home to come home to.

Shav: You didn't really want to live in a tower, did you baby?

Koreen: No. I don't know what I wanted. I guess I never did. Things didn't turn out as I imagined. That made me so angry. The angrier I got, the bigger I got. The bigger I got, the angrier I got.

Shav: Well, that's what happens.

(*Koreen weeps.*)

Koreen: What about you, Father? Could I live with you? In your globe beneath the sea?

Shav: I don't think so, baby. There wouldn't be room for you. The ceiling would crack.

[Koreen bends to the earth, digs with her hands.]

What are you doing?

Koreen: I'm digging a hole to bury my husband.

Shav: That's wise. You don't want to leave him; the birds will tear him to shreds.

Koreen: No, I wouldn't want that. I choked the life out of him. The least I could do is put him in the ground.

Go away, Father. You've answered my questions. You can't help me.

Shav: I wish I could. I better go down.

[Shav submerges. Koreen unwraps the cord from Febus' neck, puts him in the ground. She pushes sand over him and places a few of the tower's stones over his grave. She rises, turns to the sea.]

Koreen: Hopeless. Completely hopeless.

[Koreen walks to the water's edge, pauses, wades in—throws 'round her baleful eyes. Her magnificent bulk begins to harden, petrify. Her body loses human form. Her flesh is made gritty, granitic. Her features indiscernible. Thus is she rendered, immobile, a great misshapen crag. A seagull soars above her, "Erh, erh." The waves pound—their watery insults splash her stony visage—like Niobe now—all salty tears. In time, the vast persisting ocean will make silt this tower of grief. Till then she stands with fearsome aspect, fast against the crashing sea. A final blessèd curtain as light is extinguished.]

Epilogue

[And of course this Epilogue is spoken in front of the curtain by the Raconteur who is a real Character.]

Raconteur: The play is done if play it be;
        and if not play, might yet we see,
    Fate sad of those enlarged souls
        who sink expired in murky shoals.

    And yet despite the dismal,
        despite the shattered bleak;
    Despite the shorn, despite the torn,
        despite the blasted freak;
    Despite the rending garments strewn,
        the tearing out of hair,
    Despite offending varmints pruned
        (pulled fully from their lair);
    One last remark before we shuffle off
        these coils to take up pen again;
    And please consider this as you
        consider this shenanigan.

This piece, this thing that has been wrought
    and rendered as it could,
An epic, oh yes, and a burlesque,
    to know that would be good.
For Aristotle tells us
    and he tells us oh so well
That epics are a mix of form,
    a mix of say and tell.
And we have told, and we have said,
    here acted parts, here scen'ry rolled,
We ripped at certain monsters but
    with jokes have they been scold.

Sure this Gigantor drama 's lacking
    in the wisdom of Maimonides,
But still are its conventions those
    of not peculiar Comedies.
For one escapes to sing this song,
    to sing it loud and clear,
Hoping all the while at least
    that some might stay and hear.
For what if words in short life,
    fail to sell or pay?
At least one's lived and long enough
    the tale to tell and play.

And that certainly is E.O.P. (*Hiccup.*) End of piece. I thank you very much for your attendance.

An Interview with David Greenspan

This conversation took place on December 20, 2010, at David Greenspan's home in New York City. His apartment is a scene of modest personal collections. Numerous small clocks sit on shelves and tables. Handcrafted teapots line the counters and other surfaces. The walls are hung with paintings by his partner, William Kennon—many of them twilight urban landscapes, with smoke and shadow gathered around streetlamps, and yellow signs popping out of the dusk. On a desk, there are copies of Robert Gottlieb's biography of Sarah Bernhardt (Greenspan was then in rehearsal for *Jump,* a new piece about Bernhardt's performance as Tosca); Plato's *Apology, Crito,* and *Phaedo* (sources for another work in progress); and J. R. Ackerley's *My Dog Tulip.* Ackerley, the British memoirist, offers one precedent for the playwright's own intense animal sympathies. Greenspan is a famous rescuer of abandoned cats; two large-eyed, exceedingly shy adoptees beat a retreat soon after I arrived.

Robinson: Perhaps we can begin by talking about your most recent works, those written after the plays collected in this volume. One of them, *Go Back to Where You Are,* will be presented soon at Playwrights Horizons in New York.

Greenspan: Yes. It's about an actor from ancient Greece named Passalus. He has been festering in Hell for 2,000 years and is sent back to Earth by God to do one good turn. He barters with God, demanding that he be granted one final wish in exchange for this act: to have his soul obliterated. God agrees. Passalus has the ability to change his shape, so he returns to Earth in disguise. But his involvement with the other characters gets more complicated than he expected . . . he falls in love.

Robinson: I read an early version, and was especially interested in an idea that's voiced a number of times toward the end. Passalus talks about "shifting the balance" among the other characters and thereby freeing them from their own hells "into life again," as one of them puts it. Can you talk a little bit more about that narrative thread—about that "shift"?

Greenspan: I think that most of my plays are comic by nature. Well, they're often funny. A lot of my plays express what I understand to be a classical definition of comedy—the release from misery. *The Myopia,*

Dead Mother, She Stoops to Comedy, The HOME Show Pieces, this new play—all of them are about people being released from a complex of things that are holding them back.

Robinson: What kind of things?

Greenspan: Sometimes it's family. Particularly in my earlier plays it was family. Even in *The Myopia* there is a release from the trauma of family shenanigans. And that's also true of *Dead Mother* and *The HOME Show Pieces. She Stoops to Comedy* is about a release from self-involvement and imbalance in a partnered relationship. The characters in *Go Back to Where You Are* are released from a destructive family dynamic, but also from disappointment and bitterness: the bitterness of not achieving what one wanted to achieve, not realizing what one expected to realize—not realizing one's fantasies.

Robinson: Yet even as so many of your characters achieve release, they also reestablish kinship on new terms. I'm thinking obviously of Alexandra and Alison in *She Stoops to Comedy* but also of the beautiful ending of *The HOME Show Pieces* where the two men break bread and reaffirm their relationship. Many of your plays—certainly four of the five plays in this volume—seem to study different kinds of intimacy, different kinds of kinship. Sometimes they are nourishing, and sometimes they're painful, damaging, violent.

Greenspan: It's the more violent ones from which I've chosen to write an escape. And actually I think "escape" is a better word than "release" from misery—escape through a resolution of old relationships or old situations that were holding the characters back.

Robinson: Your thoughts about comic structure remind me that you openly meditate on genre in many of your plays. In *She Stoops to Comedy,* Alexandra argues that Beckett's plays "are comic tragedy not tragic comedy." Simon excuses a pun by saying it's "consistent with light-hearted nature of entertainment," and later, Alexandra says, "that's how plays work every once in a while." In *Go Back to Where You Are,* Passalus cautions us to remember that "even when there is pathos, there is not always tragedy." There are countless other examples where your characters acknowledge the conventions that shape them, or that they try, sometimes unsuccessfully or incompletely, to fit themselves into. Or that they seek to elude—another kind of release or escape? Is genre something that stands in for other forces conditioning behavior?

Greenspan: I think so. I mean, I'm kind of a theater buff. It isn't the most noble calling. I'm not as fully occupied with larger political or social movements as other writers are, like Lisa Kron (I just saw her new play, *In the Wake,* which I thought so highly of), and obviously Tony Kushner, Chris Shinn, David Grimm. My introduction to theater was *Peter Pan* on television. When I was young, I also listened to musicals my father recorded from a radio program. I've written about that in a play. So from an early age, I was an enthusiast. But theater is also a prism that I've used to examine personal, familial, and to some extent social relationships. This is true even of *The Argument,* which dramatizes Aristotle's relationship to Plato, and Gerald Else's relationship to both Aristotle and Plato.

Robinson: In that work especially, the lines between playwriting and criticism, or between theater and the theory of theater, are blurred or eroded. There's a constant interaction between analysis and action.

Greenspan: I think so. Even in *Go Back to Where You Are,* the characters comment on the play itself. They do that in *Dead Mother* (Maxine complaining that the production she saw was too wordy) and of course in *She Stoops to Comedy.* One of my favorite lines from *She Stoops to Comedy* is Alex's description of Jayne Summerhouse: "She's a treat—I mean a threat. It was a typo." I love that line because it exposes that this is a piece of writing. Also, I'm interested in the dramatic possibilities of nontheatrical texts—*The Argument,* Gertrude Stein's lecture on theater, and now Leone de' Sommi's *Four Dialogues on the Art of Staging Plays,* an Italian Renaissance text, which I have conflated with his play *A Comedy of Betrothal.* I think analysis, criticism, can be theatrical. In the musicals I found most exciting, like *Gypsy* or even some of the old MGM musicals, the characters are often putting up a show. It's a great strain in the musical theater—theatrical situations and theatrical people. *Funny Girl,* all those Judy Garland–Mickey Rooney movies, The Hot Box Club in *Guys and Dolls, Follies:* they incorporate performance.

Robinson: Rehearsal (for the actor) and revision (for the writer) are recurrent preoccupations—those moments when things can still be changed—changed on the page, changed in the rehearsal room, changed on the stage. What is it about the condition of revision or rehearsal that is so attractive to you?

Greenspan: In the earlier plays, in which there's more autobiographical material, I was trying to get it right, trying to tell the story clearly. I thought I'd like to include my process of trying to figure it out. In my more recent plays, there's a farcical element to exposing the revisions. It's as if another door opens, and before you know it, someone is talking about what's going on onstage. To some degree I've just wanted to show my hand: this is a play.

In the cinema, you're often brought into a world that's so encompassing that you forget it's a film—partly because the screen is so big that it magnifies everything, and also because it's as if we're seeing pictures in our minds. (I once read that a movie screen is a bit like the back of one's mind.) In the theater, the artificiality of the form is constantly apparent. Usually theaters are not as dark as movie theaters and so we're more aware of the audience around us, and also the theater performance is really happening in time, unlike a movie, which has been recorded. As Gertrude Stein writes, "the actors are there and they are there right away." We're not seeing something real and yet we're seeing something that's really happening at that moment. That tension between the artificial and the real I find interesting. I don't often watch movies on DVD or television. I like to go out to the movies; I like to be around people when I'm viewing. The theater, for the most part, is a communal experience, and I find that very comforting and very exciting. That awareness that you're seeing a play is something that I want to transmit to the audience.

Robinson: That helps me think about the place of artifice in your work. You consciously embrace artificiality—whether it's a highly choreographed acting style, with you often gesturing according to a set pattern, or the worked surfaces of the writing, with you drawing attention to the lyricism of certain passages, or using repetition to make us more aware of the true texture of deceptively plainer lines.

Greenspan: Or the texture of thought. We often go back and forth when we speak, which reflects the way we think.

Robinson: Earlier you mentioned wanting to get the story right when you were working with autobiographical sources for your earlier plays. Storytelling is still a preoccupation—obviously in *The Myopia,* with its Raconteur, and in *The Argument,* with its meditations on the place of plot in drama. In *Dead Mother,* the Whale speaks of Melvin's getting lost on "Exposition Boulevard," and later they both say, "we'll pretend the plot works fine." Even in other plays where you're less direct, the mechanics of narrative interest you.

Greenspan: It's funny that you mention that, because I don't think of myself as a great storyteller. In fact, in my new play, *Jonas,* there's a line, "I cannot tell a story." I think that's why other things preoccupy me—or rather, why I'm preoccupied with *trying* to tell a story. In this I'm probably influenced by Stein and Beckett. I'm just astonished by how well the playwrights I've worked with can tell stories: Adam Rapp, Sarah Ruhl, Kathleen Tolan, David Grimm. Linda Chapman and Lola Pashalinski were able to create a story from the Gertrude Stein material, and Linda and Kate Moira Ryan were able to translate the *Beebo*

Brinker Chronicles onto the stage. Since I don't find myself that facile in creating narrative, other things emerge. Sometimes your limitations are the things that you draw on. There are painters who are not great draftsmen, so other things preoccupy them, or they aren't great colorists, so other things come to the fore.

Robinson: It seems that the need to tell the story, or to get it in place, isn't just a formal concern; storytelling also exposes an emotional need. In *The Myopia,* the Orator says, "it's telling how telling a telling can be." What is being told—besides the story that may not, in fact, be told—in the attempt to narrate?

Greenspan: I admit there's an urge, and sometimes an urgency, to tell it, or dramatize it—but mostly to tell it. If I can't dramatize it, I really still want to tell the story. It might just be as basic as the need to write. In my plays, there's a great need to communicate. The great thing to me about the theater is that it's an opportunity for connection. People are there together, connecting to a story or to a theatrical experience. We say that actors connect with the audience; through them the play connects to the audience, and when actors are less than persuasive, they'll sometimes be criticized for not being particularly connected, at least to themselves, and that makes it hard to connect to the audience.

Robinson: It's interesting, though, that in many of your plays you present us with scenes depicting a lack of connection or with characters who are isolated—they're in the bathroom alone, or they're a solitary actor playing twenty-two parts. There isn't that visible community available for us. I wondered about the recurrent interest in this kind of cut-offness or solitude.

Greenspan: There's a solitude necessary to write, and perhaps my interest in it starts with that. But in my later plays, there's less isolation. *The Myopia* is an older play—I started writing it around 1991—and the isolation is more apparent. But in *She Stoops to Comedy* and certainly in *Go Back to Where You Are,* there's more of a community. *The Argument* is so much for the audience, and it's partly about my excitement and appreciation for Gerald Else's learnedness, Aristotle's learnedness. Even though I'm alone on stage, I don't think of myself as isolated.

Robinson: *The Argument,* as you said, is also about Else's own enthusiasm and appreciation for Aristotle. It's a play about a reader.

Greenspan: Oh yeah. And also Else's reading of Plato, whom he obviously loves. There's the great line that I got from Else's book *Plato and Aristotle on Poetry,* where he describes Plato as "the true dramatic poet, a comedian by virtue of the same knowledge that makes him a tragedian." Plato's turning away from poetry is taken personally by Gerald

Else, and that helps explain why he so admires Aristotle's defense of poetry, as Else calls the *Poetics.* I can't help but think of it now, just after the Smithsonian removed David Wojnarowicz's video [*A Fire in My Belly*] from the "Hide/Seek" exhibition. The hostility that art still faces from religious zealots or the right wing—people who are hostile to learning, to culture. And those among them who are educated are so arrogant, with no sense that they might not understand a work of art. So, a defense of poetry appealed to me greatly.

Robinson: It's interesting that you mention this hostility, because another recurrent feature in all your work—not just *The Argument*—is the scene of learning. The first one that comes to mind is Frank in *The HOME Show Pieces* working through the book by Spinoza, trying to make sense of it.

Greenspan: In rather a stumbling way. I don't think he really understands it.

Robinson: But that's the great thing about the scene. You're staging not-knowing again, not-understanding. The scene reminds us that incomprehension is perhaps more valuable in the world of your plays than mastery or comprehension. At least there's some kind of liveliness, questioning, alertness in that confusion, which isn't necessarily there when one understands.

Greenspan: Yes. I have a great regard for learnedness and for learned people. I sometimes wish I had the classical education that other people I know have had. I was just thinking about Lisa Kron's *In the Wake,* where the main character ultimately realizes she doesn't know—that is what the play ultimately dramatizes, a woman gaining a sense of her not knowing. I find the older I get, the less I know. When I was young, I knew quite a lot.

Robinson: Maybe that's our cue to go back and talk about your origins as a writer. You mentioned seeing musicals and movies as a child—but later on, what prompted you to make the move into writing?

Greenspan: There were a couple of factors. One, I came to New York to be an actor, and I wasn't getting a lot of work, so I thought I would just write and perform something I had written. The earliest things I did were practically out of my journal, or they were stream-of-consciousness verse monologues that I had written, inspired by emotional crises: love affairs, sexual orientation, coming out. There was just a need to write it down, so I did. And then I thought, being a performer, I'll perform them. I performed in some of the dankest little hole-in-the-wall theaters one can imagine. One of the first things I did was in the basement of a housing development across from Lincoln Center. Some of the writing I did initially was in collaboration with choreographers—

they were dance-theater pieces. But dancers are limited in their ability to deliver text. I did most of the acting in those pieces, and the dancers danced. When I returned to studying acting, I became more interested in plays, and in trying to write plays. I began to feel a greater need for actors as opposed to dancers.

Robinson: Do you think the influence worked the other way, too—that the presence of more actors changed your form? In the early works—*Principia, 2 Samuel 11, Etc.,* and *The HOME Show Pieces*—you seem to set yourself a formal problem and then show us how you work it out. *Jack,* too, seems as much about its quasi-fugal structure as it is about the title character. That style modulates as we move forward in your career. Maybe it's the overt allusions to Chekhov in *Go Back to Where You Are*—one of the characters is in a production of *The Seagull;* another is adapting the stories for the stage; one of first lines ("Mark died a year ago today") recalls the opening of *Three Sisters.* It seems that you've become more interested in tracking the emotions that flow through a group of people, marking their subtleties—an opening up of form that wasn't in the earlier work.

Greenspan: Yes. I hope there's less preoccupation with myself, more interest in things outside myself. I so admire people who do dramatize larger social or political milieus. I'm just astonished by how they're able to bring so much into a play.

Robinson: Were there models for you early on, productions you saw or plays you read that helped shape you?

Greenspan: Well, the musicals, certainly. But my experience was listening to recordings of them, not seeing them, because there wasn't much theater in Los Angeles, where I grew up. My early monologues, they're like songs in a way. Later, I read Beckett. I didn't really understand him, but the "poetry" of his prose influenced me. Thornton Wilder, too. It would seem as though I was influenced by Stein, but I only came to read her after I'd begun to write. It sounds a little highfalutin, so I'm cautious about saying it, but I was very affected by *Ulysses:* that colliding—colliding isn't the right word, but the playing of different styles, different modes I found very interesting. That influenced the writing of *Principia* and to some extent *Dead Mother.* Also Melville, his iambic language and the great breadth of his work. *The Myopia* and *Dead Mother* are kind of pendant pieces, they're very expansive. They're both epics in a way, in that they're large and episodic.

Robinson: What about your contemporaries—are there writers you feel particularly close to? I'm remembering Tony Kushner grouping you with himself in what he called the "Theater of the Fabulous."

Greenspan: I've never asked him what he meant by "the fabulous." I think of myself instead as part of a theater of the fabulist. I'm like a rhapsode, you know, telling tales. I do feel an affinity with Tony—obviously a much more accomplished writer than I—but to a certain extent I feel an affinity with everybody! All the playwrights whose work I've acted in—Terrence McNally, Bill Hoffman, Mart Crowley, Kathleen Tolan, the Talking Band—I really identify with everything! Mac Wellman, Jeff Jones, Sarah Ruhl. But I don't know if any of them have influenced me. I tend to write a certain kind of play. I mean, *She Stoops to Comedy* was going to be like *All About Eve,* and it turned into . . . what it turned into. *The Argument* was going to be a regular play about these two men, Plato and Aristotle, and then it came out the way it did. And then I wanted to write a simple play about a nightmare marriage—that grew into *The Myopia.*

Robinson: Maybe your receptiveness to everything helps explain why you can be responsive to both Stein and Aristotle. Usually people whose idea of theater derives from one are resistant to the other, yet you find a way to join them.

Greenspan: Yes. I think they have much more in common than is initially apparent. They both have a great love of analysis; there's an attempt to understand something; there's just a commitment to learning. So I don't find them mutually exclusive. As Stein puts it in "Plays," "a combination and not a contradiction." I think they both are observing theatrical phenomena, and then writing about it.

Robinson: Yes, certainly the Stein is much more about being a spectator than about being a playwright.

Greenspan: Even this Leone de' Sommi material I'm looking at. He was a practitioner—in fact he takes a different view from Aristotle. He says it's better to have a bad play produced well than a good play produced poorly. Aristotle says a great tragedy can be appreciated even if it's not performed. But, here, too I don't think they're mutually exclusive. You know, Leone de' Sommi was a director and producer and writer; Aristotle was a philosopher and critic—

Robinson: And, as you tell us in *The Argument,* a botanist.

Greenspan: A botanist. He liked to look at things—to dissect things.

Robinson: You mentioned your work as an actor in other people's work, and in general I wonder if you can see how your life as an actor has affected your life as a writer—if you're the kind of playwright you are because you were experiencing this other aspect of theater?

Greenspan: Certainly my acting work helps explain why I dramatize the making of theater so often. I've directed as well—my own plays, and on a few occasions other people's plays. But acting is my occupation, and that's reflected in my plays. *Jonas* is about three characters: myself, the character I once played, and a character that the character I once played imagines. That's based on my experience acting in *The Royal Family*—playing a character, and imagining another character that this first character is writing about.

Robinson: Are you talking about the desire and even the need to be launched out of one's circumstances into some alternative—an alternative identity, world, or narrative? The actor, or any imaginative artist, is doing that all the time. Maybe because that process is so prominent for the actor, it allows you to examine that same need in people who aren't artists.

Greenspan: I think so. I mean, I think that's something that the performer and the spectator, or the writer and the reader, have in common: they want an opportunity to see things outside themselves. Sometimes spectators, readers, and scholars notice things about a work of art that the artists themselves haven't noticed. I think all art is an opportunity for both practitioners and spectators to step out of themselves. Again, that's one of the reasons I like going to the movies or the theater as opposed to watching television: getting away, getting out of the apartment, getting out of myself.

Robinson: Yet there are many instances in your plays where characters don't get out of themselves, even as they seem to be. I'm thinking most obviously about the repeated instructions in your scripts forbidding drag when a male actor is playing a woman or vice versa—that the performer's essential appearance shouldn't change even when identity does. Can you talk about this—I think you've called it "disguiseless disguise."

Greenspan: I've done drag. I've played women or played men in drag. Why is it that the disguiseless disguise interests me? It may simply be my preoccupation with process. We've discussed how some of my plays expose the writing process. Here it's the acting process. The actor never goes away. I guess Stein said it: the actor is there and the character is there. You're getting to know the actor as well as the character. It's part of the dynamics of theater. At its most vulgar—not that there's anything wrong with vulgarity—well-known actors may receive entrance applause. Duse said that her great goal was to be immersed in her character. Every actor wants to do that, of course—you want to sink completely into the role. You want to become the character, but you're—I am, at least—always conscious. You have to be, you have to know when you're going on, you have to know when you're leaving, you have to make sure you face the right direction so the audience can hear you or see you. You have to project your voice sufficiently. You have to stop talking when your line is over. (*Laughter.*) You hope for those sublime moments when you are completely submerged in a character and the scene *and* can still function properly onstage.

Robinson: Spalding Gray once told a funny story about how he auditioned for a movie where he was to play opposite Farah Fawcett. He didn't get the part, because (the director said) he always looked like he was thinking in his scenes with Fawcett, instead of responding sexually to her. Of course, that thinking was what made him such an interesting actor.

Greenspan: It depends on the material. I remember seeing Sarah Kane's *Blasted* at Soho Rep and thinking that all three actors were submerged in their roles in astonishing ways. After the performance, I talked to Reed Birney [who played Ian] and said, "Oh God, that scene when he's being raped . . ." Reed said it was little uncomfortable at first, but after a while it was like, Let's get down to it. It was a blast. A blast in *Blasted.* So, for all I know they're thinking about dinner while they're—I don't know. But there is a great pleasure when you're just in it. You do have to emerge; you don't want to become a psychotic who can't tell the difference between the real and the imagined. You always have to be in control. You know, I tend to be rather quiet backstage, but there are people who walk offstage saying "Boy, this audience sucks," or "What a great audience!" or "I've gotta go to the bathroom." The actor is always there.

Robinson: In *The Myopia,* you were deep inside a role that asks you to stay outside whichever part you're playing in any given scene—to be at once consumed by the task of performing and conscious of the structure of the whole play. It was an amazing joining of the two styles you're describing.

Your mention of *Blasted* reminds me that when we were trying to decide which plays to put in this collection, you gave me some manuscripts from what you called a dark period in your writing. You said you didn't know what you thought of them now. We didn't talk too much about those plays, or about what prompted the writing of them—and they didn't end up in the book. But I wonder if you could talk about them now. What did you mean by "dark"?

Greenspan: Well, I'll speak frankly about it. The Public Theater [where Greenspan was a director-in-residence from 1990 to 1991] was something I was ill-prepared for, sometimes artistically, sometimes emotionally. And it was a crash. I mean, it was a high to get there, and to work with Joe Papp, but it was a crash afterwards. My work was not well received, and I was not receptive to criticism, and this was followed by a very dark period of writing. I'm not even confident about the quality of the writing. Two of those plays were produced: *Dog in a Dancing School* and *Son of an Engineer.* They're rife with a brazen—I can't call it brazen, brazen is too kind a word. Outrageous is not even the right word. Just an unrestrained sexuality, sexual perversion, disenchantment, violence—emotional and physical violence. I feel that I lost my way in those plays. I hold on to them, and maybe they have some value—I don't know. I think they were more reflections of my—again, a "dilemma" suggests that something was being worked through. They were more like reflections of a disturbance—of being disturbed by what I was experiencing, or what I was.

Robinson: I saw *Son of an Engineer.*

Greenspan: Oh God, it was so perverse—the poor actors, what I put them through. But when I did it as a solo, I think it was more successful. I sat in a chair, almost like *The Myopia,* and used the stage directions as narration. People didn't have to see what I described. It wasn't as assaultive. I think the play might be playable in that convention, although I've no interest in doing again.

Robinson: Could you talk more about the role played by the sexual content in the earlier works?

Greenspan: In *2 Samuel 11,* none of the sexual acts that are described are shown. The main character's mind is wandering, even to an old television show—I think there's something funny about it. And I found a poetry, oddly, in the language of the mind. In "Doing the Beast" from *The HOME Show Pieces,* the character I played is masturbating, but it had more to do with isolation and loneliness than sex—he was in a misguided relationship, he was compulsive.

Robinson: *2 Samuel 11* is as much about writing as anything else.

Greenspan: I agree. It's about telling the story—getting it down on paper—even if it's an inane sexual fantasy. Anything happening is worth dramatizing, is worth writing about. At least the mind can be viewed—the workings of the mind.

Robinson: Even though you're interested in the workings of the mind in those scenes that gesture toward the graphic, it does seem that some of the carnality or earthiness resists the transforming power of thought. The body in some scenes is always and only the body. I'm thinking of the many scenes in bathrooms, the preoccupation with bodily function that never recedes even when it's juxtaposed with acts of writing. You have a highly abstract sensibility on the one hand (characters counting, diagramming, charting experience on graphs), and a highly physical, almost biological, sensibility on the other. It also seems that you consciously work against an audience member's expectations for that kind of subject matter. Sex in your plays is either interrupted, unconsummated, or one of the participants is bored—I'm thinking of *The Horizontal and the Vertical,* in which the protagonist says (in so many words) "let's just get it over with" and is horrified that his partner uses the word "perky." Or it's error-filled, or solitary, or fraught in some other way. Sex is never the transporting experience that a history of clichéd depictions would lead us to expect; it's not even a relief after so many scenes of frustration.

Greenspan: There is a sense of mutual pleasure, enjoyment, in *Go Back to Where You Are.* I've had a complicated relationship to sex; perhaps most people have. Michael Feingold [the theater critic for the *Village Voice*] pointed out years ago that I dramatize sexual fantasy. I've used that aspect of my experience in a frank—and sometimes I feel brazen—way. But even the sexual fantasies in, say, *The HOME Show Pieces* are not completely divorced from the fantasies of success that preoccupy Frank in the bathroom.

Robinson: That play suggests that the carnality also springs from your theater's preoccupation with death. We've talked about *Jack,* but even in your other works there is a consciousness of mortality hovering over the action, explicitly in *Dead Mother* and *Dig a Hole and Bury You Father,* and right up to *The Myopia.*

Greenspan: Maybe that's because I experienced death at an early age. My mother died when I was relatively young. And certainly the early days of the AIDS crisis had a big impact on me: there was so much premature death. It was unanticipated, and it was unrelenting. The obituary pages were filled with people you knew, or knew of. Of course, our mortality should be a source of inspiration, in terms of what we do with our time—how we decide what makes a contribution, what's selfish, what's generous. Time is limited and our place in the scheme of things is small. When you think of yourself as a fleck of sand, I think there's much to be gained. But many writers work with this knowledge, certainly. Death may be so present in my work because of what we started talking about today—that I'm drawn to characters who are seeking, and sometimes finding, a release of some kind, even one this extreme.

Robinson: Endings—of any kind—are rarely final in your theater: they are rather preambles to something altogether different, as they are in *Go Back to Where You Are.* At the very least, endings often open onto opportunities rather than close them down, even if your characters seem unsure about them. (Something you said in another interview has long stayed with me—that you often write yourself into a corner and then choose to leave the corner intact in the finished work, finding it unexpectedly productive.) Could you talk more about that?

Greenspan: Yes, many of my plays—certainly the ones in this volume—end with the promise that something new will transpire following the action of the play. *The HOME Show Pieces, Dead Mother,* and *The Myopia* conclude with some resolution of some family involvement, family trauma, or artistic inertia: the characters in *The HOME Show Pieces* decline a Passover invitation in order to celebrate the liberation from their families, or Sylvia in *Dead Mother* says, "gotta go," or the Raconteur in *The Myopia* says, "shuffle off these coils to take up pen again." *She Stoops to Comedy* concludes with leaving the "door" open. And *The Argument* anticipates a further discourse to "take up the subject of comedy." I'm not sure why I've written those endings . . . it just seemed the right way to do it. Something always has to happen afterwards.

Chronology

1956: David Greenspan born in Los Angeles, March 17.

1978: B.A. in Drama from University of California, Irvine.

1980–85: Performed original monologues at the Limbo Lounge, P.S. 122, Medicine Show, BACA Downtown, and other small venues in New York City.

1981: *Vertices,* collaboration with choreographer DJ McDonald, presented at Westbeth Theatre Center, New York City (also acted).

1982: *The I Witness,* collaboration with choreographer David Parsons, presented by Dance Theater Workshop, New York City (also acted).

1986: *The Horizontal and the Vertical* and *Dig a Hole and Bury You Father* presented by HOME for Contemporary Theatre and Art, New York City (also acted and directed).

1987–90: Playwright-in-Residence at HOME for Contemporary Theatre and Art.

1987: *Jack* (also directed) and *Principia* (also acted and directed) presented by HOME for Contemporary Theatre and Art.

1988: *The HOME Show Pieces* presented by HOME for Contemporary Theatre and Art (also acted and directed). (Presented at New York Shakespeare Festival / Public Theater, New York City, and at Citizens Theatre, Glasgow, 1992.)

1989: *2 Samuel 11, Etc.* presented by HOME for Contemporary Theatre and Art (also directed). (Presented by Royal Court Theatre, London, 1991, and by Thick Description, San Francisco, 1992.)

Directed *Kate's Diary* by Kathleen Tolan (Playwrights Horizons, New York City, and New York Shakespeare Festival / Public Theater).

1990–91: Director-in-Residence at the New York Shakespeare Festival / Public Theater.

1990: Directed *Gonza the Lancer* by Chikamatsu Monzaemon (New York Shakespeare Festival / Public Theater).

1991: *Dead Mother, or Shirley Not All in Vain* presented by New York Shakespeare Festival / Public Theater (also acted and directed). (Presented by Stükke Theater, Berlin, 1993, and by Traveling Jewish Theatre, San Francisco, 2008.)

Directed *The Way of the World* by William Congreve (New York Shakespeare Festival / Public Theater).

1992: Performed in *Write if You Get Work* by Jeffrey M. Jones (Ontological at St. Mark's, New York City).

1993: *Dog in a Dancing School* presented by Dance Theater Workshop (also acted and directed).

1993–94: Performed solo version of *Son of an Engineer* at various small theaters in New York City and at the Red Eye Theater in Minneapolis (also directed). Fully staged production presented by HOME for Contemporary Theatre and Art (also directed).

1993–2003: Performed *The Myopia* in readings and workshops at theaters in New York City, including New York Shakespeare Festival / Public Theater, P.S. 122, and the Foundry Theatre (at the Ohio), and at the Red Eye Theater in Minneapolis.

1995: Performed in *The Mystery of Irma Vep* by Charles Ludlam (Cleveland Play House).

Began collaborating with Shapiro and Smith Dance, Minneapolis (continues to present). Pieces include *What Dark, Wee Violence, Shtick, Medea Medea,* and *Burning Air.*

1996: Performed in *The Boys in the Band* by Mart Crowley (WPA Theatre, New York City).

1997: Performed in *Second-Hand Smoke* by Mac Wellman (Primary Stages, New York City).

Obie Award for Performance (*The Boys in the Band*).

1998: Performed in *Benita Canova* by Richard Foreman (Ontological-Hysteric Theatre, New York City).

1999: Performed in *High Life* by Lee MacDougall (Primary Stages).

2001: Performed in *Lipstick Traces* by Kirk Lynn (from the book by Greil Marcus) (Foundry Theatre) and *The Wax* by Kathleen Tolan (Playwrights Horizons).

Performed in *Star Messengers* by Paul Zimet and Ellen Maddow (La MaMa, New York City).

2002: CalArts/Alpert Award in the Arts.

John Simon Guggenheim Memorial Foundation fellowship.

2003: *She Stoops to Comedy* presented by Playwrights Horizons (also acted and directed). (Presented by Evidence Room, Los Angeles, 2005; Woolly Mammoth Theatre, Washington, D.C., 2007; and San Francisco Playhouse, 2009.)

The Orphan of Zhao (from play by Ji Junxiang; score by Stephin Merritt) presented by Lincoln Center Festival / Lincoln Center Theater, New York City.

Obie Award, Special Citation (*She Stoops to Comedy*).

2003–6: Performed in *Faust* by Goethe (Target Margin Theater, New York City).

2005: Performed in *Belize* by Paul Zimet and Ellen Maddow (La MaMa) and *The Learned Ladies of Park Avenue* by David Grimm (Hartford Stage Company).

2006: Lucille Lortel Playwriting Fellowship.

2007: *The Argument* presented by Target Margin Theater (also acted).

Performed in *Some Men* by Terrence McNally (Second Stage Theatre, New York City), *Dinner Party* (from Plato's *Symposium*) (Target Margin Theater), and *The Beebo Brinker Chronicles* by Linda Chapman and Kate Moira Ryan (from novel by Anne Bannon) (Hourglass Group, New York City).

Obie Award for Performance (*Faust* and *Some Men*).

2008: *Old Comedy* (from Aristophanes's *The Frogs*) presented by Target Margin Theater.

Obie Award, Special Citation (*The Argument*).

2009: *Coraline* (from novel by Neil Gaiman; music and lyrics by Stephin Merritt) presented by Manhattan Class Company, New York City (also acted). (Presented by San Francisco Playhouse, 2010.)

Performed in *Cornbury, or the Queen's Governor* by William Hoffman (Theatre Askew, New York City) and *The Royal Family* by George S. Kaufman and Edna Ferber (Manhattan Theatre Club).

2010: *The Myopia, an epic burlesque of tragic proportion* (also acted) and *Plays* (from lecture by Gertrude Stein) presented by the Foundry Theatre (also acted and directed).

Performed in *Rescue Me* by Michi Barall (Ma-Yi Theatre, New York City), *The Metal Children* by Adam Rapp (Vineyard Theatre, New York City), and *Orlando* by Sarah Ruhl (Classic Stage Company, New York City).

Obie Award for Sustained Achievement.

2011: *Go Back to Where You Are* presented by Playwrights Horizons (also acted).

Jonas presented by Transport Group, New York City (also acted and directed).

Performed solo version of *The Patsy* by Barry Conners (Transport Group).